MW01618253

Vilhelm Hammershøi

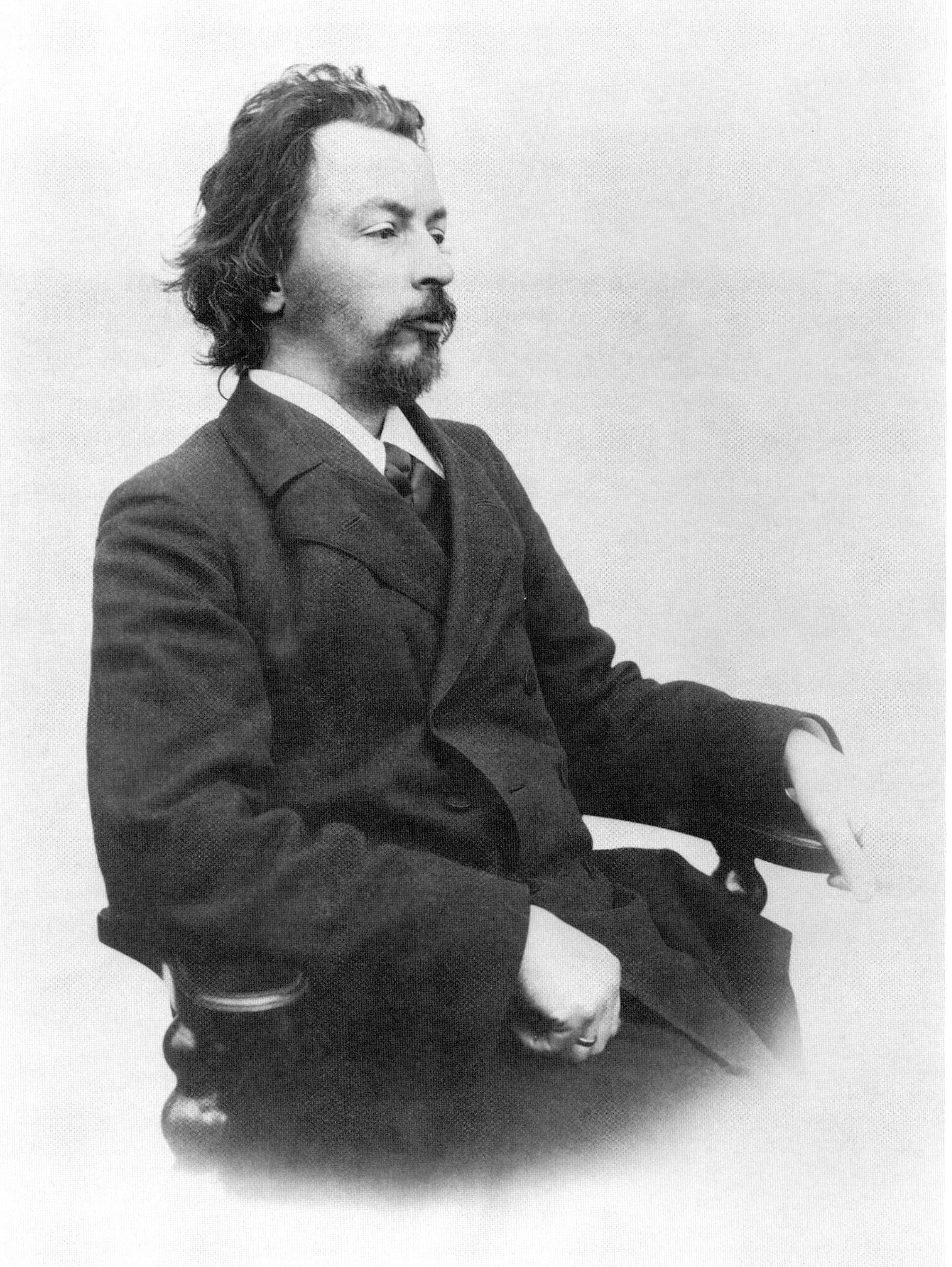

Vilhelm Hammershøi

1864 - 1916

Danish Painter of Solitude and Light

Anne-Birgitte Fonsmark,
Director, Ordrupgaard

Mikael Wivel,
Curator, Ordrupgaard

in collaboration with

Henri Loyrette,
Director, Musée d'Orsay

Robert Rosenblum,
Curator of Twentieth-Century Art,
Guggenheim Museum

ORDRUPGAARD

•

GUGGENHEIM MUSEUM

This book has been published on the occasion of the exhibition *Vilhelm Hammershøi (1864–1916): Danish Painter of Solitude and Light*, curated by Anne-Birgitte Fonsmark and Mikael Wivel.

Ordrupgaard, Copenhagen,
August 15 – October 19, 1997

Musée d'Orsay, Paris,
November 18, 1997 – March 2, 1998

Solomon R. Guggenheim Museum,
New York,
June 19 – September 7, 1998

The exhibition is jointly organized by Ordrupgaard, Copenhagen, and the Musée d'Orsay, Paris.

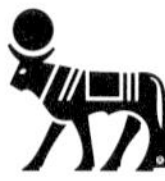

The major sponsor of this exhibition is Novo Nordisk.
Significant support has been provided by the Danish Ministry of Culture.

ISBN (hardcover) 0-8109-6913-0
ISBN (softcover) 0-89207-208-3

Guggenheim Museum Publications
1071 Fifth Avenue
New York, New York 10128

Hardcover edition distributed by
Harry N. Abrams
100 Fifth Avenue
New York, New York 10010

General editors: Anne-Birgitte Fonsmark
and Mikael Wivel
Editor, English-language edition:
Stephen Robert Frankel
Translator: W. Glyn Jones
Designer: Michael Jensen
Production: Edition Bløndal,
DK 2900 Hellerup, Denmark

Printed in Germany by Waterless Bløndal 1998

LENDERS TO THE EXHIBITION:

Individual lenders:

H.M. Queen Ingrid of Denmark
Jane Abdy, London
Warren Adelson, New York
Ambassador John L. Loeb, Jr., New York
C. W. Obel A/S, Copenhagen
and several anonymous lenders

Public institutions:

Denmark
Åbenraa: Kunstmuseum Brundlund Slot
Århus: Aarhus Kunstmuseum
Copenhagen: Davids Samling;
Den Hirschprungske Samling;
Ny Carlsberg Glyptotek;
Ordrupgaard;
Statens Museum for Kunst
Elsinore: Helsingør Bymuseum,
Marienlyst Slot
Maribo: Storstrøms Kunstmuseum
Odense: Fyns Kunstmuseum
Randers: Randers Kunstmuseum
Vejen: Vejen Kunstmuseum

France
Paris: Musée d'Orsay

Germany
Berlin: Staatliche Museen zu Berlin,
Preussicher Kulturbesitz,
Nationalgalerie*
Schleswig: Schleswig-Holsteinisches
Landesmuseum, schloss Gottorf*

Great Britain
London: Tate Gallery*

Sweden
Malmö: Malmö Konstmuseum
Stockholm: Nationalmuseum;
Thielska Galleriet*

United States
Cambridge, Mass.: The Busch-Reisinger
Museum, Harvard University

*NOTE: *The works lent by those institutions marked with an asterisk are not in the New York exhibition but are included in the catalogue.*

Cover: Vilhelm Hammershøi, *Interior* [with young woman seen from behind, Strandgade 30], [ca. 1903–04], oil on canvas, cat. no. 32 (detail)

Frontispiece: Vilhelm Hammershøi, ca. 1891. Det Kongelige Bibliotek, Copenhagen

Contents

Foreword

When we chose to mount a comprehensive retrospective of the work of the Danish painter Vilhelm Hammershøi (1864-1916) in collaboration with the Musée d'Orsay, Paris, in 1997–98, it was not only because he was one of the most original artists of his day, but also because today his works look strikingly contemporary. Hammershøi's œuvre consists of exquisitely composed pictures that often border on the abstract, with a particular focus on the interiors of the apartments in which he lived. The mysterious and almost dream-like atmosphere of these pictures evokes a deeply personal artistic world. Behind the empty interiors' stillness and timelessness, we frequently sense an element of disquiet, but the pictures are devoid of any real action or narrative and should perhaps be regarded as a series of existential statements.

Hammershøi's paintings were controversial in his time, and made him a loner in Danish artistic life. He did not receive support from official institutions, but rather from private art collectors, especially Alfred Bramsen, a dentist who became a patron early in Hammerhøi's career, and also from Wilhelm Hansen and Heinrich Hirschsprung, the founders of Ordrupgaard and Den Hirschsprungske Samling, respectively. However, he did gain some recognition, particularly outside Denmark—partly as the result of a number of exhibitions—and his singular talent attracted the interest of outstanding figures in the world of international culture such as Sergei Diaghilev, French critic Théodore Duret, and Austrian poet Rainer Maria Rilke. But not long after Hammershøi died, his name began to fade into the oblivion that was typically the fate of artists who did not conform to the narrow ideological strictures of the avant-garde—a trend that only began to change many decades afterward. We hope that this exhibition marks a major turning point in Hammershøi's revival.

The exhibition brings together most of Hammershøi's principal works, the first time such a comprehensive retrospective has been seen outside Denmark. Our gratitude goes especially to those who have so generously agreed to lend their pictures—museums as well as private collectors in Denmark, Norway, Sweden, France, Britain, Germany, the United States, and Canada.

Our thanks to Henri Loyrette, director of the Musée d'Orsay, for his partnership with us in organizing the original Hammershøi exhibition at Ordrupgaard and bringing it to Paris.

We would like to express our gratitude to the Solomon R. Guggenheim Museum for the opportunity of bringing the works of Hammershøi to the United States, where it can find new appreciation by an American public. To all those at the Guggenheim who were involved with the exhibition and the catalogue, we extend our warmest appreciation. In particular, we would like to thank Thomas Krens, director of the Guggenheim; Professor Robert Rosenblum of New York University, for initiating the project of bringing the exhibition to the Guggenheim; and Anthony Calnek, the Guggenheim's director of publications, for overseeing the production of the English-language version of this catalogue.

To the two art historians who have contributed their essays to the catalogue, Poul Vad and Robert Rosenblum, we offer our sincere thanks.

Finally, we would like to express our heartfelt thanks to the Danish Ministry of Culture and Novo Nordisk for their generous support.

Anne-Birgitte Fonsmark

Director, Ordrupgaard

Foreword

The Solomon R. Guggenheim Museum's presentation of *Vilhelm Hammershøi (1864–1916): Danish Painter of Solitude and Light,* marks the first occasion that the American public will have to view a comprehensive survey of paintings by this artist. Organized by the Ordrupgaard, Copenhagen, and the Musée d'Orsay, Paris, this exhibition gathers a notable body of Hammershøi's work from collections in Europe and the United States, and allows for a concentrated look at the endeavors of this relatively little-known painter.

In recent years, the Guggenheim Museum has embarked upon a more expansive exhibition program, a major part of which has been devoted to investigating the late nineteenth century in order to better understand the origins of twentieth-century art. Indeed, within our own permanent collection, the works housed in the Thannhauser galleries offer an in-depth look at many canonical images from the nineteenth century. In presenting *Vilhelm Hammershøi*, the Guggenheim is doing something it has rarely done before: hosting an exhibition dedicated to a single artist who was active primarily in the nineteenth century. Fittingly, this Danish artist's interiors and landscapes—best characterized as melancholy, atmospheric, and often stark—have been connected to the paintings of such twentieth-century artists as Georgia O'Keeffe, Edward Hopper, and Andrew Wyeth, to name but a few. It is our sincere hope that this exhibition will inaugurate the first of many shows to examine artists of the nineteenth century and contextualize their works within our own times.

Vilhelm Hammershøi could not have traveled to the United States without the support of several pivotal individuals and organizations. We are tremendously indebted to the sponsors of the exhibition, the Danish Ministry of Culture and Novo Nordisk—their generous support has made the New York presentation of *Vilhelm Hammershøi* possible. A special thanks must be extended to the curators: Anne-Birgitte Fonsmark, Director, Ordrupgaard; Henri Loyrette, Director, Musée d'Orsay; and Mikael Wivel, Curator, Ordrupgaard, for realizing this ambitious undertaking and bringing to fruition an exhibition of seminal importance to our understanding of Vilhelm Hammershøi's oeuvre. Furthermore, we are grateful for the indefatigable efforts and unflagging enthusiasm of Fonsmark and Wivel, as well as those of our own Curator of Twentieth-Century Art, Robert Rosenblum, as they were the driving forces responsible for bringing the exhibition to New York. Finally, the institutions and collectors who have magnanimously lent their beloved paintings to this exhibition deserve our deepest gratitude. We are honored to have this opportunity to acquaint the museum audience in the United States with Hammershøi's achievements.

Thomas Krens

Director, The Solomon R. Guggenheim Foundation

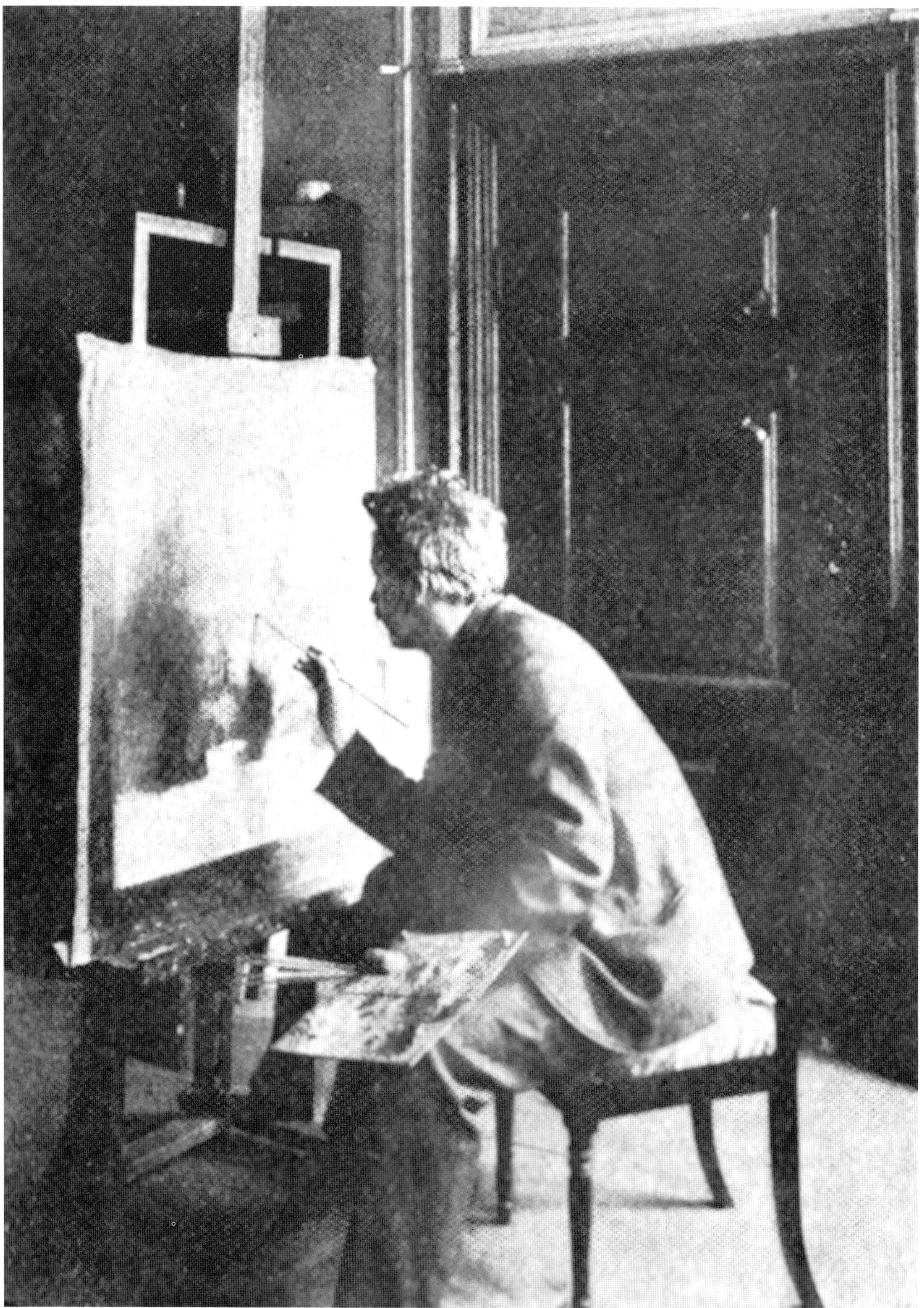

Vilhelm Hammershøi – An Introduction

Poul Vad

When Carl Dreyer directed his first feature film, *The President*, in 1918, his cinematic pictorial composition and set design were clearly indebted to Vilhelm Hammershøi's paintings. Dreyer found in Hammershøi a combination of emotional intensity and austere, classical pictorial structure that corresponded to his own creative objectives, which he achieved with ever greater clarity throughout his life's work—perhaps most clearly in his very last film, *Gertrud* (1964), which to a Dane is scarcely imaginable without Hammershøi. It can be argued that Dreyer became Hammershøi's most important—and maybe even his only—heir, which indirectly suggests the isolated position Hammershøi occupied and ultimately still occupies in Danish art—and presumably beyond it, too.

When Dreyer made *The President,* Hammershøi had been dead for two years. He died at the height of his fame, and that same year a memorial exhibition of his work was organized in Copenhagen, bringing together more Hammershøi pictures than ever before or since.

When Hammershøi died, it was not only a great artist who died, but a phenomenon in Danish and European art. In the midst of the great upheaval brought about by modernism, the apparent conservatism of his art made it seem like a mutation, though one that was impossible to dismiss; but once he was gone, it was soon considered irrelevant, allocated to an obscure corner of the history of art and only discussed with a kind of unenthusiastic, obligatory respect.

Hammershøi's death in 1916 gave rise to lengthy articles in Danish newspapers and was noted in both the German and French press. During the 1920s, Hammershøi was still discussed with respect in German and French art histori-

Vilhelm Hammershøi at work on the portrait of Ida (cat. no. 52) at Strandgade 30 in 1907. Det Kongelige Bibliotek, Copenhagen

ans' writings on modern European art (for example, in André Michel, *Histoire de l'Art*, vol. VIII, 2 [Paris, 1926], p. 719, and Henri Focillon, *La Peinture aux XIXe et XXe Siècles* [Paris, 1926], pp. 441–42). But 1916 was the very year in which Dada was born: after the much-needed revolt against academicism and the art of the Salon that had been set in motion by the Impressionists and continued into the early twentieth century, the rallying cry of the avant-garde became entrenched as an ideology, which in the following years—especially after World War II—took hold among many artists as a fundamental part of their identity, and among art historians as the framework within which the development of modern art was described. Hammershøi was a victim of this way of looking at things and disappeared from international art histories, while in Denmark a reevaluation of his work and its significance was long in coming.

Hammershøi was modest and unpretentious to the point of self-effacement, but as a painter, he repeatedly challenged deeply ingrained norms and expectations in a way that many people found deeply unsettling. In his work, quietness and a radical sense of being different mingle so subtly that the understanding of them and the evaluation of his work have alternated between extremes. Writing of Rodin, Rainer Maria Rilke maintained that "fame is ultimately only the embodiment of all the misunderstandings that congregate around a new name." Hammershøi's fame has primarily been linked to his paintings of interiors which, together with his rigorous use of a range of grays—a limited palette that many found shocking, and confused with an absence of color—suggested *quietness* as Hammershøi's special characteristic and artistic domain. This led people to disregard or refuse to acknowledge the radically different quality that became quite evident in his two great figure compositions *Artemis* (cat. no. 10) and *Five Portraits* (cat. no. 26), which astonished his contemporaries, and that is present in everything he touched, even the simplest interiors, where it can have a particularly disturbing quality.

Hammershøi was born in 1864 and made his debut at the age of twenty-one with a picture that at a single stroke made him a well-known and controversial name in Danish art: the portrait of his sister (1885; cat. no. 2). In order to understand the stir created by this picture, one must remember that the dominant taste of the time demanded and expected a composition that was meticulously planned, richly detailed, and, in the most conventional terms, faithful to nature. In this work, Hammershøi completely ignores this dominant taste, as though the young artist possessed a strange innocence that allowed him to find an original approach without seeming self-consciously blatant.

The assurance he demonstrated in that picture had its foundation in many years of artistic training. Hammershøi received professional instruction in drawing from the age of eight. Then, in 1879, at the age of fifteen, he began studying at the Kunstakademiet (Royal Academy of Fine Arts), starting at the most elementary level and, over the next five years, taking classes in all disciplines related to drawing and painting, while continuing his private lessons. Finally, from 1883 to

1885, he studied at De frie Studieskoler (the Independent Study Schools). These schools, modeled on art schools run by French painters—especially that of Léon Bonnat, who had had many Danish pupils—were established in 1882 to give budding young artists an alternative to the teaching offered by the Kunstakademiet, which was profoundly conservative and rejected all new ideas. Hammershøi's teacher at De frie Studieskoler was the most sensational younger painter of the time, the French-influenced Peder S. Krøyer—who is said to have admitted that he did not understand this strange pupil, but also that he did not try to influence him either.

Hammershøi had distinguished himself as an artist at an early age; even his sketches of models attracted attention for their rich gradation of tones extending from white to black. A number of his small oil paintings from these early years, especially the landscapes, reveal a determination and an ability to develop the surface in a painterly fashion, and to conceive the motif as a whole, omitting all inessential details.

These qualities were fully apparent in the portrait of his sister, which inaugurated a compositional idea—a dark figure against a grayish-white background—that he continued to develop. It was also Hammershøi's first intensive exploration of the theme of femininity, to which he continually returned. The tender young girl's slightly forward-leaning body is caught in a kind of unstable balance between rest and movement, which he emphasized with her arms and hands. In 1885, this picture's slightly oblique axes, blurred painterly treatment, and apparent paucity of color, which were regarded as an almost unhealthy deviation from the norm, made it provocative and incomprehensible to many viewers. Hammershøi had painted it as an entry for a competition held by the Kunstakademiet; and when it did not win, a number of the leading younger artists staged a protest. Hammershøi's picture thus unleashed their simmering dissatisfaction with the academy, which a few years later led to a real revolt, again with a painting by Hammershøi as the catalyst. This was the establishment in 1891 of Den frie Udstilling (The Independent Exhibition), which broke the Kunstakademiet's monopoly on mounting exhibitions and had a lasting influence on the artistic life of Denmark.

Hammershøi's works in the second half of the 1880s coincided with a trend away from plein-air painting in more recent Danish art and toward pictures of interiors, intimate domestic life, a somber palette, melancholy subjects, and even themes related to death—occasionally given a clearly symbolic setting. However, with their combination of sensual refinement and a completely original composition in which line plays a crucial role, Hammershøi's pictures had a different quality right from the start—for example, the portrait of his sister might make one think of a painter such as Degas (although Hammershøi did not know his pictures) rather than Hammershøi's own Danish contemporaries.

Hammershøi's next major effort, a life-size painting that he called *Job* (preliminary study, ill. p. 13) and exhibited in 1888 after having struggled with it for a year and a half, was in the spirit of the age, but in a ferociously uncompromising way. The painting is like a mysterious, inaccessible key to Hammershøi's psyche and artistic development during these critical years, for it no longer exists in the form in which Hammershøi exhibited it: it was already dark by then, with a Rembrandt-like chiaroscuro, but soon after that it darkened so catastrophically that it became nearly impossible to see the image. The picture caused a considerable stir in 1888, but the composition is now best known through a preparatory drawing: a naked man, seated and stiffened in pain and almost swallowed up by the darkness surrounding him—the incarnation of suffering. That the picture's ruin was perhaps built into it can be seen as symbolic of Hammershøi's insufficient human or artistic understanding for the great painterly and existential demands of this task. What is important here, though, is that he took up the struggle, thus giving an indication of his heroism and drive to take things to the ultimate extreme that became more apparent later on, but which are not usually associated with this artist who is regarded as the master of the interior, of silence, and of intimacy.

The figure of Job, positioned along the central axes of the rectangle it occupies, recalls a figure from Egyptian sculpture; but the painterly treatment is unthinkable without Rembrandt—and it was in the same year Hammershøi did it, 1887, that he went on his first study trip to Holland. At this point in his career, the two determining poles in Hammershøi's artistic orientation emerged clearly: the strictly formal art of early antiquity, and Dutch painting of the seventeenth century, in which the ordinary everyday world is endowed with an almost mystical intensity. Nevertheless, from the very beginning, Hammershøi carried with him artistic baggage that tied him to a particular Danish tradition: the so-called Golden Age of Danish painting, which refers to the work of artists who created a distinctive Danish culture of visual art between about 1820 and 1850. When, in later years, Hammershøi was given the opportunity of establishing a modest collection of works of art, he selected only paintings and drawings by Danish Golden Age artists for his walls—not a single painting or drawing by him or any of his contemporaries. His works contain fairly clear references here and there to pictures by those earlier Danish artists, but what is most important is the entire foundation on which his painting rests, intellectually and aesthetically: a respect for reality, a striving for harmony, a pictorial structure of almost crystalline clarity, combined with intimacy of feeling. From these essential characteristics, one could easily assume that Hammershøi might have considered himself a late pupil of the founder of that school, C. A. W. Eckersberg (1783–1853), whose art had been decisively influenced by studying with Jacques-Louis David from 1811 to

Vilhelm Hammershøi, Study for *Job*, [1887]. Charcoal on paper, 47 x 27 cm. Private collection

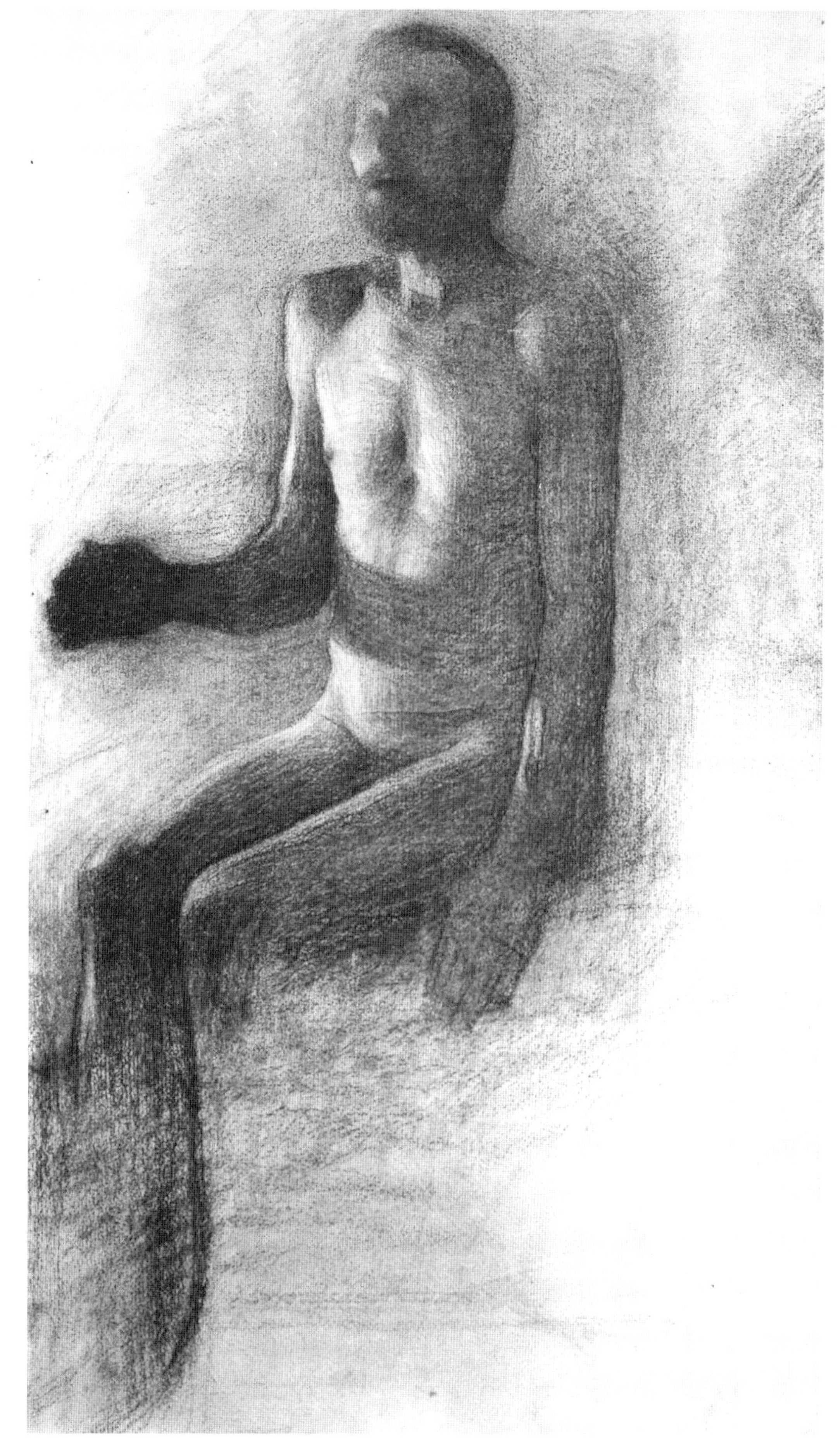

1813. But a *very* late pupil: one need go no further than Hammershøi's picture of Job, showing a tormented, fearful awareness of which there is not even a hint in the paintings of the Golden Age artists—an awareness that testifies to the fact that the "conservative" Hammershøi belongs to the modern era.

The second half of the 1880s was a productive period for Hammershøi: he introduced new motifs (interiors, female nudes, and, around 1890, his first architectural motifs) and tried out various pictorial possibilities. He based the structure of some pictures on the vertical and horizontal axes, occasionally slightly oblique, and eliminated the sense of depth between the picture plane and the planes within the picture, as in the large painting of a baker's shop (1888; cat. no. 4). His ideas about color were already firmly established, focusing on a range of grays that during these years attained a rare degree of refinement. As already stated, the visit to Holland in 1887 was important; and in 1889 Hammershøi went to Paris for the first time, to attend the World's Fair, where he was represented in the Danish art section. There, he had his first opportunity of seeing contemporary art outside Denmark, although there is nothing to suggest that it made any impression on him—he undoubtedly preferred to visit the collections in the Louvre! Even Whistler, with whom Hammershøi has been compared, and some of whose pictures he saw here for the first time, seems not to have left any trace in his art.

But Hammershøi was not unaware of what was taking place in contemporary French art. That same autumn of 1889, an exhibition of Impressionist paintings was mounted in Copenhagen, organized by Karl Madsen, the leading young Danish art critic of the time, who in 1911 would become director of the Statens Museum for Kunst (Royal Museum of Fine Arts). Hammershøi was a close friend of his (it was in Madsen's home that Hammershøi painted the first of his "empty rooms," in 1888), and from the first he gave strong, though not uncritical, support to Hammershøi. The exhibition included pictures by the leading French Impressionists from the collection of Mette Gauguin (i.e., Paul Gauguin), as well as works by Scandinavian Impressionists. It is not known what Hammershøi thought of these pictures; perhaps his experience of them left discreet traces in a single portrait. But that same year he painted his first self-portrait, and it is in a visual language completely different from both the Impressionists and his own immediate Danish predecessors. It is a dark portrait of head and shoulders modeled almost sculpturally, like a bust seen in three-quarter profile, with one eye barely visible (but not looking directly at the viewer) and the other entirely in shadow. Hammershøi has created a sense of commanding presence by giving a feeling of weight to the upper body and neck in the lower half of the picture, and setting off the raised head in the upper half, a formal arrangement that suggests heroism subtly (made all the more powerful by the absence of external attributes to convey it). This impassive portrait reveals a strong, self-confident, but isolated man. Stylistically, the picture combines a static, sculptural concept rooted in antiquity and a painterly chiaroscuro that recalls the seventeenth-century Dutch masters, creating a perfect synthesis of these elements.

This is the stage the still young Hammershøi had reached around 1890–91: he had established his reputation as one of the most talented painters of his generation; he had acquired opponents who found his art outré or even unhealthy; he had instigated revolutionary changes in Danish artistic life; and he had also been “discovered” by a collector, Alfred Bramsen, a dentist who gradually acquired an extensive collection of Hammershøi’s works and became an enthusiastic, perhaps even somewhat fanatical, advocate of his art.

Hammershøi had grown up in an affluent, cultured middle-class Copenhagen family, at the center of which was his mother, a strong and gifted woman. He had three siblings, two of whom—his younger sister, whose portrait he had painted in 1885, and his younger brother, Svend, who also became a painter (and ceramic artist)—played important roles in his life. His mother must have understood at an early stage that Vilhelm was special: as described above, he was given the best artistic training imaginable; and early on she began to save all evidence of his talent, and after he began to exhibit his work she collected newspaper clippings and other relevant material, which she meticulously pasted into scrapbooks and carefully annotated. She continued to keep these scrapbooks until a few months before her death at the age of seventy-six, only two years before that of her son. In 1890 Hammershøi became engaged to Ida Ilsted, the sister of one of his friends from the Kunstakademiet, and in 1891 they married. She was a rather ordinary girl from the provinces, shy and unaffected, with fine, bright blue eyes and delicate nerves. Their marriage, which remained childless, was not only a major part of Hammershøi’s personal life but also came to play a part in his art: his wife appears in the many of the interiors featuring a lone female figure (even from the back she is easily recognizable, with her swept-up hair and bare neck).

Ida accompanied him on his many journeys abroad, starting with their honeymoon trip to Paris, where they stayed six months, from September 1891 to March 1892. Those months in Paris shed much light on Hammershøi’s relationship with the art of his own time and on the self-confidence with which he judged it. His choice of Paris for his first prolonged visit abroad suggests that he was aware of its role as the contemporary art capital of the period, and that he was prepared to let himself be challenged (and then there was also the Louvre!). This was not common knowledge in Denmark then. Except at the end of the 1870s, when several Danish painters had gone to Paris (where they had attended Léon Bonnat’s school), no regular contact had been established with artistic life there or with modern French art (which was especially associated with Bastien-Lepage, Gauguin’s stay in Copenhagen in 1885 really being of significance only to Hammershøi’s most important Danish contemporary, Theodor Philipsen). When one of Hammershøi’s friends from the academy, J. F. Willumsen, headed for Paris in March 1890, followed by Hammershøi in 1891, their doing so indicated a radi-

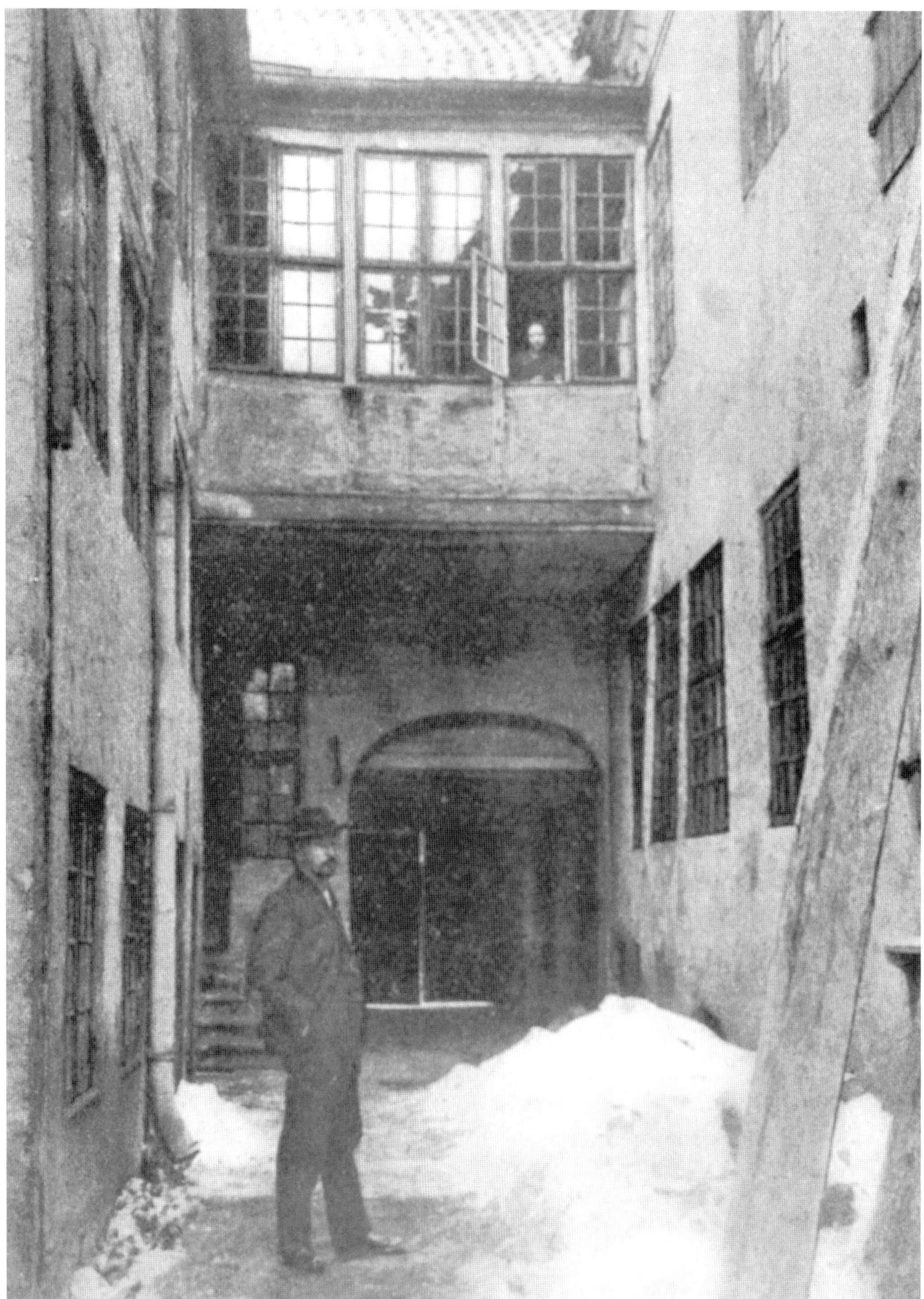

cal desire to go in a different direction from their peers. Some comments by a leading French critic might have been decisive for Hammershøi: in July 1890 Théodore Duret, a friend of the Impressionists and Whistler, visited Copenhagen to become acquainted with recent Danish art. He had Karl Madsen as his "guide," and the only Danish painter who really awoke his interest was Hammershøi. He visited Hammershøi's parents, after which Hammershøi's mother noted in her scrapbook that Duret "expressed his opinion of Vilhelm's art in very flattering terms."

A splendid portrait of Ida that Hammershøi had painted in 1890 was—presumably on the recommendation of Duret—sent to the leading Parisian art dealer Paul Durand-Ruel in autumn 1891. Hammershøi saw it there one day that December, and on the same day visited Duret. In a letter, Hammershøi recalled that Duret received him extremely courteously and encouraged him to come back on one of the days when artists such as Whistler and Monet were dining with him. But Hammershøi, whose French was not very good, probably felt like a stranger in this milieu; he did not visit Duret again. And the possibility of selling the picture to Duret, who was apparently interested, came to nothing. However, several French artists are said to have seen the picture at Durand-Ruel's.

After a little over a month in Paris, Hammershøi wrote to his mother: "You must not be afraid that I shall lose my independence, there is no chance of that, but of course I have come here to Paris to see a great many things and also preferably to learn something, but I think I shall learn more from the older art than the new."

That he was not at all pleased with modern and contemporary art when he did manage to see it emerges from a letter that he wrote to Danish painter Johan Rohde in January 1892, one of the few times that Hammershøi comments on works he had seen, which he does in the most scathing terms: "There is a small exhibition of Impressionists and Symbolists here at the moment, and it is rubbish. I hope for the Symbolists that it is a very poor exhibition. Most of the paintings look like jokes. There is one with a checkered lady in which the blades of grass and the leaves on the trees are oblongs, and then another by the same painter—I don't know his name—showing a woman with round coins on her dress, and in this one the leaves and the grass are all round, even a tiny puppy dog is round. It has such style! And there are also paintings on such touching subjects as a man hurrying into a pissoir. I liked that one a lot!"

How did Hammershøi respond to this radical art and its formulaic search for a "style," which he ridicules here?

After about a month in Paris, Hammershøi began to copy an ancient Greek relief in the Louvre (cat. no. 7) depicting the Three Graces, and he worked with great concentration on the picture for two months. To copy as though he were a

Vilhelm Hammershøi in the courtyard at Strandgade 30, winter 1907; Ida can be seen at a window in the gallery. Private collection

novice in the realm of art might look like a retrogressive act on the part of a mature artist like Hammershøi; yet, it must be said that he did not lack artistic ambition, and that in his own reverse approach he was just as radical as the artists who saw themselves as radical artistic innovators. The copy he made, the same size as the relief, was not a copy in a strict sense, but a painterly paraphrase in which light—which is not inherent to the artistry of the relief—plays a crucial role. The short, sporadically applied brushstrokes, typical of Hammershøi, were the means by which he gave the surface of the picture a painterly consistency *without* seeking to imitate the texture of the marble. And finally, he related to the relief not only as an exemplary work of art, but as a sheer *object* in that the irregular edges of the block of stone are reproduced just as meticulously as the three figures and thus contribute to the unity of the picture.

In the 1890s, the placement of secondary figures in the foreground, an organizational principle in much ancient and sacred art, was one of the striking features in that decade's search for style and a new sacral expression—it is found in the work of Symbolists in many countries. The copy that Hammershøi made shows that he was also looking to ancient art as a source of renewal, but that at the same time, with his objective view of his model, he was indicating the distance that must separate modern man from the culture and sphere of experience that underlay the work and the style. The copy was thus also an implied criticism of the seductive worship of the past and of the formulaic "style" that Hammershøi saw all around him; or, it might be said, an expression of critical awareness on the part of an artist who did not adopt an intellectual stance toward the problems of the day, but combined intuition and artistic intelligence. And his humble picture has turned out to possess the durability of things classical.

Hammershøi and his wife viewed not only the most recent art but also life in the nineteenth-century French metropolis with the eyes of strangers, visitors to a world that was not theirs. Ida, who had been catapulted there almost straight from the tiny Danish provincial town where she had been born and bred, wrote in a letter to her mother-in-law: "When we have had our dinner, we sometimes walk out along the elegant boulevards, and in truth there are indeed Parisian women to be seen there. It is dreadful to see how painted and powdered they are, and how dressed up."

Hammershøi's next journey abroad, in the autumn of 1893, was to northern Italy and Florence, where especially Giotto and the early Renaissance painters (such as Fra Angelico) made a profound impression on him. Shortly after returning home, he started the great figure painting *Artemis* (cat. no. 10); in its life-size figures one can see an echo of Masolino's frescoes (1424–26) in the Brancacci Chapel in the church of Santa Maria del Carmine in Florence, as well as echoes of ancient sculpture. This picture, with its single, almost androgynous standing male figure and three female figures, is like an enigmatic poem about sex; and the composition is light and airy, with the large, strangely weightless figures spread across the surface of the picture, displaying almost no depth, and drawn in an awkward manner, as though Hammershøi were unable to unite ideal and reality. When he exhibited it in 1894, Hammershøi again attracted attention, and once more opinions were strongly divided—even friends of his art, such as Karl Madsen, did not understand the picture, which they considered a failure; but in *Taarnet*, the periodical of the young literary Symbolists, it was highly praised. In the posthumous sale of Hammershøi's effects in 1916, Madsen bought the picture for the Statens Museum for Kunst: he realized that, despite his reservations, *Artemis* had a place in the history of Danish art.

Especially with regard to *Artemis*, attempts have been made to see a link between Hammershøi and the archaic figure compositions of Pierre Puvis de Chavannes—a notion that has not been properly thought through. It is possible to see *Artemis* as a free paraphrase of classical art, but as in *A Greek Relief*, the painterly content is inseparable from the subtle treatment of light; and despite the two artist's shared predilection for subdued, neutral colors, their fundamental ideas about color are entirely dissimilar. When Hammershøi built up his pictures slowly and laboriously by means of small, sporadically applied brushstrokes, it was in order to capture the tiniest vibrations of light, to balance the different areas of the picture surface in terms of the intensity of light and the color values, and to ensure that the paint was applied evenly and firmly over the entire surface. It was a technique he had taught himself—one cannot find it in the work of any other Danish painter of the time—and it forced him to work so meticulously that at times it tested his patience.

Although it might seem illogical to compare Hammershøi and Georges Seurat, since their use of color could hardly be more different, there is on a deeper structural level a certain similarity between the two artists: they combined their depiction of the tiniest nuances of light with a notion of the objects in a space as fixed, beautifully modeled bodies, clearly defined in a linear sense, and ideally oriented to horizontal and vertical axes parallel to the picture plane—this applies at any rate to early works by Seurat. Both wanted to anchor painting in classical formal values again, and in their landscapes they also combined a refined depiction of light with strict linear composition.

Hammershøi's particular ideas about color were of course also determined by the Danish weather and light with which he had grown up and in which he still lived: summers with blue skies and changing cloud formations; cloud cover;

Following pages:

Ida Hammershøi in front of the double doors in the living room at Bredgade 25, ca. 1912. Det Kongelige Bibliotek, Copenhagen

Vilhelm Hammershøi in front of the double doors in the living room at Bredgade 25, ca. 1912. Det Kongelige Bibliotek, Copenhagen

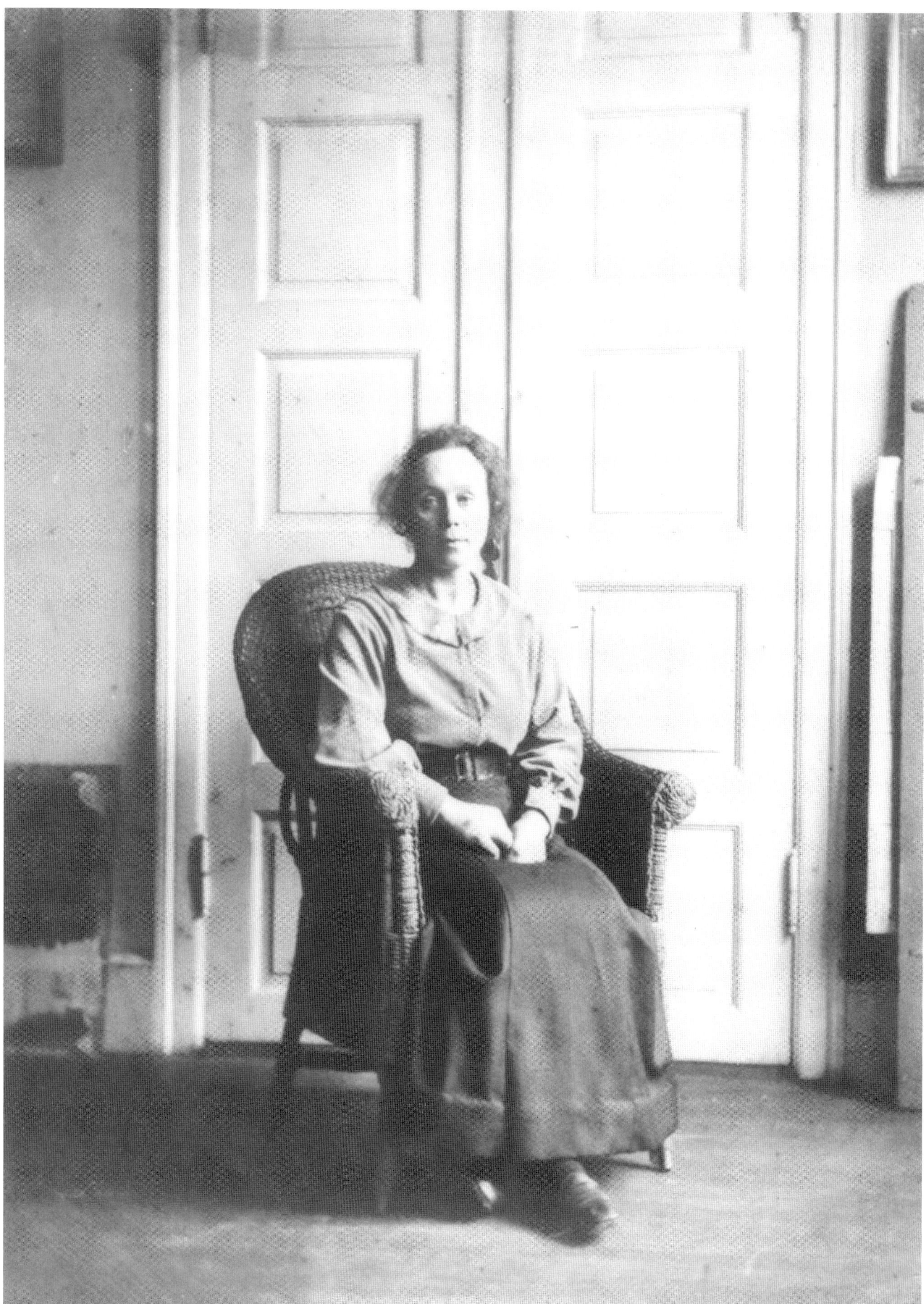

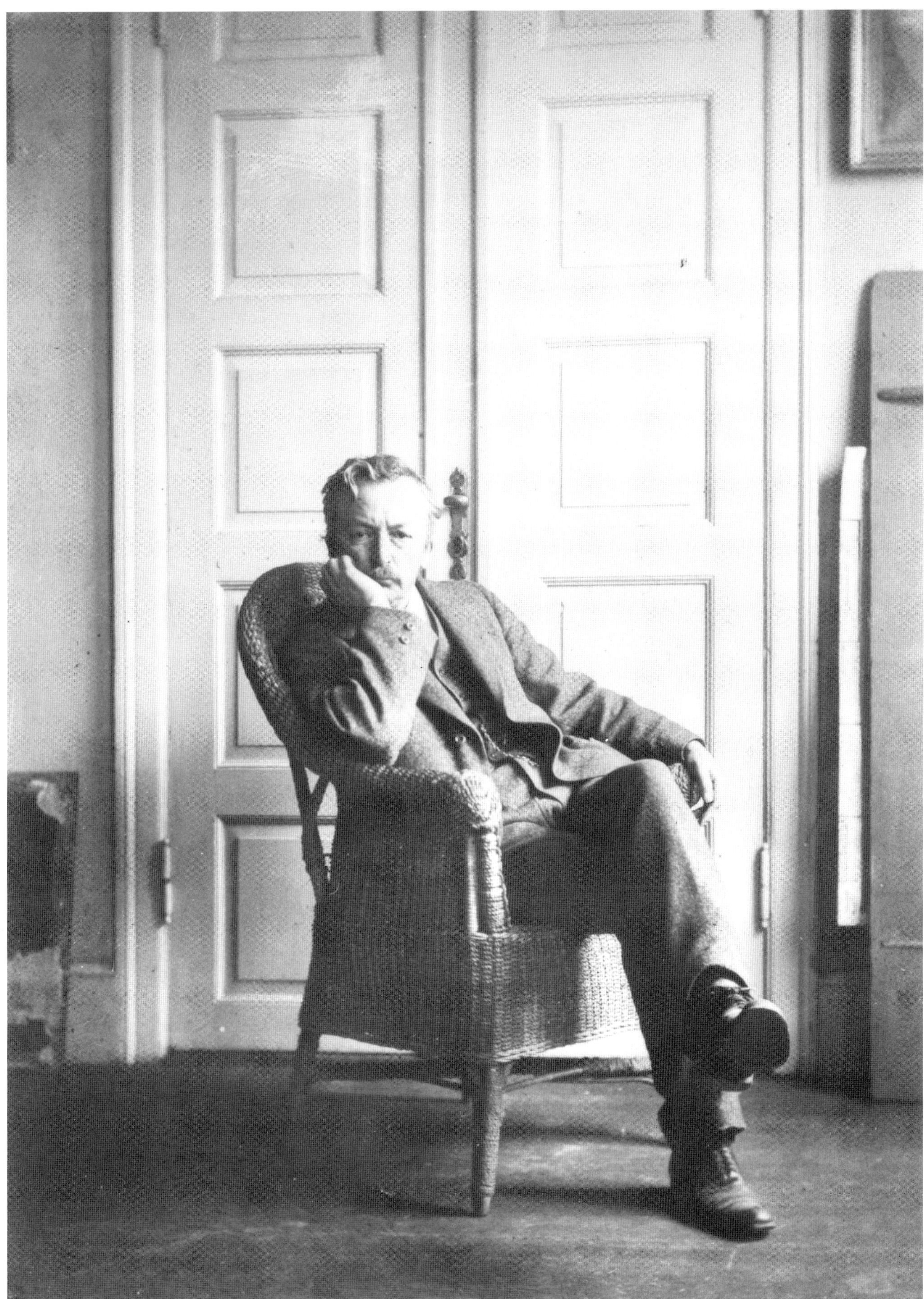

the crystalline clarity of September giving way to long autumn months with heavy, low rain clouds; winter days when snow is transformed from sparkling clarity to a dead, white mass; the spring sunshine that has to struggle for weeks before finally taking over. Hammershøi was a town-dweller, but he usually spent a month or two during the summer painting landscapes out in the countryside, especially in the area around Copenhagen and in intensively farmed and cultivated areas further away, just as the Golden Age painters had done. In his pictures of open landscapes, such as *Landscape* [Kongevej near Gentofte], [1892] (cat. no. 8), and *View of Gentofte Lake,* also called *Sunshower,* 1903 (cat. no. 31), he used a horizontal line—perhaps a road going right across the picture plane, or perhaps the horizon—as his basic compositional principle: the articulation of the picture's width, from one edge of the frame to the other, rather than a dynamic movement into the internal space of the picture (which had dominated northern European landscape painting since the Dutch painters of the seventeenth century), and in contrast to the suggestive depths that in the Romantics—most obviously Caspar David Friedrich—express a vast longing with religious overtones. Depth in Hammershøi is suggested by the brilliantly portrayed aerial perspective in the space before us. But Hammershøi's landscapes and forest scenes have an idiosyncratic, almost purged quality—the foreground is often slightly blurred, containing no detail, as if the painter has not entered the space he is depicting, whereas the middle ground and the delicate cloud formations can stand out with exquisite clarity on the canvas. The landscapes are highly sensual, but they also border on the unreal. Firmly anchored in the present, Hammershøi never renounced the precision of observation—he extracted an essence that is more real than reality, but also alien and at times almost immaterial.

But Hammershøi is first and foremost a town-dweller, and he became Denmark's most important architectural painter. He had grown up and spent his entire life in Copenhagen, which as an architectural milieu, with its stylistically pure neoclassical burgher houses from the eighteenth and early nineteenth centuries, can in general be seen as an intrinsic source of his sense of style. However, in his architectural paintings, Hammershøi concentrated almost exclusively on monumental buildings—castles, mansions, churches—often of great historical and symbolic national significance. And it was precisely this aura of tradition that Hammershøi broke down or at least disregarded, through an eye for and a preoccupation with form that interpreted the buildings primarily as monumental, spatial objects. Through his choice of viewpoint, cropping, and lighting, he gave them a whole new life, replacing their faithful representation with a kind of sublime neutrality and a subtle sense of strangeness produced by slight distortions of their extent and their overall spatial reality. In his enormous painting *View of Amalienborg Square* (cat. no. 12), he depicted that mid-eighteenth-century jewel of Danish architecture with a surprising shift of the center that rudely interrupts the palace's façade. In his architectural pictures, Hammershøi manipulated spatial shifts to extend parts of a building or bring them surprisingly close in a way that is similar to modern cameras' wide-angle lenses and zoom optics. For a few of his architectural pictures (such as *View of the Old Asiatic Company*, 1902; cat. no. 28), where it was impossible for him to work directly in front of the motif from beginning to end, he used photographs to complete them.

The 1890s were also the decade when Hammershøi began to focus on painting interiors, which had been a flourishing genre in Danish painting at the end of the nineteenth century. The bourgeois rooms, the intimacy, the quiet life indoors had been much-loved subjects—especially cultivated, it must be admitted, by painters with rather conservative taste who never achieved any significant status in the history of art. A couple of the best were Hammershøi's friends Carl Holsøe and Peter Ilsted, his brother-in-law.

Hammershøi, who depended for subjects almost entirely on the rooms around him, moved during the autumn of 1898 into an apartment in one of the oldest of Copenhagen's burgher houses, built in about 1636 in the district of Christianshavn, which had just been newly constructed. Christianshavn's docks, street canals, and seventeenth- and eighteenth-century buildings have something about them of the old Dutch urban culture that Hammershøi loved. He found architectural motifs there, but the apartment was the richest source for his picture-creating imagination. The rooms, in various dimensions and with late Baroque and neoclassical details, and with light streaming into them in different directions, offered him an inexhaustible supply of motifs on which he never tired of producing variations during the eleven years he lived there. The result was a series of important works throughout the entire period. They were to him what fruit arrangements were to Cézanne: the artistic meditations on these rooms and the light in them were preoccupied with the essence of things. But while Cézanne used color to fuse light, volume, and space together into a dynamic whole, Hammershøi sought the fleeting quality of light amidst the static geometry of the different planes.

Around the turn of the century, the typical home was filled with furniture, lamps, bric-a-brac, window curtains, door curtains, and pictures. In contrast, the rooms in Hammershøi's apartment were spartan in their furnishings, with a few select pieces of Empire furniture on the large and otherwise empty floors, a small number of exquisite pictures on the walls, a single piece of eighteenth-century Copenhagen porcelain, and beautifully bound books (Hammershøi was a book collector). Thus, through a conscious aesthetic choice, he put his personal stamp on the circumscribed reality that served as the starting point for his pictures: these rooms were his studio.

In his depictions of the play of light on the walls, floors, and doors, or as back light entering the room, Hammershøi reached a pinnacle of tonal refinement. Despite the pictures' obvious debt to seventeenth-century Dutch paintings of interiors, especially to Vermeer and Gerard Terborch, they are anything but a Romantic cult of a vanished epoch. Hammershøi was a cool observer, a pictorial phenomenologist, who explored not only the play of light on the expansive surfaces and the sparse furnishings but space itself, which appears to become larger in both depth and breadth in his pictures. He conveyed an impression of a pervasive emptiness, partly by leaving the foreground empty in many pictures: the bare floor crying out for someone to walk on it, but never being walked on.

The black-clad female figure who is occasionally seen, often with her back to the viewer, does not fill the emptiness but instead emphasizes it. She has the same neutral quality of an object as a chair or a table has; but she is no doll, no mannequin like the figures in Balthus's strange pictures. This comes across most clearly in the works in which a half-length female figure with her back to us is the principal motif, while the interior is merely suggested by a wall plus the corner of a table or a picture. These undemanding and apparently uncomplicated pictures, which radiate female sensuality, are among the most beautiful in Hammershøi's oeuvre.

In a painting from 1898, Hammershøi seriously turned the third dimension, depth, into a primary expressive element in his art—and he continued to explore it in the interiors he painted around the turn of the century. During a visit to London in 1897–98, Hammershøi painted a picture which he called *Two Figures (The Artist and His Wife)* (cat. no. 16), which is really the start of a new chapter in his artistic development: it represents in the right foreground a male figure with his back to us and, on the other side of a table covered with a white cloth, a woman against a dark, almost black background. The horizontal plane of the table separates the two and at the same time appears to form a base on which the female figure rests; she has the ideal beauty of a fifteenth-century Florentine bust. The way in which the picture is cropped close around the figures, especially the husband leaning into the picture, can, together with the extreme simplification, remind one of Japanese woodcuts (see also *Landscape in Snow* [Søndermarken], 1895–96, cat. no. 11). But the confined space creates a sense of claustrophobia, and is filled with a darkness that eats its way into the figures as though about to engulf them. The striking green color, particularly in the faces—which can also be seen in many of his pictures from later years—is like the very negation of blood pulsating in our veins and of the vital warmth that comes from the sun.

Hammershøi himself rated this picture very highly and must have realized that it was a landmark in his oeuvre. There is a direct line of development leading from *Two Figures* in 1898 (cat. no. 16) to the monumental masterpiece *Five Portraits* in 1902 (cat. no. 26) and the two moving portraits of Ida in 1907 (cat. nos. 52 and 53).

Five Portraits, which has the character of a grand and somber vision, can again be seen as a paraphrase of older art: seventeenth-century Dutch group portraits (classical representations of the Last Supper have also been suggested), subjected to a ruthless reinterpretation replacing the theme of fellowship with that of mutual isolation. It is a picture that is full of unease and mysterious, stimulating paradoxes: the large feet sticking up in the foreground; the figure at the far left turning his back on the others; the fixed eyes staring at us. The picture is surreal: the sources of light do not explain the long, uniformly illuminated surface of the table, the slight tilt of which seems to make the room appear dangerously unstable, despite the solidity conveyed by the large male bodies dressed in black. The models were Hammershøi's friends, but the picture cannot be equated with a genre that was popular in European painting around the turn of the century—that is, the group portrait of artists gathered together because they constitute an artistic community. In that sense, there is no particular program that Hammershøi's picture is meant to express, and, in any case, it would have been completely alien to him to think in terms of a "group," for he was an individualist, and so were the men portrayed—thus the title!

Five Portraits was considered quite shocking when it was first exhibited in Copenhagen in 1902—especially the large feet, which upset many people. But it attracted positive attention at the Venice Biennale in 1903; and in 1904, when it was exhibited in the Secession in Berlin, Lothar Brieger-Wasserfogel wrote in his review of the exhibition in the *Gazette des Beaux-Arts* (Sept. 1, 1905, p. 258): "The Dane Hammershøi, a brand-new painter, only exhibits a single work, but it is a masterpiece."

With its claustrophobic space, its nocturnal darkness, and its two shining candles, *Five Portraits* expresses a melancholy that is also part of European tradition; and it combines a modern, individualistic sensibility with a classic striving for form. Although Hammershøi is a Scandinavian artist by definition, his painting is in many respects fundamentally different from contemporaneous painting in Norway and Sweden. This is partly because of Denmark's special painting tradition and partly because, as the capital city in a populous small country, Copenhagen is more closely related to Amsterdam than to Oslo or Stockholm—and it is the culture of Copenhagen that forms Hammershøi's intellectual background. And because northern European or perhaps even central European urban culture underlies Hammershøi's *Five Portraits,* it is not surprising that his art should speak powerfully to a major central European writer.

In the autumn of 1904, Austrian poet Rainer Maria Rilke (1875–1926) spent a lengthy period in Skåne (in southwestern Sweden just opposite Copenhagen). He visited Copenhagen several times with the principal objective of studying Hammershøi's art, which had made a deep impression on him. He met Hammershøi and planned to write an essay on the Danish artist, whom he considered to be a genius. Rilke must have regarded him as an artist whose aims were parallel to, or confirmed, his own during these years when he was working on his greatest prose work, *The Notebooks of Malthe Laurids Brigge* (the principal character of which is a Dane), and his celebrated cycle of *New Poems* that strove to achieve objectivity with "thing-poems" (*Dinggedichte*) and thus marked his break with Germanic Romantic idealism. In a letter from Paris a year later,

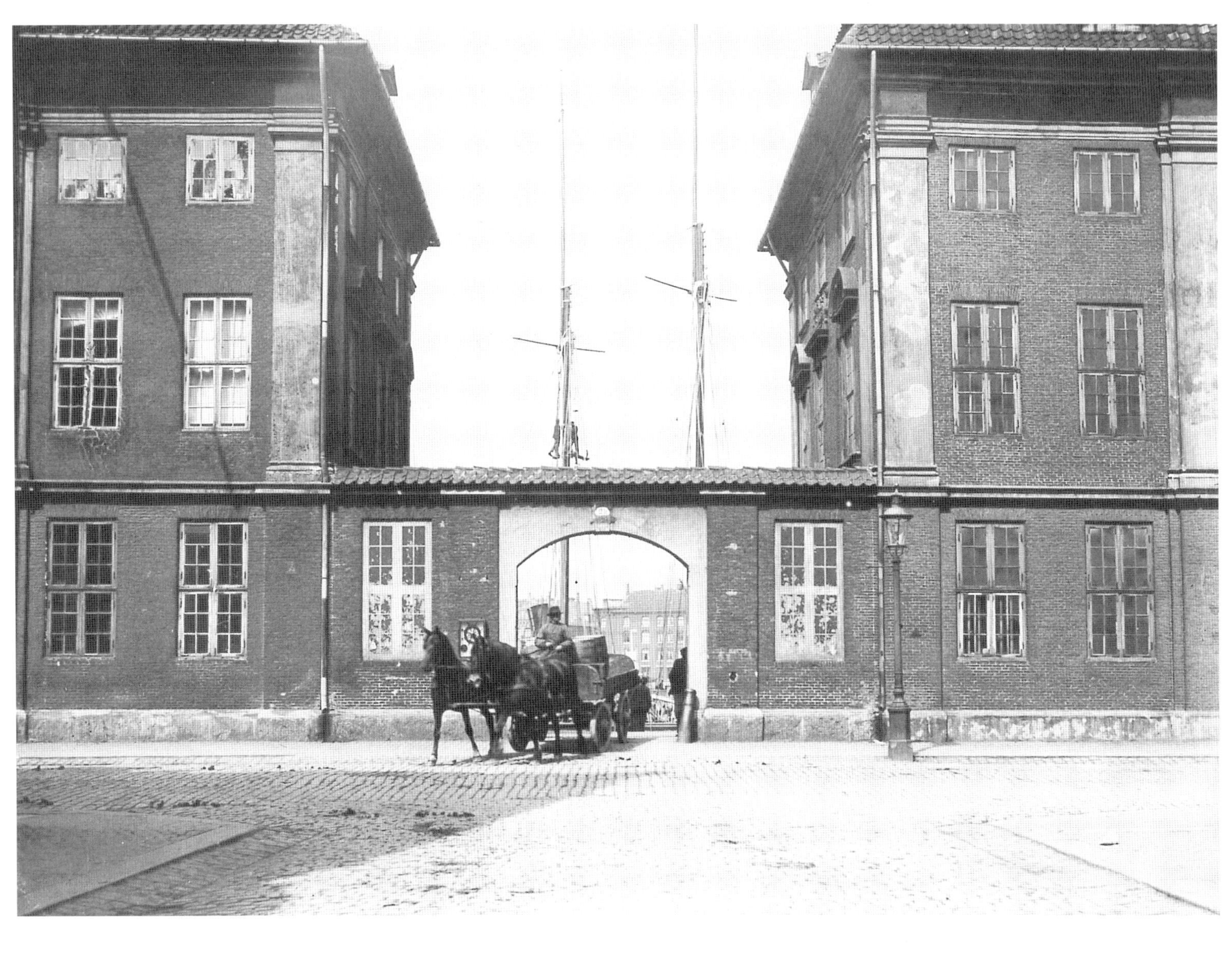

The entryway to the Asiatic Company dock, Strandgade 25, 1902. Københavns Bymuseum, Copenhagen

he still expressed his firm intention to write about Hammershøi—but his nomadic life as a poet never took him back to Copenhagen and Hammershøi.

Hammershøi's journeys abroad always involved visits to major cities: he sought culture, not nature, on these trips. And it is characteristic of his work's dependence on light and on his experience of the "spirit of the place" that during his visits to foreign countries he found his motifs indoors and in the storehouses of artistic inheritance: the collection of Greek antiquities in the Louvre in Paris in 1891 (cat. no. 7), and one of the rooms of ancient Greek art in the British Museum in London in 1897 (cat. no. 15), although he eventually stopped working on the latter picture because the room had become too dark; and when he was in Rome in the winter of 1902–03, he found his motif—typically enough, after searching for several weeks—in the fifth-century church of Santo Stefano Rotundo (cat. no. 30) and painted a wonderfully subtle and poetic picture of the light and the circular movement in the static space.

Hammershøi developed a very special relationship with London. He had visited there in 1897–98 (his reason for doing so remains unknown); and after making the acquaintance of English concert pianist Leonard Borwick in Copenhagen in 1903, he returned to London more often. Borwick admired Hammershøi's art, and at his invitation Hammershøi again visited London in 1904 (accompanied, as always, by Ida). Further visits, some short and some longer, followed in 1905–06 and on several occasions between 1911 and 1913. During the visit in 1905–06 he painted his first London motif, a sure sign that he now felt at home with the city and its light. He found an apartment from where he could look out toward the British Museum and painted a strikingly foreshortened view of its façade (cat. no. 44), and a view of Montague Street (cat. no. 43) that includes a corner of the museum, the long row of houses facing the side of the museum, and autumn trees—the only street scene in the whole of his oeuvre, permeated with true urban melancholy and just as subtle in its depiction of the street as his evocation of indoor space in his interior scenes.

In 1907 an eminent English critic of art and literature, Arthur Clutton-Brock, wrote what was perhaps the most clear-sighted critical evaluation of Hammershøi to appear during his lifetime. It was published under the title "A New Master" in a review of a major Danish art exhibition in London. Clutton-Brock perceived the influence of Vermeer in Hammershøi's work, but also had a sense of Hammershøi's originality ("His light is even cooler and more silvery than Vermeer's"), of his sophisticated execution and his unforced sensitivity:

> His little picture, "Resting" (cat. no. 39), a picture of a girl with her back towards us, is a miracle of just and simplified drawing. There is no emphasis in it anywhere, no attempt at a graceful pose, and yet no dullness or ugliness. Like Vermeer's finest works, it seems to be taken direct from Nature, yet it has all the distinction of a beautiful style. Like Vermeeer, he seems to solve a mathematical problem, so exact and lucid is his design; and yet he does not treat objects as if they were merely there for the light to play upon them.

In an interview that same year, Hammershøi described in simple, straightforward terms what he emphasized when painting a picture, and his account supports Clutton-Brock's observations:

> What makes me choose a motif is as much the lines in it, what I would call the architectural stance in the picture. And then the light, of course. It is naturally also very important, but the lines are almost what I am most taken by. Color is not of secondary importance, I suppose; I am not indifferent to how it looks in color, I work very hard to make it harmonious. But when I choose a motif I think I mainly look at the lines.

As Hammershøi did not allow himself to change the lines in the motif in front of him—whether it was architecture or an interior—his choice of viewpoint, and thus the way in which the motif was to be cropped, was crucial to achieving the perfect dynamic balance he always sought. This also explains why he often painted a motif on a bigger canvas than the simple reproduction of it demanded, so that while working on a picture he could extend his field of vision if the harmony he was striving for made it necessary.

A couple of important pictures from 1907 show Hammershøi engaged on adding a new aspect to his art. In the two portraits of his wife from that year (cat. nos. 52 and 53), he modeled the volume of the head and the body as well as the white cup three-dimensionally. It is typical of Hammershøi that he devoted equal attention to each element: Ida's disillusioned face, portrayed earnestly but tenderly, is no more important than the cup and saucer, which glow with a luminous beauty. The classically inclined artist invests feeling in perfection of form and thereby makes both the figure and the inanimate object grow in significance.

Hammershøi's emphasis on volume culminated around 1909–10 in two pictures of a standing nude female model that proved to be Hammershøi's last large-scale works. In 1889 he had painted a seated model (cat. no. 5), a major early work, in which the full body's sensuality contrasts with the awkward and uncomfortable black chair; and the head, with the hair gathered up and the eyes half closed, is the very image of undeveloped sexuality. The standing nude model in an interior (cat. no. 64) has lowered her head and moved an arm across her breasts to conceal them, as though painfully aware of the observing eyes in the adjoining room—which only further emphasizes her dark pubic hair (which is beautifully and carefully painted) as the focal point of the picture. But it was the first time that Hammershøi, who had painted numerous seated figures, portrayed a large-scale standing figure. (*Artemis* does not count, because its figures are not shown in a real space.) In changing to an upright format, he brought a new dimension into his art, both literally and figuratively. Hammershøi has given magnificent painterly expression to the interplay between the hard, black door frame—which extends from the top to the bottom of the picture—and the body's sensual outline; and the weight of the heavy door curtain on the right makes the woman seem to float, at the same time that she remains standing solidly on the floor.

In 1909, Hammershøi and Ida had to leave the apartment at Strandgade 30, but after moving in and out of a couple of other apartments—still in the central part of Copenhagen—they returned to the same street in 1913, this time to a beautiful apartment in the Baroque building belonging to the Asiatic Company, the façade of which had provided the motif for several pictures (cat. nos. 27, 28, and 51). In this apartment, he painted yet another series of beautiful interiors, including one of a view through the open doors of four rooms, in which the light from the large windows on one side of the high-ceilinged rooms is conveyed by a lighter, sometimes chalky shade of white that is new in his art. And in 1914, Hammershøi began a large-scale picture with Ida as his model. Through a more dynamic composition that pointed toward other potential new developments (which were never realized), it suggests undiminished sensual excitement as well as a freer movement in space.

The opposition from conservative forces in Danish artistic life that Hammershøi had encountered in his youth had long been overcome. By 1905 he had already had a successful solo exhibition in Berlin and other cities in Germany, where his fame had continued to grow. The award of first prize in an international art exhibition in Rome in 1911 increased it further, although Hammershøi appeared to care as little about such successes as he had the disappointments and adversity that he had experienced during his youth. His final years, though, were very difficult. His mother's death in 1914 and the outbreak of World War I that same year had a profound effect on him. On top of that, he felt increasingly fatigued, a condition that turned out to have a fatal cause: cancer of the throat. And after a long and painful illness, he died on February 13, 1916, at the age of just fifty-two years old. Ida survived him by many years, and finally died in 1949.

Hammershøi's untimely death, together with the long-term political and cultural repercussions of World War I—one of which was to break the hitherto fruitful links between Denmark (and the rest of Scandinavia) and central Europe via Germany—destroyed any possibility of widespread public awareness and understanding of his art for decades afterward. He was isolated in a time pocket and in a local tradition that was defined as peripheral in relation to a small number of normative centers, which made it impossible to see his art for what it was: a distinguished, independent contribution to the culture of visual art in Europe at the turn of the century and during the early decades of the new century.

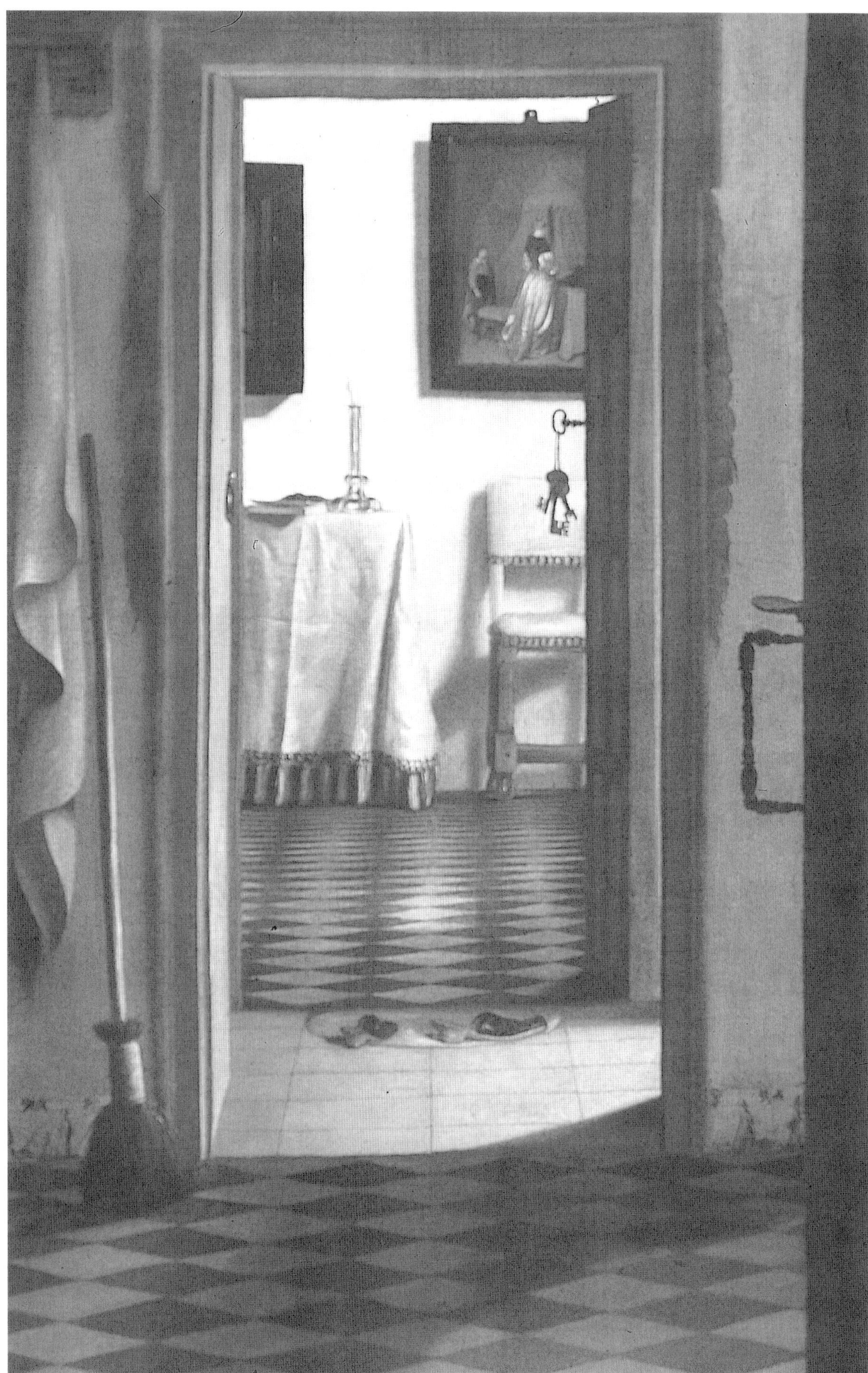

Vilhelm Hammershøi, at Home and Abroad

Robert Rosenblum

It has long been believed that late-19th-century Scandinavia produced only one artist, Edvard Munch, whose work held an emotional power so gripping that his vision, like Freud's explorations of the unconscious, appeared to transcend national boundaries. Anyone anywhere who had ever experienced the melancholy of solitude, the anxiety of urban pressures, the slow death of a family member, or the fires of sex could respond to Munch, and the fact that he came from Norway seemed almost incidental to his achievement.

But in the late twentieth century, the question of art as a universal language versus art that has distinctive national accents has come into focus again as we begin once more to value the regional and the personal, and perhaps to raise them above the universal. Can it be that our planet's growing uniformity, with its global chains of shops, hotels, restaurants, and airports, has reawakened the need for cultural diversity, and that instead of feeling that Coca-Cola, McDonald's, and Holiday Inn are making the world less daunting to travelers, we long for a time when crossing national borders meant entering totally unfamiliar territories? Politically speaking, there are, of course, frightening aspects to these efforts at resurrecting cultural roots. Whether in the United States or Canada, Bosnia or the Baltic, Spain or Ireland, such assertions of ethnic differences can quickly turn into hatred. But in the less violent domain of art history, the consequences of this revived interest in nationalism have produced not wars, but a greater awareness both of the international orchestration of modern art as well as of the national voices of individual players. Kandinsky and Mondrian may have elevated

Samuel van Hoogstraten, *Interior*, or *The Slippers*.
Oil on canvas, 103 x 70 cm. The Louvre, Paris

us to a new kind of extraterrestrial space, but these days we are also concerned with their Russian and Dutch roots.

Our growing fascination with national diversity has been particularly fruitful for art of the nineteenth century, an epoch that marked some of the most exalted as well as the most bloody resurgences of cultural identity; and in the last twenty years, traveling exhibitions have brought to foreign audiences a broad sampling of what nineteenth-century painting looked like in, for example, Hungary, Belgium, Italy, Poland, and Portugal. Among these many efforts to broaden awareness of national traditions, two exhibitions of Scandinavian painting loomed large: first, *Northern Light: Realism and Symbolism in Scandinavian Painting 1880–1910*, which traveled around the United States in 1982–83;[1] and then, *Dreams of a Summer Night: Scandinavian Painting at the Turn of the Century*, shown in London, Düsseldorf, and Paris in 1986–87.[2] Featuring painters from Iceland, Norway, Denmark, Sweden, and Finland, both these exhibitions increased audience awareness of a world of Scandinavian art beyond Munch, and made clear that Munch's work, though towering in its genius, nevertheless emerged from a large community of artists who often shared his themes and passions. Among these artists, several were instantly singled out by new spectators as creating private domains of unforgettable power that fit closely into a general Scandinavian mood of lonely confrontations with an irrational world, whether of nature or of buried human emotions. At the same time, these artists showed notable affinities with their contemporaries working in many other countries. One of them, Swedish playwright August Strindberg, was a passionate amateur painter capable of expressing the infinity of nature's chaos in small but turbulent landscape and marine paintings. Another, a Dane, was Vilhelm Hammershøi, an artist with an uncanny ability to re-create the Dutch realist tradition of immaculate and prosperous domestic interiors in modern spaces so chillingly silent and empty that their lone residents seem to be entombed—as if the women who once graced the paintings of Jan Vermeer or Pieter de Hooch had become widowed or depressed, never again to leave their four walls.

Well-known in Denmark,[3] where his stature now rivals that of the most famous Danish painter of the early nineteenth century, Christen Købke (who also moved recently from national to international recognition in art history and whose work is also being acquired by foreign museums), Hammershøi is a painter whose intensely personal achievements were only first recognized here in 1983, with two small-scale exhibitions in New York and Washington, D.C.[4] Yet the work surely merits full-scale exposure beyond his native realm.

Because Hammershøi's best-known works are meticulous renderings of the late-eighteenth-century interiors of an historic, seventeenth-century house at Strandgade 30, where he lived from 1898 to 1900, we may at first think of him as a hermit in the midst of Copenhagen. Indeed, the paintings suggest an artist who has isolated himself in a monk's cell and taken vows to remain at home and look at nothing but his own doors, walls, windows, and, on occasion, a gloomy view of the narrow courtyard. But this image of an ascetic recluse is belied by his biography and his international exhibition record. By the time of his first trip to Paris in 1889 on the occasion of the Exposition Universelle, which included four of his paintings, he had already made several visits to the major art cities of Germany, Holland, and Belgium; and in 1891–92, he spent six months back in Paris. Soon after, what must have been a rich exposure to the old masters as well as to contemporary art of the 1880s and 1890s expanded further. In the fall of 1893, he traveled to Italy on a scholarship from Copenhagen's Kunstakademiet, returning in 1902–03 for a longer sojourn in Rome. In addition, he made repeated visits to London, the residence of one of his idols, James Abbott McNeill Whistler, whose work taught him much about the nuances of grisaille and the aestheticizing of plane geometry. One of his primary goals in London was to meet this modern master,[5] whose mixture of realist observation and abstract pattern was more sympathetic to him than much of the chromatically rich and seductive avant-garde painting he had seen in France,[6] but this encounter never took place. Hammershøi's London sojourns began during the winter months of 1897–98, when the gray, sunless skies cast the same melancholic spell they did in Copenhagen. He returned to these skies in the winters of 1905–06 and 1912–13, each time taking up residence near the British Museum, whose façade and nearby streets he depicted without a single pedestrian in sight (cat. nos. 43 and 44).

Just as his frequent travels must have acquainted him with the broadest range of old and new art, so, too, did they help to spread his fame internationally. His work appeared in many European exhibitions, some thoroughly international, as in Paris (Expositions Universelles, 1889 and 1900) Munich (Jahresausstellung, 1891, and Sezession, 1904), Berlin (Sezession, 1900), Venice (Biennale, 1903), and Rome (Esposizione Internazionale de Belle Arti, 1911), and others restricted to Scandinavian art (St. Petersburg, 1897, and New York, Buffalo, Toledo, Chicago, Boston, 1912–13) or to Danish art (London, 1907). In 1912 he was invited by the Uffizi to add his own self-portrait to their venerable encyclopedia of artist's self-portraits, an honor he shared with his own Danish teacher Peder Krøyer and the French painter with whom Krøyer had studied, Léon Bonnat. It is telling that some of his most distinguished admirers were foreigners with pan-European taste: Austrian poet Rainer Maria Rilke; Russian ballet impresario Sergei Diaghilev; and French critic Théodore Duret. If Hammershøi gives the impression of having been trapped with his wife, Ida, for endless winters in his bleak Copenhagen apartment, he might also fit Degas's characterization of Gustave Moreau as a hermit who knew the railway schedules.

So it is that, while recognizing the Danish accent of Hammershøi's insular universe, we may also locate him within a surprisingly varied community of international artists, especially when we realize that his ambitions occasionally reached far beyond the constraints of depicting Copenhagen interiors to embrace a world of ideal nudity and ancient narrative. Already in 1887, he essayed the biblical theme of Job in a painting, which, because of Hammershøi's use of bitumen, apparently darkened to near invisibility. However, its impact may be glimpsed in a related drawing (ill. p. 13) that explores the psychological potential of casting a Caravaggesque light on this naked symbol of human suffering and endurance. Hammershøi may well have been offering a personal response to a famous painting of Job by his own master's teacher, Bonnat, which was shown at the Salon of 1880 (ill. p. 37).[7] But in place of that French artist's theatrical hyperrealism of anatomy, emotions, and chiaroscuro, Hammershøi has substituted curiously archaic stylizations that, as in Egyptian or early Greek sculpture, impose rudimentary geometric patterns upon the nude body and the raking light, with results that give this immobilized figure a mysterious aura of remote antiquity and psychological seclusion. And as with so many of Hammershøi's drawings, we may also discern here affinities with Georges Seurat's granular light and schematic planes and volumes—affinities that, as Kirk Varnedoe has suggested,[8] can be expanded to include many other parallels between the Dane and his French contemporary. Both artists, for instance, reveal a taste for what were considered "primitive" phases of art history—Egyptian art, archaic Greek art, early Italian Renaissance painting. In this context, Hammershøi provides an extraordinary document of the late-nineteenth-century search for stylistic regression. During his 1891 stay in Paris, the art that he selected for prolonged scrutiny at the Louvre was not the Venus de Milo but a pair of archaic Greek reliefs depicting *Apollo and the Nymphs* and *Hermes and the Three Graces*.[9] Choosing a part rather than a whole, he replicated the trio of gift-bearing figures at the left of the Hermes relief—the personifications of beauty, charm, and grace (cat. no. 7).[10] Copying art in a museum was, of course, the most familiar of academic practices, but Hammershøi's painting is something totally different, a personal reincarnation of the ancient marble's ritualistic magic, a meditation comparable to Rilke's poetic response in 1908 to another archaic sculpture at the Louvre, the torso of a *kouros*. Muffled in Hammershøi's painting by a diffuse, gray light, the marble relief takes on the quality of a melancholic dream, capturing that mood of nostalgia for a lost classical world which so often inspired the revival of Greek art in northern Europe, particularly in Denmark, with its strong tradition for seeking a fundamental purity in the earliest forms of antique sculpture, painting, and architecture. Predictably for a Dane, Hammershøi had already in 1882 copied one of Bertel Thorvaldsen's neoclassical reliefs, *Priam Begging Achilles for the Body of Hector*[11] and he naturally knew that touchstone of nineteenth-century architectural archaism, Gottlieb Bindesbøll's Thorvaldsen Museum in the heart of Copenhagen. And in the summer of 1911, he rented a house, Spurveskjul, that had been designed by Denmark's most prominent neoclassical painter and interior designer, Nicolai Abildgaard. Hammershøi's totally faithful but equally imaginative veneration of the archaic relief in the Louvre extends this Danish neoclassical tradition still further.[12]

Surprisingly, this Parisian painting of 1891 contains echoes of the art of Seurat, who had died in February of that year. In works such as the *Grande Jatte*, Seurat had demonstrated how a modern painter could absorb from Egyptian and Greek antiquities at the Louvre a new sense of grave, ceremonial procession measured by figures whose profiled bodies transform empirical fact into evocative symbol. Two years later, Hammershøi's own archaizing dreams became even more complex, as expressed in the ostensibly minimal but densely layered figural fantasy of 1893–94, titled *Artemis* (cat. no. 10). Now, these solemn, slow rhythms reawaken not only the beginnings of Greek art, with postures recalling parts of the Louvre relief not included in his copy, but also of Italian art, paralleling Seurat's attraction to the lucid geometries of such Quattrocento masters as Piero della Francesco. Here, the inspiration is clearly the Adam and Eve cycle by Masaccio and Masolino in the Brancacci Chapel, which Hammershøi had seen in Florence in 1893 and had preserved back home in his collection of art photographs.[13] Reviving the fundamental simplicities of the Italian fresco tradition as defined by Giotto (whom he considered the greatest of all), Hammershøi here strips his background to the barest trinity of flat planes and resurrects for his figures the primordial clarity of Masolino's and Masaccio's vision of the first man and woman. But as with the earlier re-creation of an archaic Greek relief, what we see here is a private meditation on the elemental mysteries of a remote and dead world, experienced in a modern reverie of nostalgia and desire. Sharing the Symbolist goals that dominated so much of Western art in the 1890s, Hammershøi hoped to attain a new territory of fragile, ambiguous evocation in which nothing could have a fixed meaning. The figures themselves, which at first echo the sculptural modeling of a Florentine fresco, are dimmed by the pervasive pale tones of beige and gray, giving them the weathered look of a painted relic that has survived over the centuries and that, in view of the cropping of the figures' arms, left and right, suggests a fragment of a much wider frieze.

No less elusive is the narrative. It is only the minimal attribute of a crescent moon over the head of Artemis, the central nude referred to in the title, an identity that in turn would make the nude male object of her gaze correspond to Endymion, who, standing rather than sleeping, is nevertheless totally self-absorbed, averting his somnolent eyes from the goddess. But references to the first temptation in the Garden of Eden, enforced by allusions to the Brancacci Chapel, are equally present, not only in the pairing of the central figures, who evoke Masaccio's *Expulsion*, but above all in the male nude, whose posture is oddly identical with Masolino's Eve and who conveys, with his ample chest and minimized genitals, an aura of androgyny familiar to the sexual blurring of much Symbolist art. And moving from classical and biblical narratives of sexual desire, Artemis also enters the more generalized world of erotic awakenings, best known in Munch's many variations on the themes of puberty or the three stages of a woman's life, an unfolding sequence of sexual magnetism also suggested by the postures of what might be called Hammershøi's Three Graces. But characteristically, Hammershøi's exploration of what appears to be a sexual narrative remains on a subliminal level, immersing us in a twilight dream of unfulfilled longings, the equivalent of the emotions we might project into the lonely, earthbound figures forever trapped in the austere enclosures of a Copenhagen apartment.

Hammershøi's treatment of the nude in *Artemis* deserves comment, too. Generally speaking, it belongs to an international community of efforts to express the inexpressible through new variations of posture, gesture, and thought as conveyed through the traditions of the ideal nude. Painters as diverse as Pierre Puvis de Chavannes and Ferdinand Hodler (both of whose works Hammershøi must have seen in Paris) come to mind, with their mural ambitions and heraldic figure groupings; and looking ahead, one may even be reminded of Picasso's neoclassical nudes, with their enigmatic physical and psychological weight. But Hammershøi's treatment of the naked body also has a distinctly Danish inflection that is found as well in his more conventional studies of the nude, such as the seated female figure of 1889 (cat. no. 5). Looking backwards, the introspective stillness of these figures, as well as their peculiar stylizations of swollen, rounded volumes and cold, abstract surfaces, can be seen in the many academic studies of nudes by Christoffer Wilhelm Eckersberg and his students or, looking ahead, in the Machine Age nudes of Vilhelm Lundstrøm.[14]

Of course, a comparable Danish ancestry can also be traced for Hammershøi's best-known canvases—not timeless nudes, but time-bound and space-bound domestic interiors. Many little paintings from Denmark's so-called Golden Age of painting (the first half of the nineteenth century) by such artists as Wilhelm Bendz or Christen Dalsgaard had already presented Biedermeier versions of this dollhouse world of immaculate rooms, at times with window views to a beckoning, luminous outdoors. Ultimately, this tradition harks back to seventeenth-century Dutch painting, from which Hammershøi derived a rich variety of motifs. But the uncanny silence and inertia of Hammershøi's interiors have the closest affinities not with Dutch or Danish painting, but with the work of a German Romantic master, Caspar David Friedrich. In this context, it is revealing to look at one of Friedrich's most famous canvases, *Woman by the Window*, 1822 (ill. p. 37), and to realize how much of Hammershøi's spatial and emotional world is prefigured here. Friedrich's image is also based on the most closely observed personal realities. The room is part of his home in Dresden (An der Elbe 33) where he had been living for two years, and the woman seen from behind is not anonymous but his wife, Caroline Bommer, whom he had married four years earlier. We might almost be at Strandgade 30 with Hammershøi's new wife, Ida Ilsted, whom Hammershøi painted in 1890 in a virtual reprise of Friedrich's image (ill. p. 41).[15]

Léon Bonnat, *Job*; exhibited in the Salon of 1880, Paris.
Oil on canvas, 162 x 130 cm. Musée des Beaux-Arts, Bayonne

Caspar David Friedrich, *Woman at a Window*, 1822. Oil on canvas, 44 x 130 cm.
Staatliche Museen zu Berlin, Preußischer Kulturbesitz, Nationalgalerie

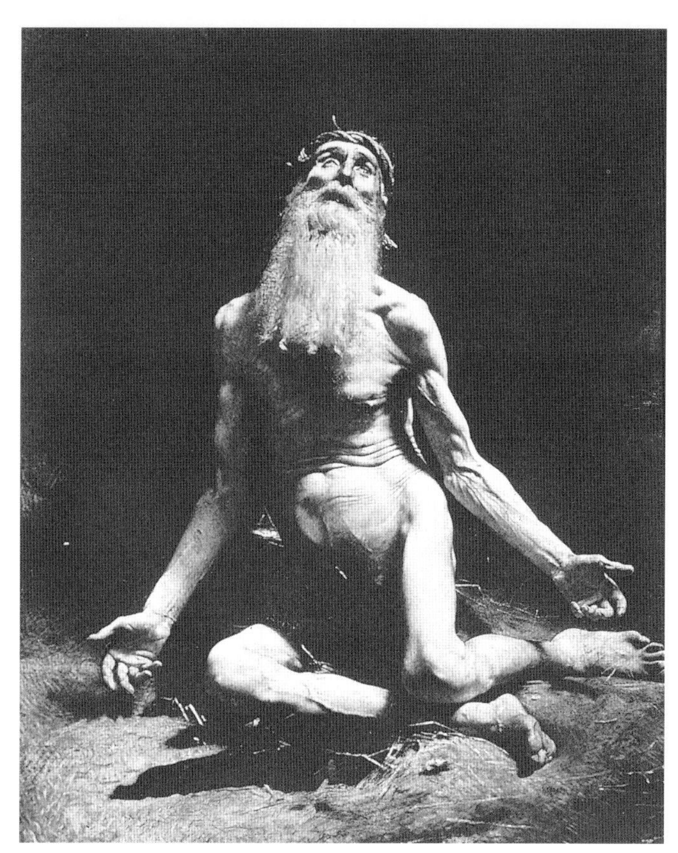

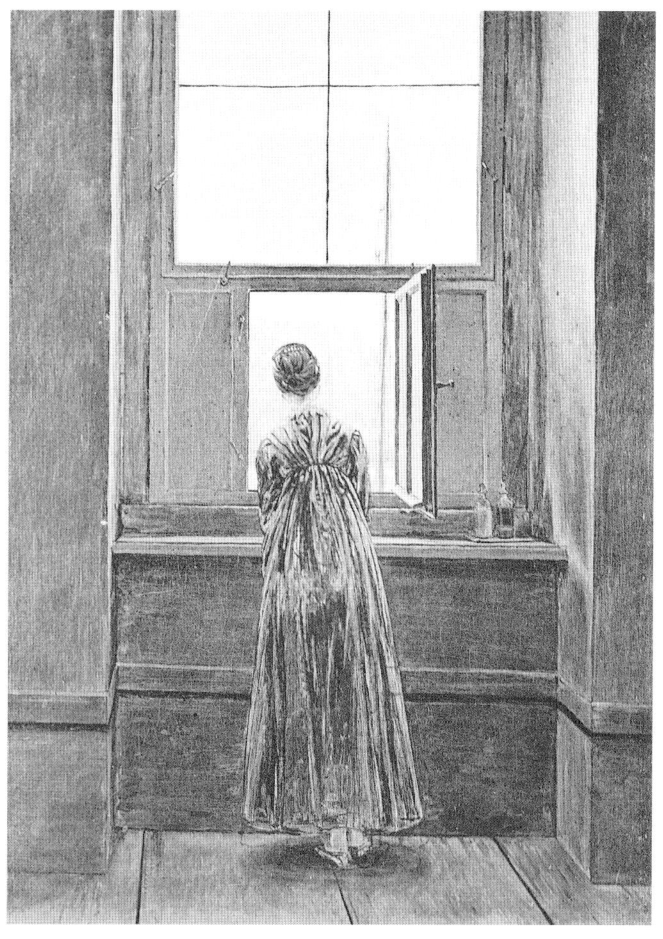

What we see of the bare room seems at once a protective shell and a prison, a construction underlined by the window view that discloses the fragment of a boat's mast and rigging on the river outside, an evocation of a voyage that may take place only in the woman's imagination. Moreover, the oblique cropped view familiar to most Dutch domestic interiors has been replaced by a frontal view, framed by the near symmetry of the walls and windows. This important shift of axis further immobilizes the figure and creates a poignant gulf between near and far, between the palpable world of the enclosing room and a dreamlike beyond that lies across the threshold of reality. As Poul Vad suggested in his monograph on Hammershøi, Friedrich's symmetry and symbolic use of a window view are related to our understanding of the late-nineteenth-century artist.[16] Indeed, both painters succeeded in transforming the conviviality and material pleasures of Dutch seventeenth-century interiors into shrines of private melancholy. A lone figure seen from behind, whose presence in a Terborch or a de Hooch might seem casual and psychologically neutral, can become for both Friedrich and Hammershøi a mysterious psychological void meant to be filled by our own fantasies. And the cheerful, prosperous interiors of the Dutch are turned into monastic cells with bare windows pierced by pure rectangles of cold sunlight. The children the Hammershøis never had would be impossible intruders in these silent spaces.

In the way that many aspects of Symbolist art revive Romantic goals, it is worth noting, too, how often Hammershøi's city views and landscapes re-create Friedrich's mystical aura. In the objective, yet almost ghostly rendering of the Asiatic Company buildings just outside Hammershøi's home (1902; cat. no. 28), we almost feel that we have stepped out of Friedrich's window view onto the street to confront yet another confining threshold that fills the spectator with unfulfilled longings. Once more, the frontality and symmetry of these maritime buildings force the viewer into a fixed position, as if before an altar whose central motif is an arch which, in turn, blocks us from the ship, visible only as a cropped fragment of mast and rigging that extends above the upper frame. Living in cities filled with ships and waterways, both painters must have seen such sights every day, yet both had the imaginative power to turn their local harbors into docks that crossed the boundary between public facts and private fictions. Even the more fully descriptive view of the Greenland Trading Company Dock at Christianshavn (1908; cat. no. 59) revives Friedrich's spirit. As rendered by Hammershøi, this site of busy commerce now discloses, through a foggy, crepuscular light, a pair of deserted ships moored at empty docks that resemble a cemetery more than a thriving port.

Similarly, Hammershøi shares Friedrich's genius for instilling a rapt mystery into landscape. A pair of oak trees (1907; cat. no. 54)—one mature, one young—are presented on the brink of nothingness, a lonely couple whose poignant isolation provokes an empathic response in the viewer. A similar sense of desolation can be found in other views of the Danish countryside, where low horizons, vast skies, and flat earth parallel the kind of Dutch landscape recorded by such seventeenth-century painters as Jacob von Ruisdael and Philips de Koninck. But just as Friedrich emptied the Dutch tradition of its sense of constant, pulsating animation, whether from the vital energies of nature or of man, so too did Hammershøi choose from his native landscape the most unpopulated, barren territories that elicit stillness and reverie. Views of Refsnaes, Lake Gentoft, and Lejre (cats. nos. 22, 31, 42) defy our sense of scale, time, and space, diminishing trees to the size of ants, opening voids in all directions, and leaving us immobilized in the midst of a new kind of nature that seems as alien to human life as another planet. For all their expansive spaces, these landscapes are ultimately as imprisoning as the rectangular enclosures of the artist's rooms or, for that matter, of his views of Copenhagen's buildings. His rendering of Amalienborg Square (cat. no. 12), enclosed by four royal palaces and dominated by Jacques-François-Joseph Saly's equestrian statue of King Frederik V, is no less drained of life than his landscapes and domestic interiors. On the one hand, the image, in typically achromatic tonalities that can associate it with the documentary world of photography, appears as impersonal as the work of a scrupulous architectural draftsman; but it can also look like a hallucination, as if the city had been evacuated, and time had stopped. Amalienborg Square, of course, seldom has much pedestrian traffic; but this center of Danish royal history now seems as dead and uninhabited as medieval Bruges, which Baudelaire described as a "mummy city," and which Fernand Khnopff depicted in a series of touristic views (see ill. p. 41) that are both as architecturally exact and as emotionally sepulchral as Hammershøi's views of Denmark's famous monuments.[17] Looking ahead to the next generation, one step further would take us to the haunting urban spaces of Giorgio de Chirico, such as his *Pink Tower* (1913; Peggy Guggenheim Collection), where the sunbaked, brilliantly colored relics of an Italian city, with its arcades, fortress, and equestrian statue, offer the Mediterranean version of Hammershøi's bleached and chilling vision of an urban tomb.

The deathly silence and emptiness of Hammershøi's landscapes and city views reach their maximum concentration in his interiors, which become the ultimate retreat from society. "I lock my door upon myself," a line from a poem by Christina Rossetti, which in turn inspired Khnopff to make a painting of a woman—his sister—almost entombed in her home (1891; Munich Neue Pinakothek), pinpoints this late-nineteenth-century phenomenon of a growing withdrawal from the public world behind the closed doors of a domestic sanctuary; but Hammershøi takes this isolation to unfamiliar extremes, often representing totally empty interiors, as if the tenant had died and the furniture had all been removed, leaving nothing but bare walls and floors: gray and white planes occasionally accented by a cold, antiseptic patch of window-shaped sunlight.

Looked at more objectively, these interiors can also be viewed as fascinating documents in the growing rebellion against the excesses of Victorian furniture and decoration, a movement that can be seen already in the paintings of

Whistler, whose discreet gray tonalities and delicately balanced arrangements of rectilinear planes (dados, picture frames, wall panels, doorways) left a deep impression on Hammershøi. By the end of the century, such reformers of architecture and design as C. F. A. Voysey and Charles Rennie Mackintosh in Britain or Adolf Loos and Josef Hoffmann in Austria had fully realized this reversal of Victorian taste, propagating a style of minimal ornament and purifying whiteness compatible with Hammershøi's pristine clarity. Indeed, compared to his interiors, those painted by many of his Danish contemporaries, whether by his own brother-in-law Peter Ilsted or by such other minor artists as Carl Holsøe or Christian Vilhelm Mourier-Petersen, still belong to a late Victorian world of gilded frames, richly patterned carpets, grandfather clocks, and abundant flowering plants.[18] But apart from considerations of his purist design as part of the history of interior decoration, Hammershøi's bare rooms have gripping psychological power, both when a single figure is present and, even more, when there is nothing left but the domestic skeleton without its living flesh.

The motif of an empty room is one of particular importance to the nineteenth century. In seventeenth-century Dutch painting, the depiction of a household devoid of people was extremely rare, one familiar exception being in the Louvre, Samuel von Hoogstraten's *The Slippers* (ill. p. 30).[19] But like Hoogstraten's trompe l'oeil peepshows, this factual account of a sequence of rooms presents the spectator with the agreeable illusion of entering a prosperous, well-regulated home as a welcome guest. Predictably, it was not until the Romantics that empty rooms could become charged with private, secret feelings. Friedrich's drawings of the window wall of his studio (1805–06; Vienna, Belvedere) are virtually surrogate self-portraits, filled with concealed symbols that mirror the sanctity and loneliness of his vocation; and Eugène Delacroix's view of a corner of his own studio (1825; The Louvre) where the fires of a stove offer an almost human warmth, again makes us feel that we are looking at an entry in a personal diary. By the end of the century, depictions of rooms without their human occupants had become a familiar theme, subject to a widening range of different and often contradictory interpretations. Van Gogh's *Bedroom at Arles* (1888; Amsterdam, Van Gogh Museum) is probably the most famous example—an image of a humble utopia that seems steeped with the artist's restless personality, a virtual self-portrait that would later have joyous descendants in, for example, Matisse's unpopulated rooms and studios. Other artists, however, could convey a more theatrical ambiance of domestic spaces in which we may feel, as in an early painting by Munch of a bourgeois living room (1881), that we are looking at a

Fernand Khnopff, *Deserted City*, 1904. Colored chalk, charcoal, and pastel on paper, 76 x 69 cm. Musées Royaux des Beaux-Arts, Brussels

Vilhelm Hammershøi, *Bedroom*, [1890]. Oil on canvas, 53 x 58 cm. Private collection

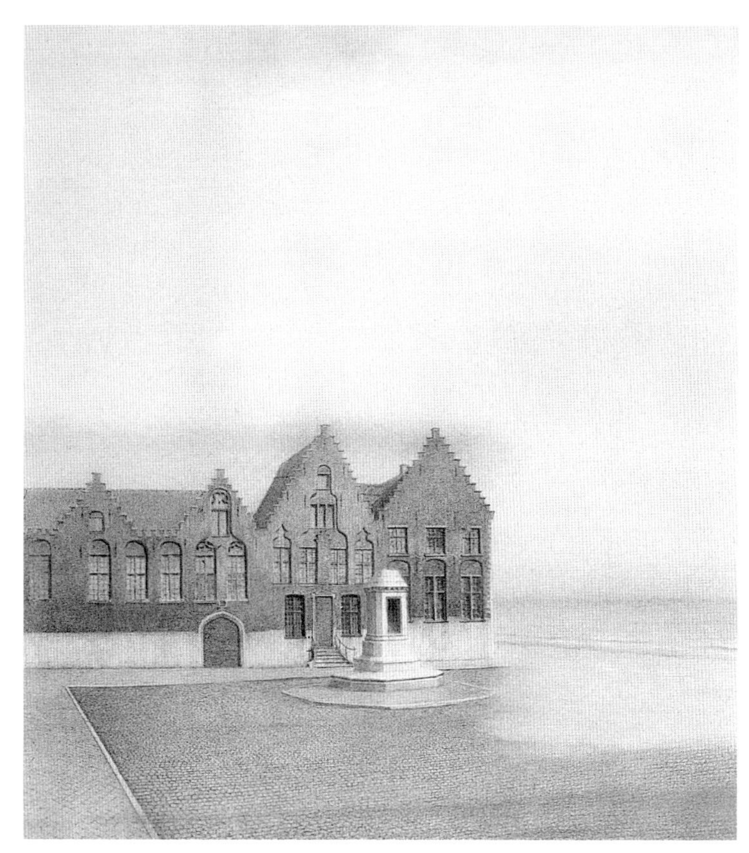

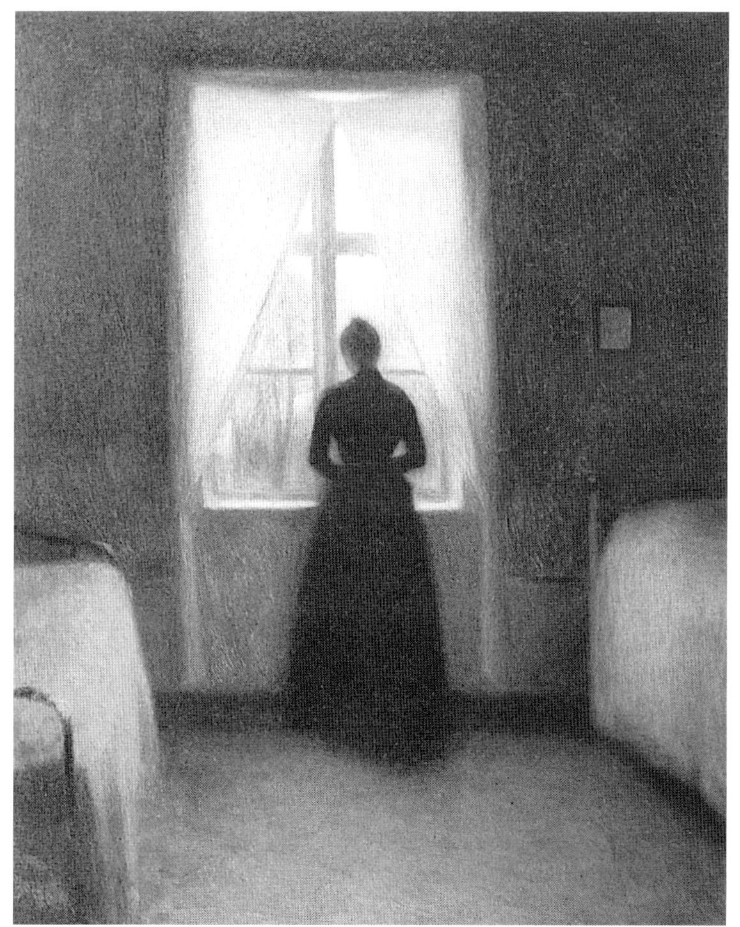

stage set in which a modern drama might suddenly unfold—perhaps *Hedda Gabler* or *A Doll's House*. That mood of intimate domesticity where modern dramas of life, love, and death can be enacted is particularly prevalent in Parisian painting of the 1890s, especially in the work of Édouard Vuillard and Félix Vallotton, both of whom had close connections with contemporary stage production, frequently of plays by Ibsen and Strindberg. And there is also a burgeoning new category of what might be called "portraits of rooms," best exemplified by the hugely successful expatriate American painter Walter Gay,[20] who painted detailed but casual glimpses of elegant historic interiors, whether French chateaux, Venetian palazzi, or the homes of Boston patricians.

But the mood of melancholy and often eerie confinement prevalent in Hammershøi's empty interiors is perhaps closest to that found in works by many of his contemporaries, especially in Belgium, a point clearly demonstrated in the major international Symbolist exhibition *Lost Paradise*, 1995, where Hammershøi's *Dust Motes Dancing in the Sunbeams*, 1900, was included with a group of gloomy interiors by Xavier Mellery, George Lebrun, and Léon Spilliaert, and immediately fit into this community of fin-de-siècle artists who, with their doors locked to the street outside, explored the morbid mysteries that could be found in the corners of their homes.[21]

Yet even within this odd company, Hammershøi remains distinctive, his extremes of pristine austerity cutting closer to the bones of painting and of feeling. This distillation of plane and light and this renunciation of the sensuous are so intense that we may think ahead to many twentieth-century directions, whether the abstractions of Piet Mondrian or, retaining Hammershøi's domestic theme, the paintings of an American, Edward Hopper, who could also transform the light-flooded, bare white walls of an empty room into a no-man's land, the ultimate stop on the voyage of the lone self (see ill. p. 44).[22]

When people *are* found in Hammershøi's interiors, they are, like Hopper's figures, totally silent and static, helplessly subordinate to these immaculate, rectilinear spaces. But still more remarkable, when Hammershøi painted pairs or larger groups of people, each individual remains locked into a private world. This can be seen, for instance, in the unusual double portrait of Hammershøi and his wife (1898; cat. no. 16), in which everything conspires to separate rather than to unite the couple. They sit on opposite sides of a table covered with a virgin white cloth as devoid of objects as the artist's rooms are devoid of furniture; but rather than facing each other across the table, they sit at opposite ends. Ida, her hand with its wedding ring resting on the cloth in an almost sacramental way, averts her eyes from us and from her husband. As for Vilhelm, we see only his back, thereby obliging us to imagine what we intuit to be an expression of equal self-absorption. Yet surprisingly, this couple still seems spiritually united, as if they were joined by a mood of such silent introspection that it verges on communal prayer.

This mood was amplified to astonishing dimensions in one of the most unexpected and unforgettable paintings of Hammershøi's career, *Five Portraits*, 1901–02 (cat. no. 26).[23] Its startling size (3.4 meters wide) belies the usually intimate format of his interiors, so that its ability to cast a spell of almost occult privacy is all the more disarming. The life-size sitters are all close friends from the Danish art world and all promoters of Den frie Udstilling (the Independent Exhibition). They begin at the left, with architect Thorvald Bindesbøll, and continue on the near side of the table with Hammershøi's younger brother, Svend, also a painter. Then comes Karl Madsen, a Rembrandt scholar and passionate supporter of Hammershøi's art, followed by Symbolist painter J. F. Willumsen. Closing the group at the right is Carl Holsøe, another painter of interiors, shown with his legs up; his foreshortened and seemingly huge shoe soles jut abruptly outward at the viewer like the bare feet of Mantegna's *Dead Christ* and draw us back into his isolated corner of the painting. The mood is of a secret society holding a séance, with a cultlike solemnity replacing the conviviality of a shared meal or drink and with a still life so spare—two thin candles and three empty gin glasses on a spotless white tablecloth—that the world of the senses seems to have been banished from this inner sanctum, which, in fact, is the artist's living room at Strandgade 30. Tensions are further underlined by the extreme compression of the figures in this shallow space, the upper edge of which is so close to the tops of their heads that, even in the most relaxed of their seated positions, they look eternally imprisoned.

Many sources can be suggested for this unique fraternity. Given Madsen's art-historical specificity, Rembrandt's group portraits may all be relevant, whether of the syndics, of the Conspiracy of Julius Civilis or of the fragment of an anatomy lesson given by Dr. Joan Deyman (which has a comparably obtrusive pair of corpse's feet). And there is also a nineteenth-century background of Danish group portraiture, well-known in such an example as Constantin Hansen's *Assembly of Danish Artists in Rome* (1837; Copenhagen, Statens Museum for Kunst).[24] But much closer in time and spirit is the brooding group portrait by Finnish painter Akseli Gallen-Kallela (1894; private collection) that presents the artist together with a trio of like-minded young men, musicians (including Sibelius) who also yearned to resurrect the heritage of their Russian-ruled nation.[25] The painting's first title, *The Problem*, was then changed to *The Symposium*, in reference to Plato's mixture of drink and intellectual communion; but this mood takes on a mystical dimension as a vision of the winged Egyptian god Osiris suddenly appears above a still life of liqueurs and coffee far more casual and earthbound than Hammershøi's minimal tableware. Nevertheless, there is clearly a kinship between these two Scandinavian group portraits, in which youthful compatriots in the arts seem to bear the weight of the world on their shoulders. Yet Hammershøi's painting also proclaims its artist's uncanny originality. Even without an airborne vision, its ambiance is deeply mystical, as if we had entered the chambers of a spiritualist. Typically, each of the five men seems locked in a private world, avoiding

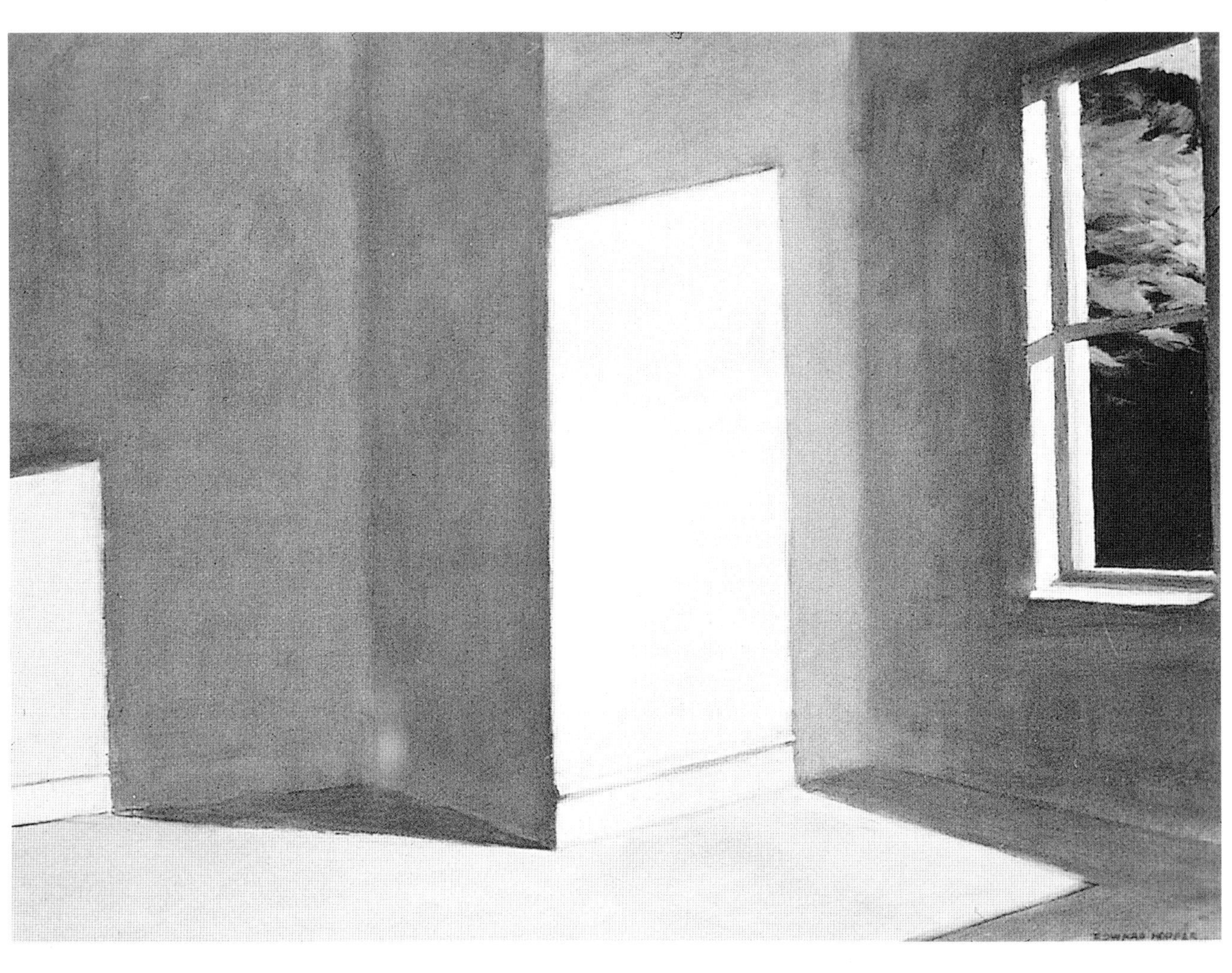

Edward Hopper, *Sunlight in an Empty Room*, 1963.
Oil on canvas, 73.5 x 101.5 cm. Private collection, United States

contact with his neighbor, while, at the same time, all of them direct their gazes to the viewer, who must look up at them. The effect is like standing before a tribunal, which comes into fixed, frontal focus with the hypnotic stare of Willumsen. And once more, Hammershøi's Symbolist gift of stirring memories from beneath the surfaces of his ostensibly cool, objective descripton of hard facts opens unexpected vistas. As in his *Artemis*, this group is haunted by intimations of more familiar narratives, especially such mystical Christian themes as the Last Supper or the Supper at Emmaus.[26] What might at first be mistaken for a group photograph of the members of a private club turns into a new kind of sacred communion.

Hammershøi's otherworldly group portrait, one of the highest moments in the history of Danish art, can also be fitted into a broader international pattern that would immediately include another unforgettable group portrait, of five avant-garde Parisian artists by Swiss-born Félix Vallotton, *The Five Painters* (Winterthur, Kunstmuseum). Born in 1865, one year after Hammershøi, he had also developed by the late 1880s a style of comparable precision and economy in which the realist premise familiar to nineteenth-century paintings of genre scenes, landscapes, portraits, and studio nudes was distilled into hard-edged, simple shapes, both modeled and flat, in a spotless environment that prefigures the international revival in the 1920s of a cool, sharp-focus realism. It is probably a question of parallel tracks rather than direct influence that makes Vallotton's portrait of five Nabi painters, himself included, look like a pendant to Hammershøi's group portrait of 1901.[27] Begun the following year, 1902, this Parisian painting, while looking back to a long tradition of more relaxed and crowded group portraits of artists by, among others, Henri Fantin-Latour and Maurice Denis, now isolates and immobilizes the individual sitters, whose frozen hand gestures seem to connect them in a mysterious ritual. His hands clasped before him in a posture of total self-absorption, the red-bearded Vuillard replaces Willumsen's magnetic stillness in the earlier painting. And the restriction to an almost colorless world again recalls Hammershøi's penchant for monochrome painting. Despite wrong-headed suggestions that the Danish artist might have been color-blind[28] (a diagnosis equivalent to a French endocrinologist's suggestion that the swollen necks of Ingres's women could be explained by what the doctor deduced was a thyroid disorder), this preference was, in fact, shared by many fin-de-siècle painters, including Whistler, Carrière, and Picasso.

Like all artists, Hammershøi is not only an individual with unique characteristics, but someone nurtured in a national culture that both natives and foreigners recognize. So it is that in looking at Hammershøi we may choose to be reminded of Købke or Eckersberg or Thorvaldsen. But the uncommon intensity of his art also drives us far beyond Danish borders, compelling us to locate him within a loftier United Nations of artists. There, with neighbors from all over the world—France, Belgium, Britain, Germany, the United States—his full stature may begin to be measured.

Notes

1. Kirk Varnedoe, *Northern Light: Realism and Symbolism in Scandinavian Painting, 1880–1910* (New York: The Brooklyn Museum, 1982). This exhibition catalogue was later expanded into a more inclusive book: idem, *Northern Light: Nordic Art at the Turn of the Century* (New Haven and London: Yale University Press, 1988).
2. *Dreams of a Summer Night: Scandinavian Painting at the Turn of the Century* (London: Hayward Gallery, 1986).
3. Even in Denmark, however, Hammershøi's reputation waned considerably after World War I, to be revived there as well as abroad in the 1980s. The fullest account of his life, art, exhibition record and bibliography is found in Poul Vad, *Vilhelm Hammershøi and Danish Art at the Turn of the Century* (New Haven and London: Yale University Press, 1992)—an English translation of the monograph's first Danish edition, 1988. The specialized bibliography in English is particularly informative, and I have drawn heavily from it for the facts and ideas in this essay. Other sources included the catalogue notes by Emily Braun in Varnedoe, *Northern Light*, 1982; the text, notes, and biography in Finsen Raaschou-Nielsen, *Vilhelm Hammershøi*; the catalogue notes by Hanne Westergaard in *Dreams of a Summer Night*; and, above all, an essay that, like mine, attempts to expand Hammershøi's achievement internationally: Kirk Varnedoe, "Private Light: Hammershøi," *Art in America*, March 1983, pp. 110–17.
4. Hanne Finsen and Inge Vibeke Raaschou-Nielsen, *Vilhelm Hammershøi: Painter of Stillness and Light* (New York: Wildenstein 1982; and Washington, D.C.: The Phillips Collection, 1983).
5. On this failed ambition, see Vad, *Hammershøi*, pp. 168–70.
6. Vad (in *Hammershøi*, p. 105) cites Hammershøi's negative remarks about an Impressionist and Symbolist show that he saw in Paris, which must have been the 1892 exhibition at Le Barc de Boutteville, which included works by a broad range of Neo-Impressionists, Symbolists, and Nabis, including Bonnard, Bernard, Angrand, Filiger, Sérusier, Signac, Cross, and Ranson. Apparently most of these paintings looked like jokes to him, offending his profound sense of truth to observed fact as well as his penchant for subdued understatement.
7. It should be said that a case has been made for the painting's title, *Job*, being an afterthought of the artist, or, in another interpretation, that the painting was a response to his friend Kristian Zahrtmann's earlier painting *Job Being Comforted by His Friends*, 1887. But Bonnat's painting is also legible without its biblical reference, as a generic statement of human suffering.
8. See Varnedoe, "Private Light," p. 111.
9. Hammershøi's attraction to this particular relief is borne out by the diplomatic efforts he had to make in order to receive permission to copy it (see Vad, *Hammershøi*, p. 103).
10. Vad (in *Hammershøi*, pp. 110–11) suggests the analogy with the Symbolist theme of a cycle of three women, a motif of equal relevance to Hammershøi's later work *Artemis*.
11. See ibid., p. 28 and fig. 24.
12. For further remarks about the particular character of Danish neoclassicism, especially as revealed in painting, see my essay "Danish Golden Age Painting: An International Perspective," in *Thorvaldsens Museum Bulletin 1997* (Copenhagen: Thorvaldsens Museum, 1997), pp. 45–58.
13. The Quattrocento sources that have been suggested for *Artemis*, including works by Perugino and Luca Signorelli, are discussed at length in Vad, *Hammershøi*, pp. 123–30. To this may be added the generic similarities to the trio of archaic nymphs in the archaic relief at the Louvre that are omitted in Hammershøi's copy. As for the Brancacci Chapel, it is worth mentioning that an image of Masaccio's *Expulsion*, clearly of importance to Hammershøi, appears in an earlier Danish painting, Ludvig Find's *Portrait of Thorvald Erichsen*, 1897, together with images of Trecento paintings.
14. I have discussed this Danish inflection of the nude in my essay "Danish Golden Age Painting" (see n. 12, above). For the fullest presentation of the nude in Danish nineteenth-century painting, see the exhibition catalogue *Den nøgne guldalder; Modelbilleder: C. W. Eckersberg og hans elever* (Copenhagen: Den Hirschsprungske Samling, 1994).
15. Illustrated in Vad, *Hammershøi*, p. 349.
16. Ibid., p. 119.

17. Varnedoe (in "Private Light," pp. 114, 116) already mentioned the affinity to the depictions by Khnopff of the Belgian Symbolist idea of "Bruges-la-Morte," illustrating that artist's view of Notre Dame de Bruges.
18. I have discussed some of these canvases in another essay, "Art: In a Northern Light; Penetrating Interiors in Danish Painting," *Architectural Digest*, August 1985, pp. 126–30ff.
19. The slippers of the title, like the partial view of a painting of a woman by Terborch on the far wall, provide surrogate human presences in this unusual interior.
20. See *Walter Gay: A Retrospective* (New York: New York University, Grey Art Gallery and Study Center, 1980), an exhibition catalogue that includes a particularly informative essay by Gary A. Reynolds on the tradition of painting empty rooms as well as on some literary parallels in the novels of Gay's friend Henry James.
21. See Jean Clair, "Troubling Places," in *Lost Paradise: Symbolist Europe* (Montreal: Montreal Museum of Fine Arts, 1995), pp. 164–95.
22. Hammershøi's broad affinities with two twentieth-century American painters, Georgia O'Keeffe and Edward Hopper, were already briefly suggested by Varnedoe (in "Private Light," p. 113) and can provide many fascinating transatlantic comparisons that would also include works by Sheeler and Wyeth.
23. Apart from the long discussion of this painting by Vad (in *Hammershøi*, pp. 213–34), the catalogue entries by Emily Braun (in Varnedoe, *Northern Light*, 1982, cat. no. 30) and Hanne Westergaard (in *Dreams of a Summer Night*, cat. no. 32) are particularly informative.
24. Hansen's group portrait was shown in Copenhagen in 1897. (See Westergaard, ibid.)
25. Gallen-Kallela's painting is discussed in detail in both Scandinavian painting catalogues cited above (*Northern Light*, where it is cat. no. 26, and *Dreams of a Summer Night*, where it is cat. no. 22).
26. Vad goes so far as to suggest, quite convincingly, that Eckersberg's *Last Supper* altarpiece at Frederiksberg Church (1839–40) left its mark on *Five Portraits*.
27. To my knowledge, this comparison was first suggested by John Klein in his "Portraiture and Assimilation of the 'Very Singular Vallotton,'" an essay in Sasha M. Newman, *Félix Vallotton* (New Haven: Yale University Art Gallery, 1991), p. 110. Of all foreign artists, Vallotton may offer the closest parallels to Hammershøi, a comparison worth exploring further.
28. This diagnosis was made in 1981 by Dr. Ib Ostenfeld. See Vad, *Hammershøi*,, pp. 374–75.

Plates

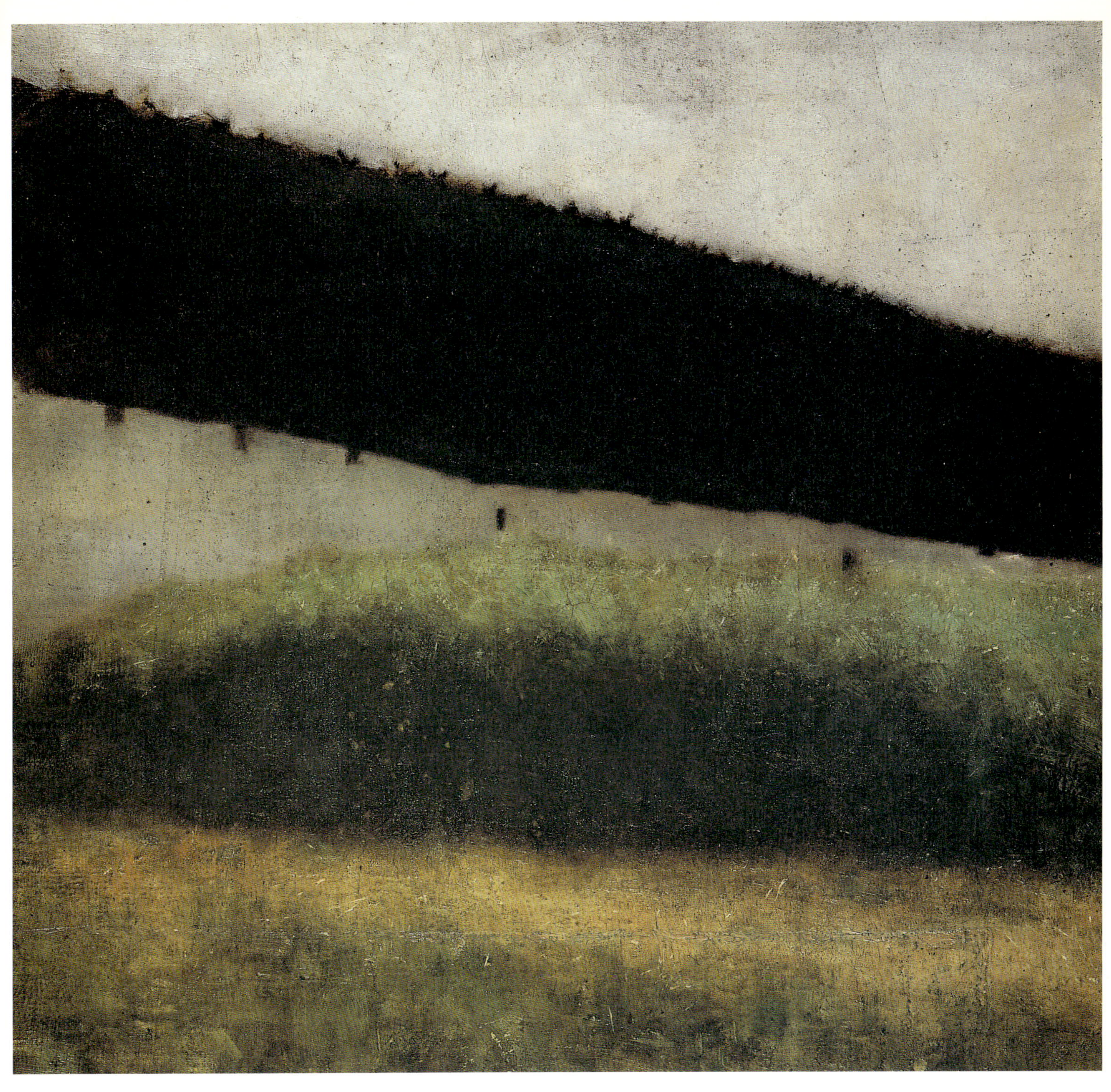

Farm Building, [1883]
Cat. no. 1

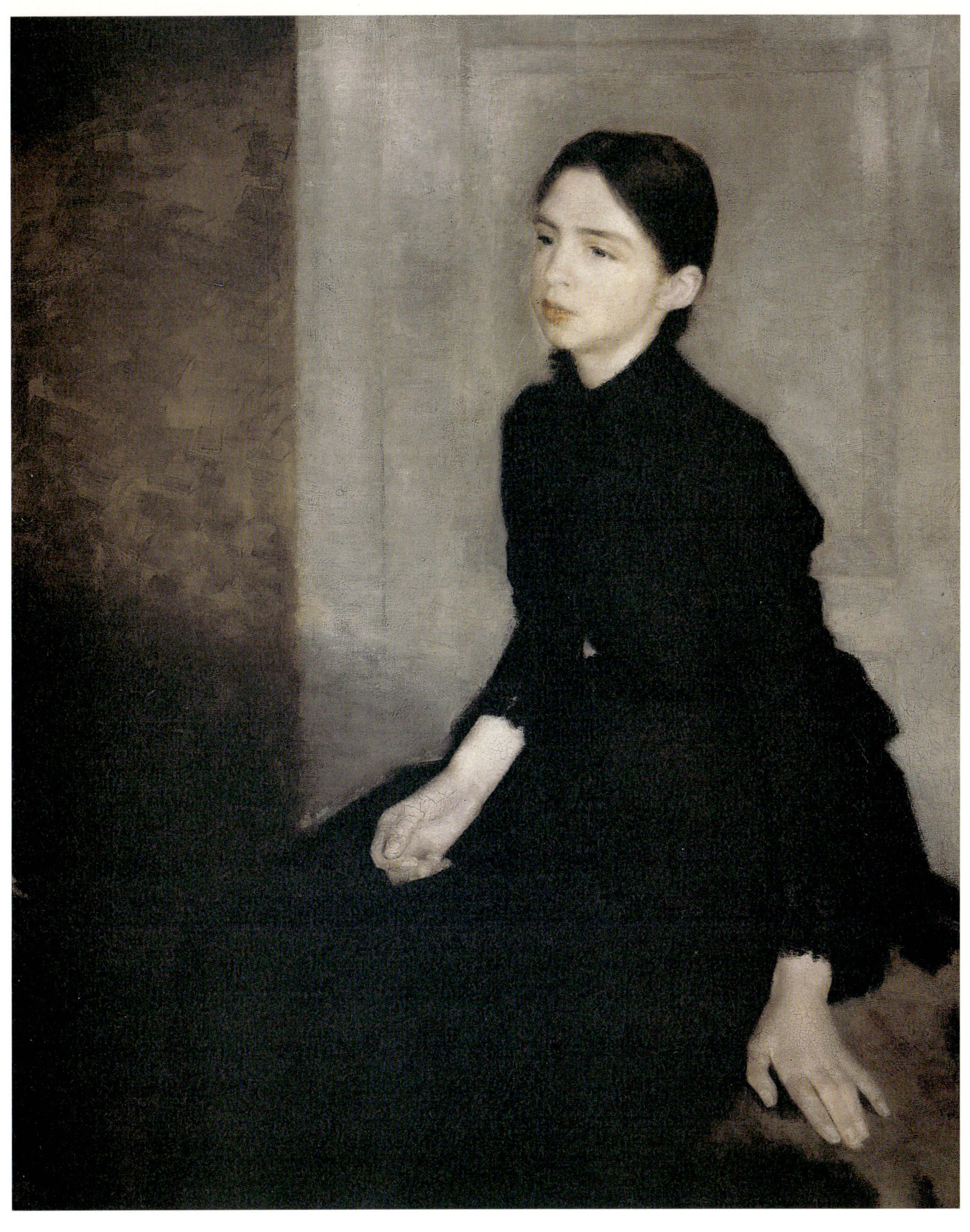

Portrait of a Young Girl [Anna Hammershøi], [1885]
Cat. no. 2

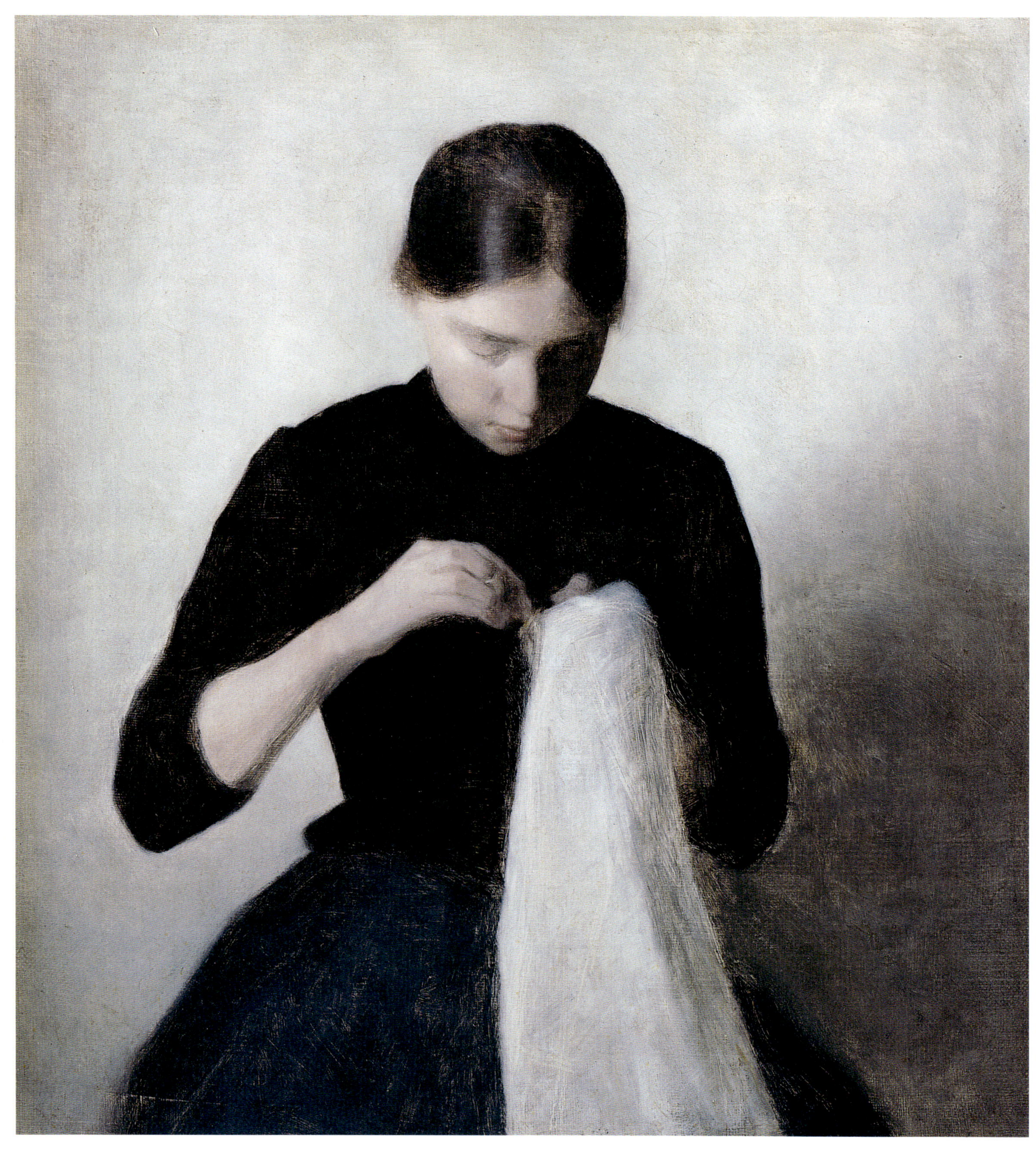

Young Girl Sewing [Anna Hammershøi], [1887]
Cat. no. 3

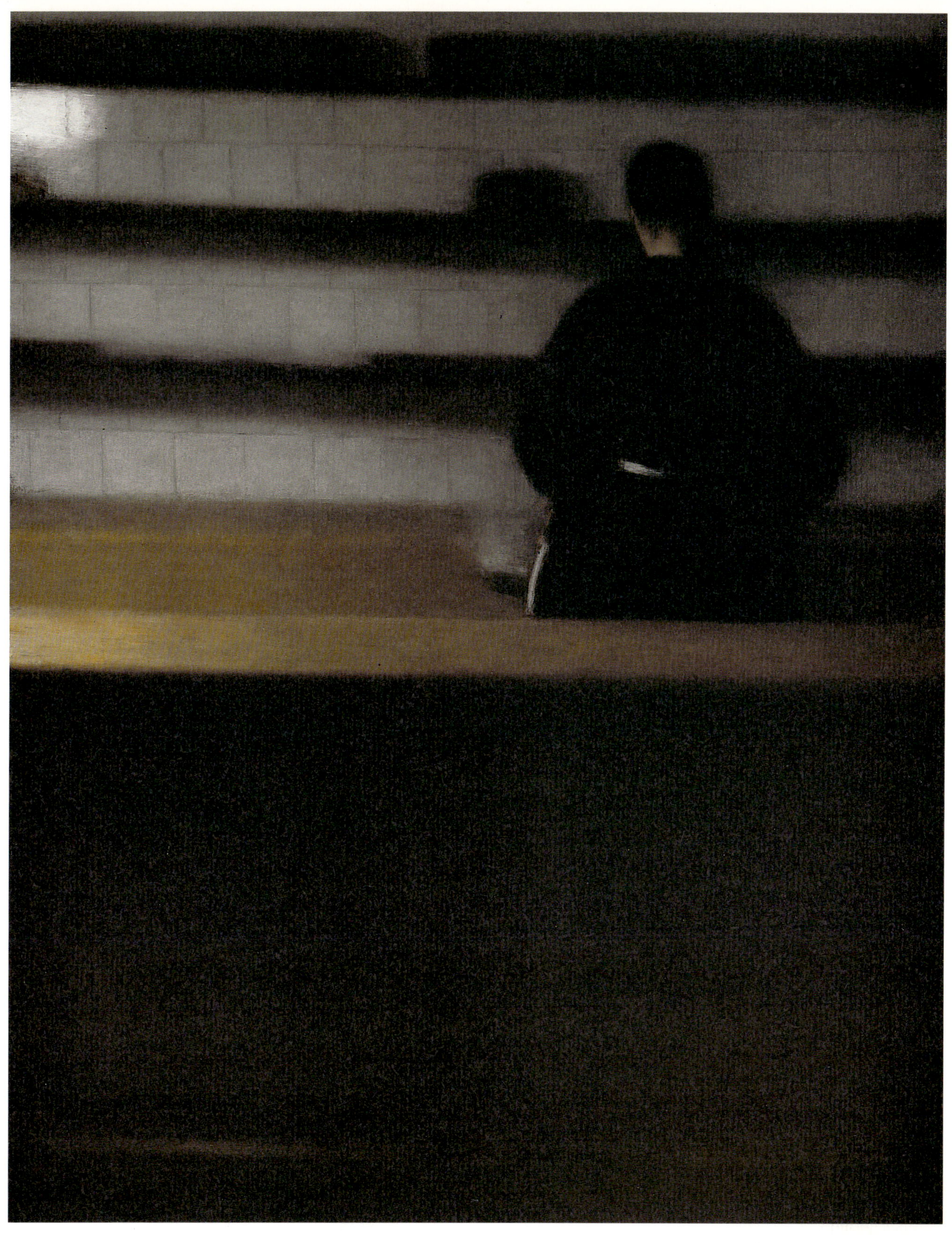

Study: Baker's Shop, [1889]
Cat. no. 4

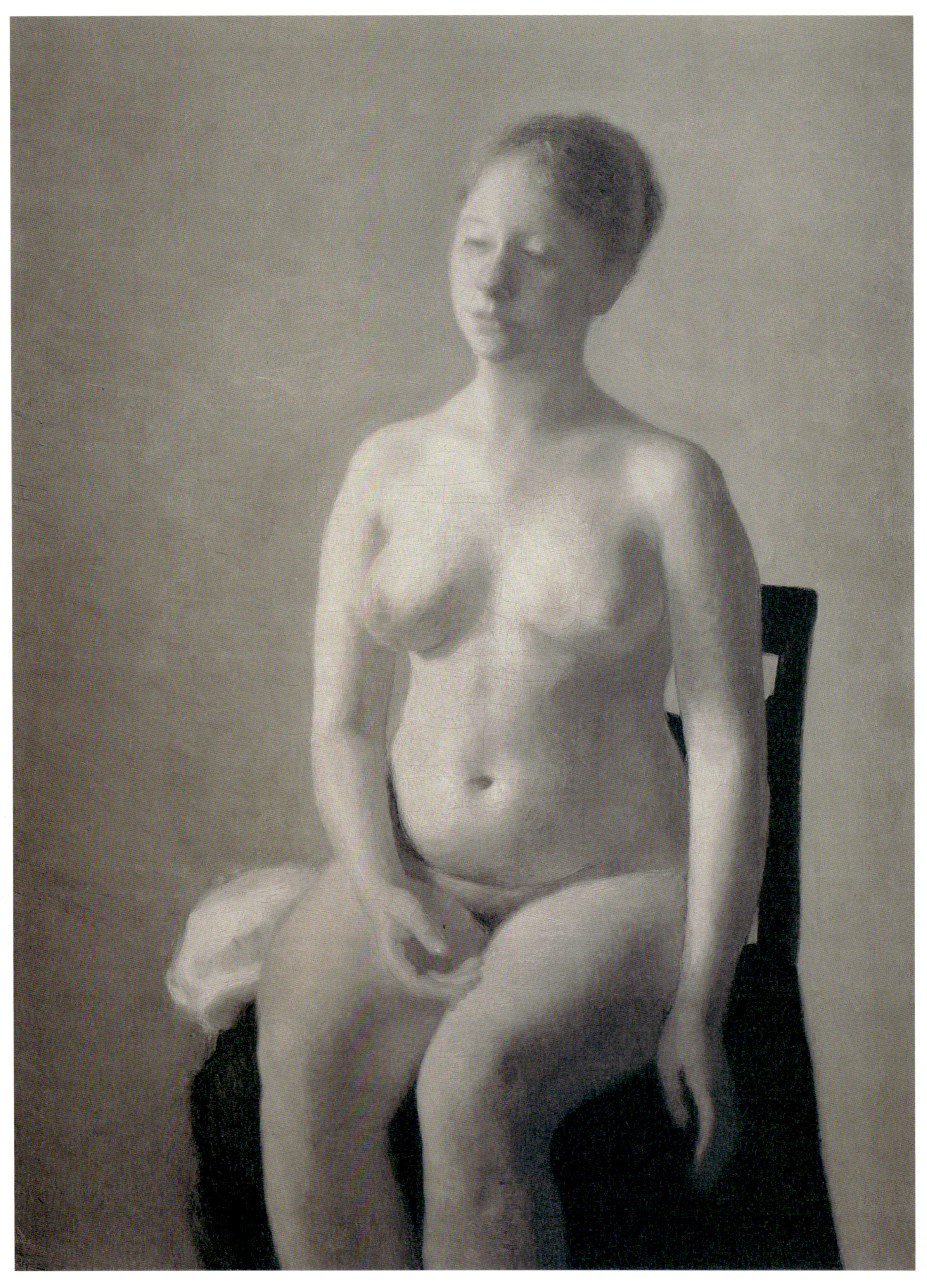

Study of a Model, or *Nude Female Model*, [1889]
Cat. no. 5

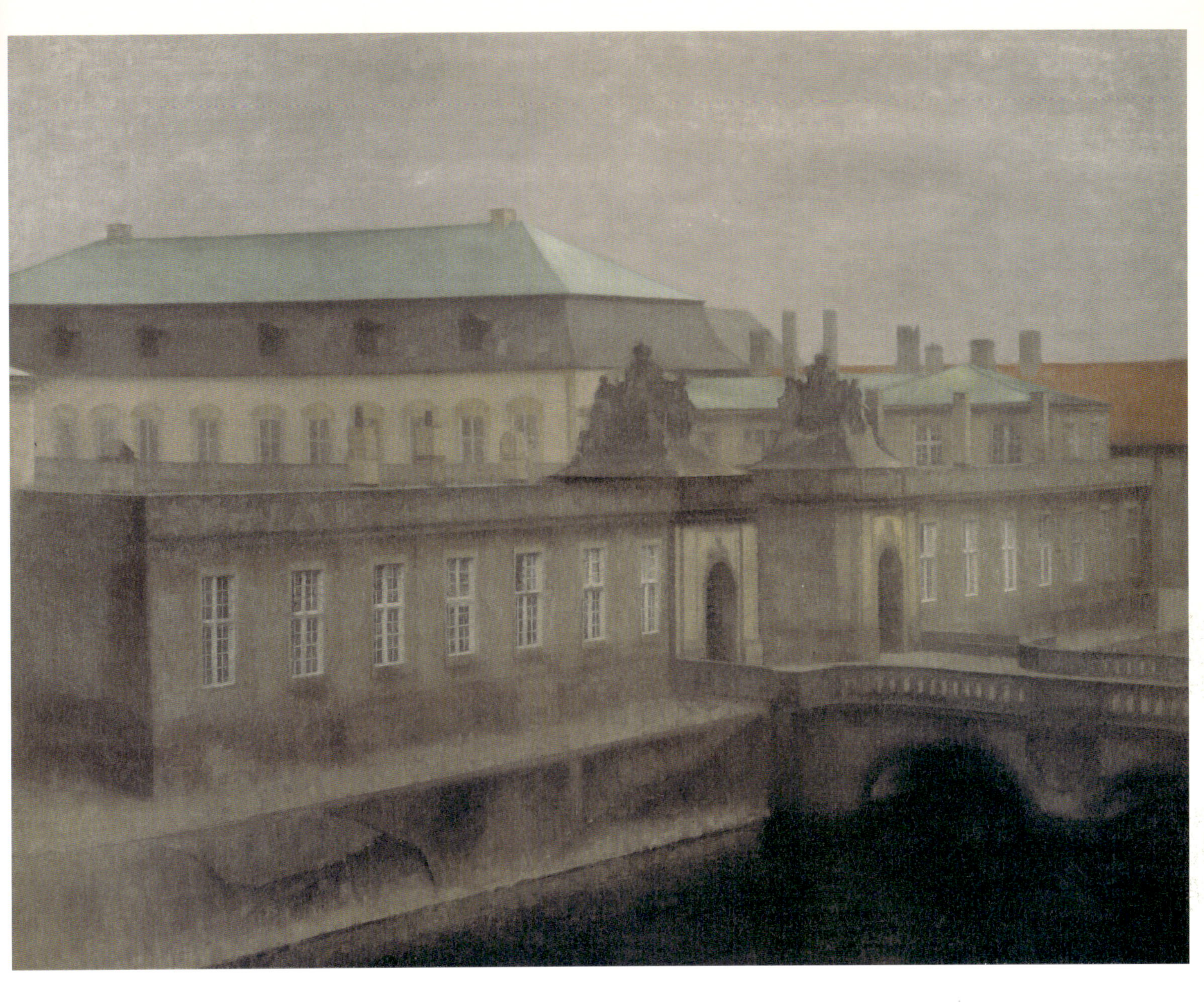

View of Christiansborg Palace, [1890–92]
Cat. no. 6

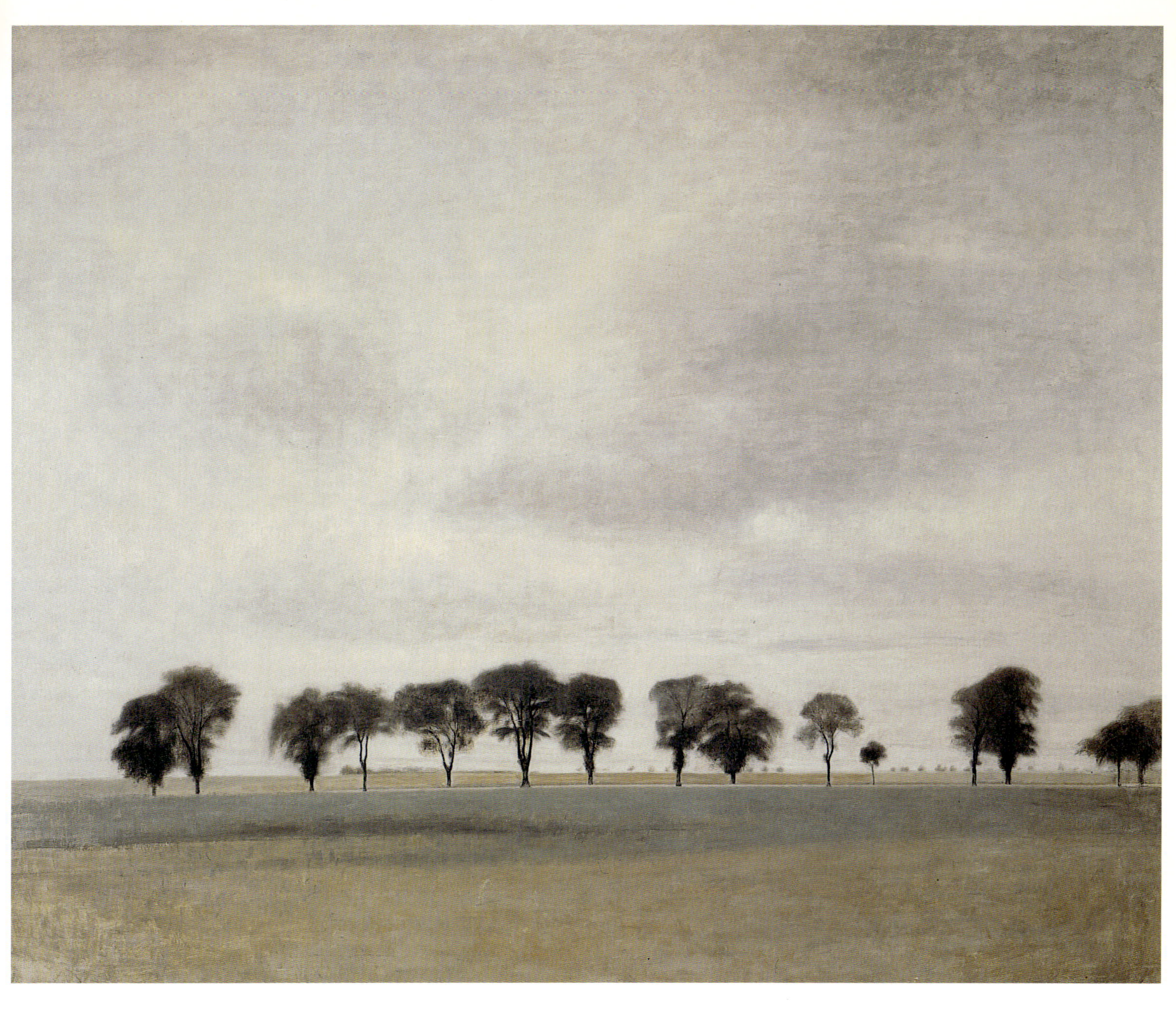

Landscape [Kongevejen near Gentofte], [1892]
Cat. no. 8

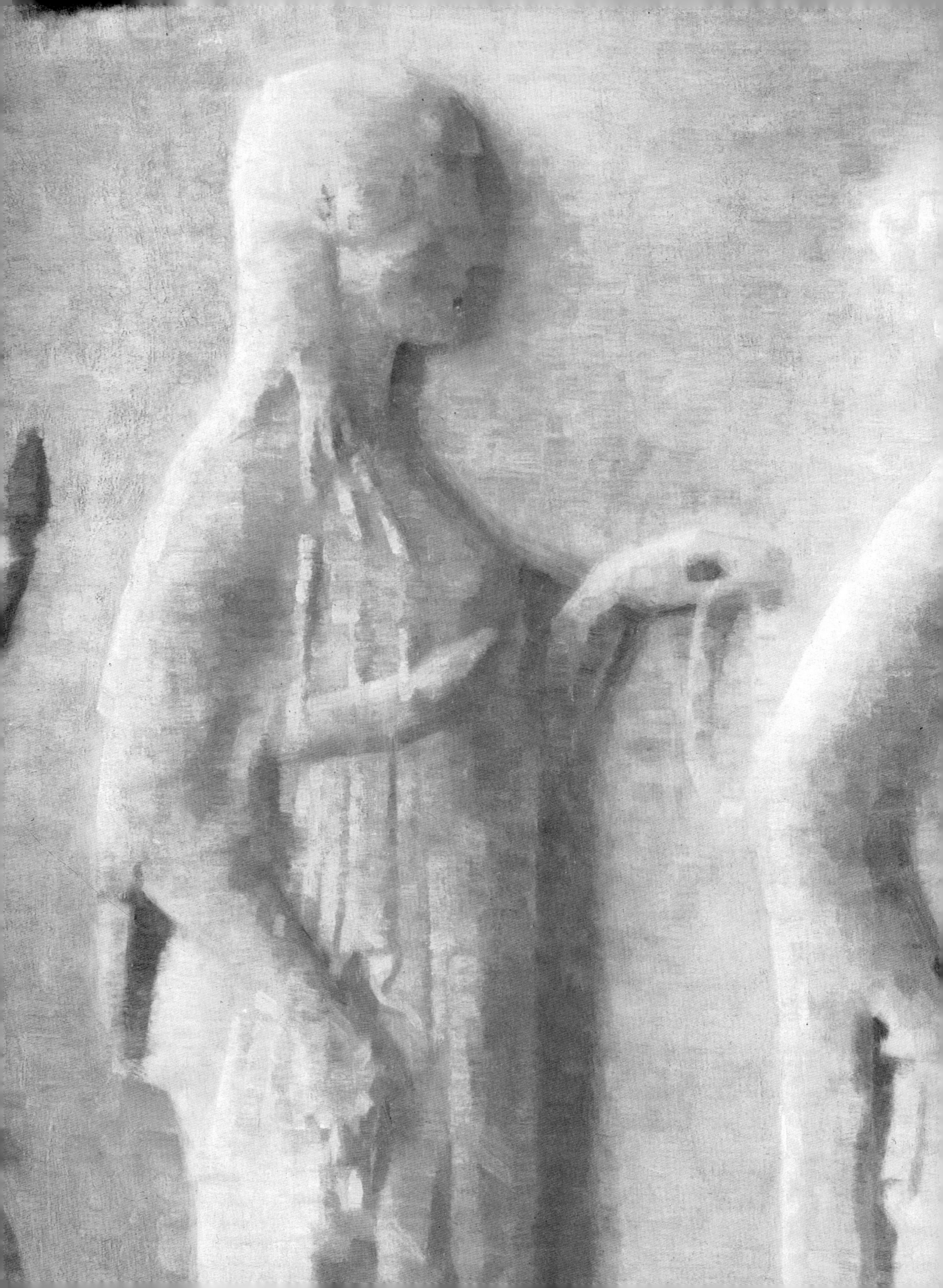

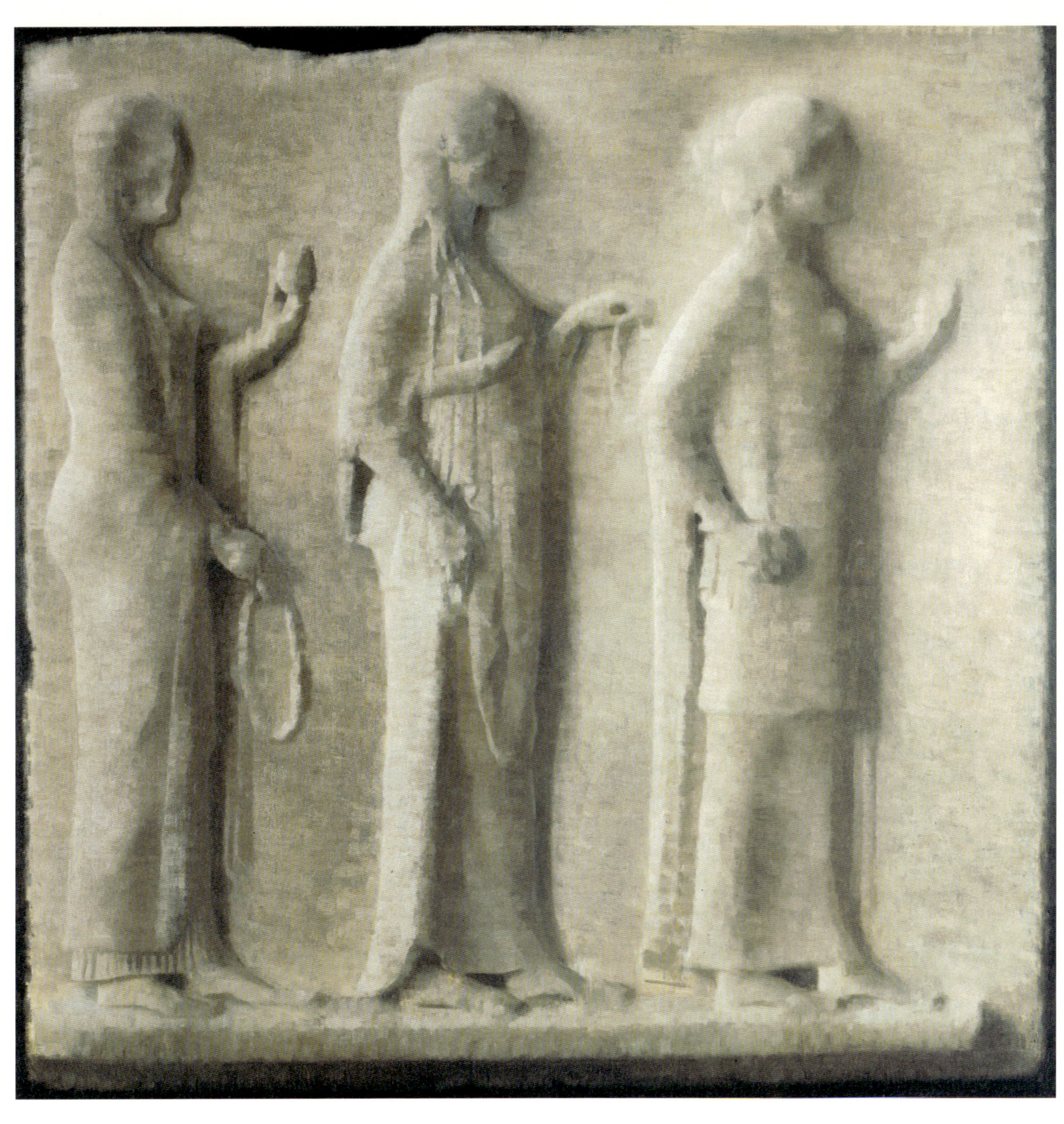

A Greek Relief [Paris], [1891]
Cat. no. 7

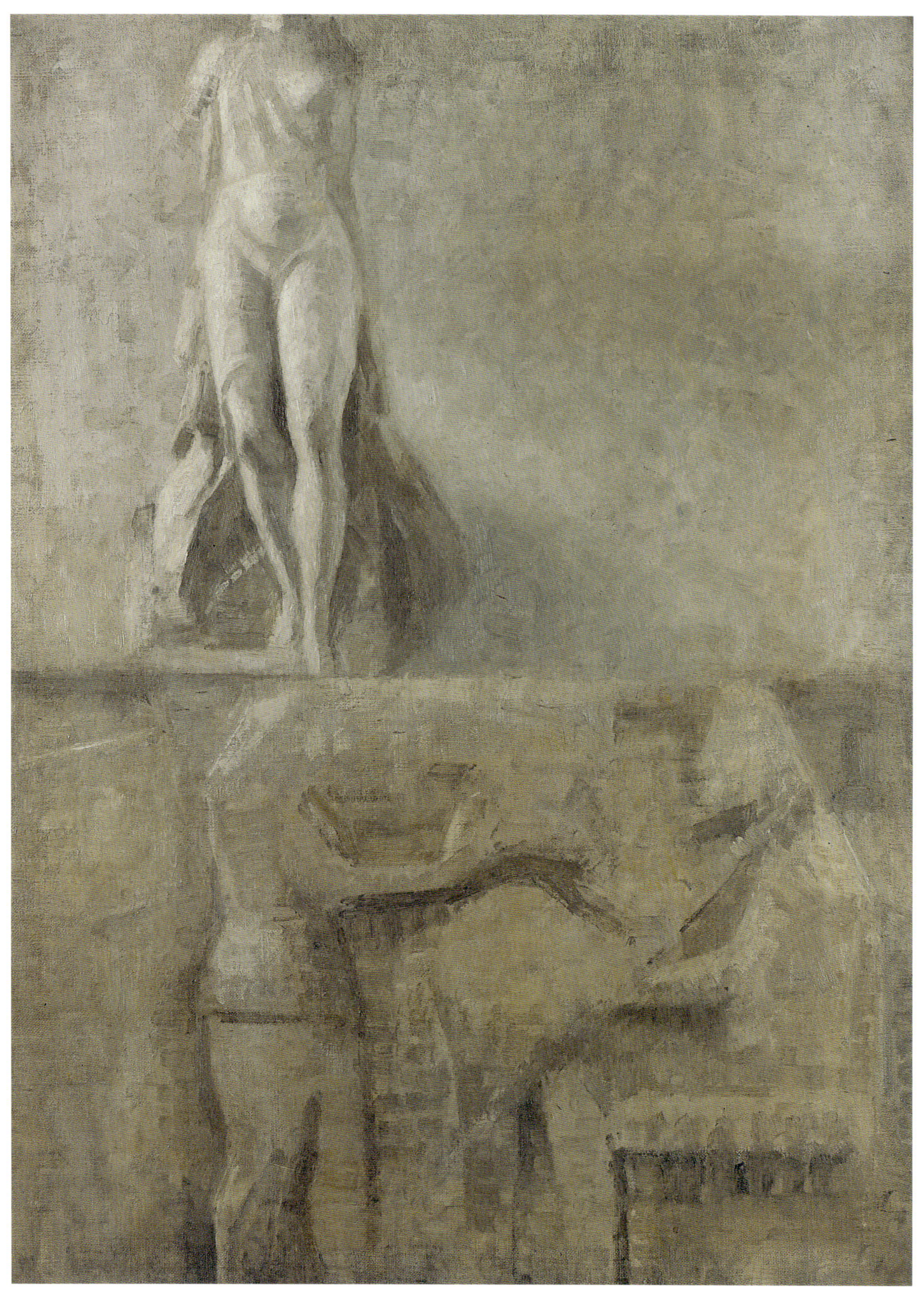

Sketch Done in a Room of Ancient Greek Art
in the British Museum [London], [1897]. Cat. no. 15

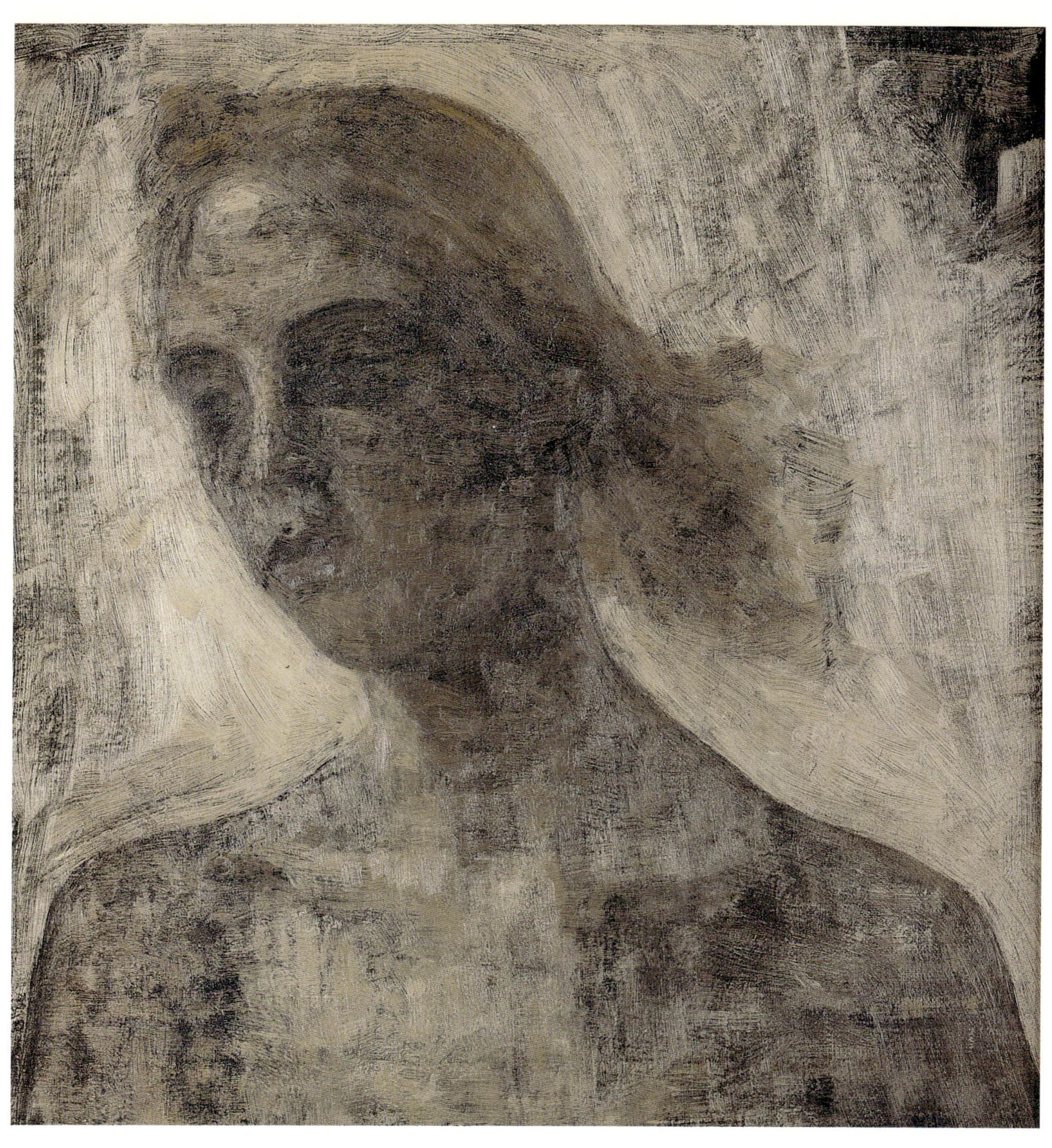

Study of a Head, [1893]
Cat. no. 9

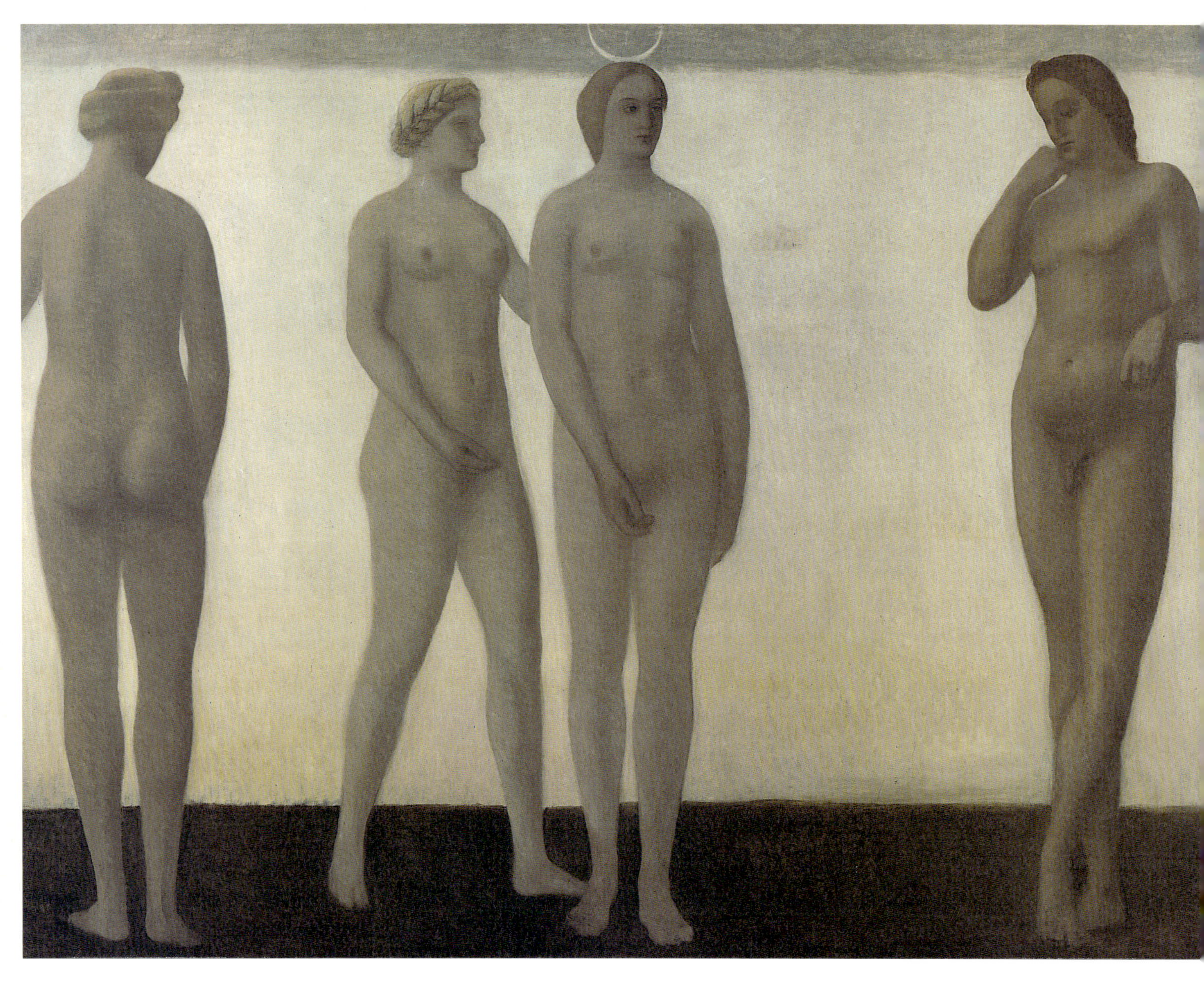

Artemis, [1893–94]
Cat. no. 10

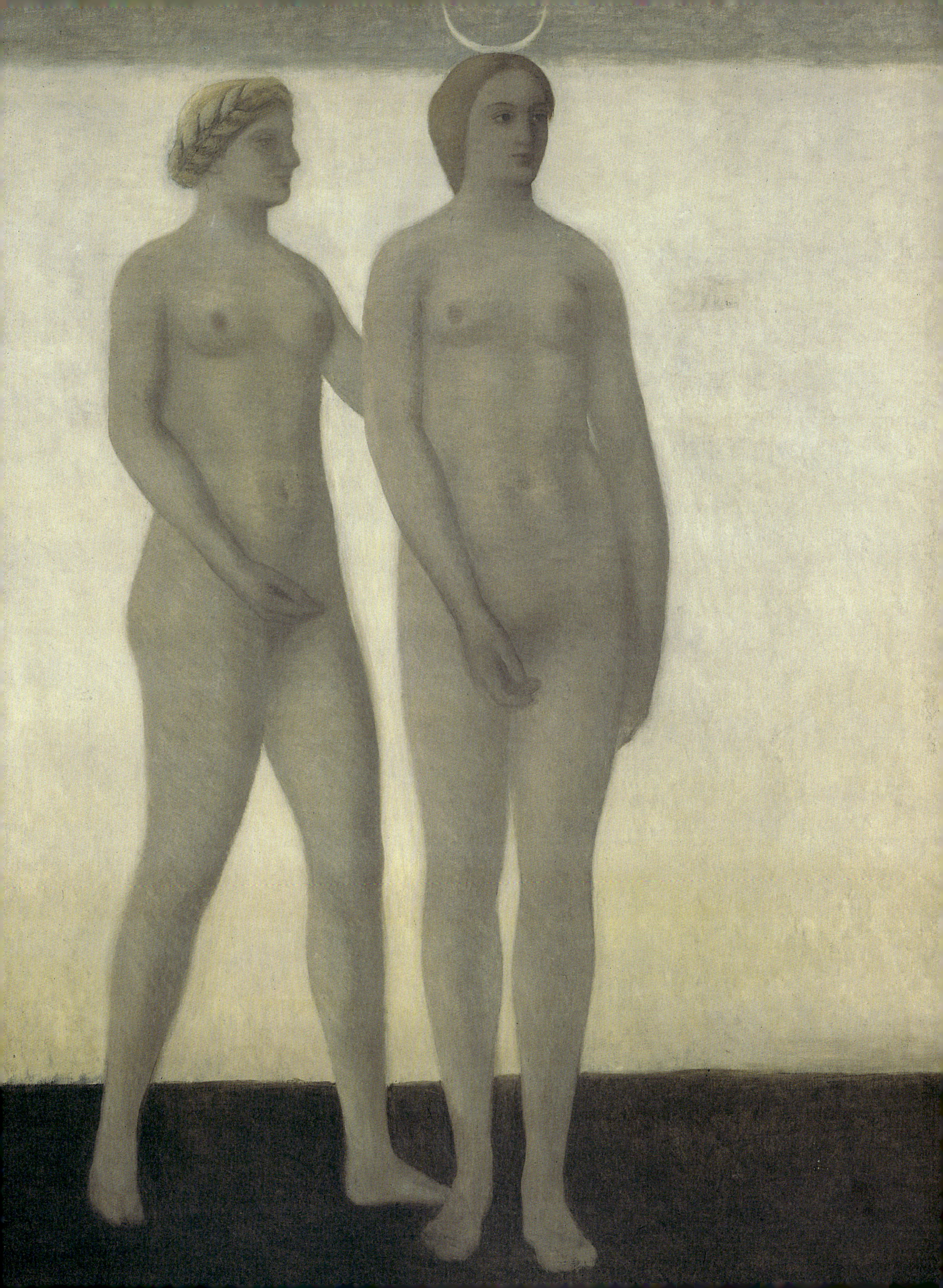

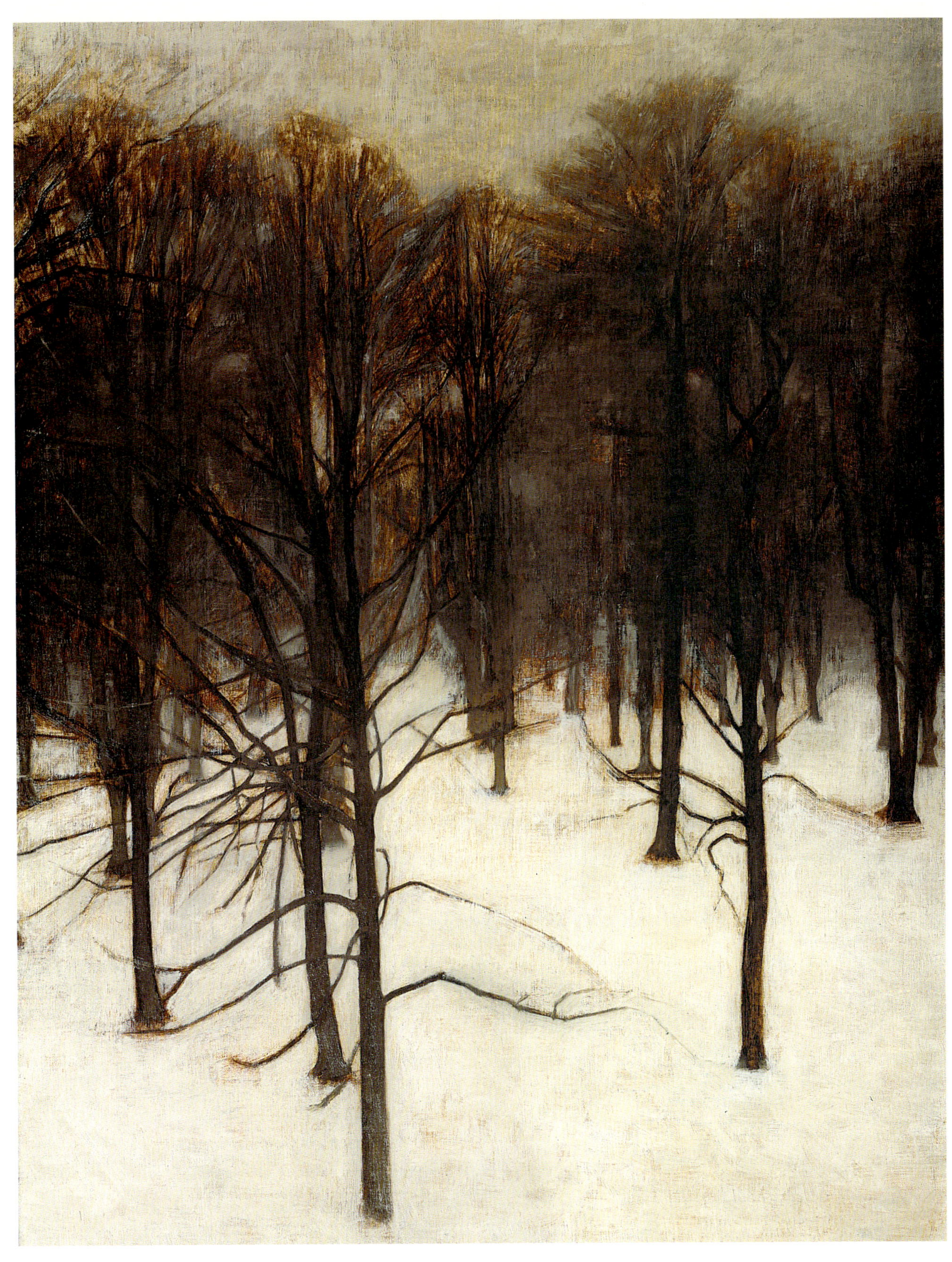

Landscape in Snow, [Søndermarken], [1896]
Cat. no. 11

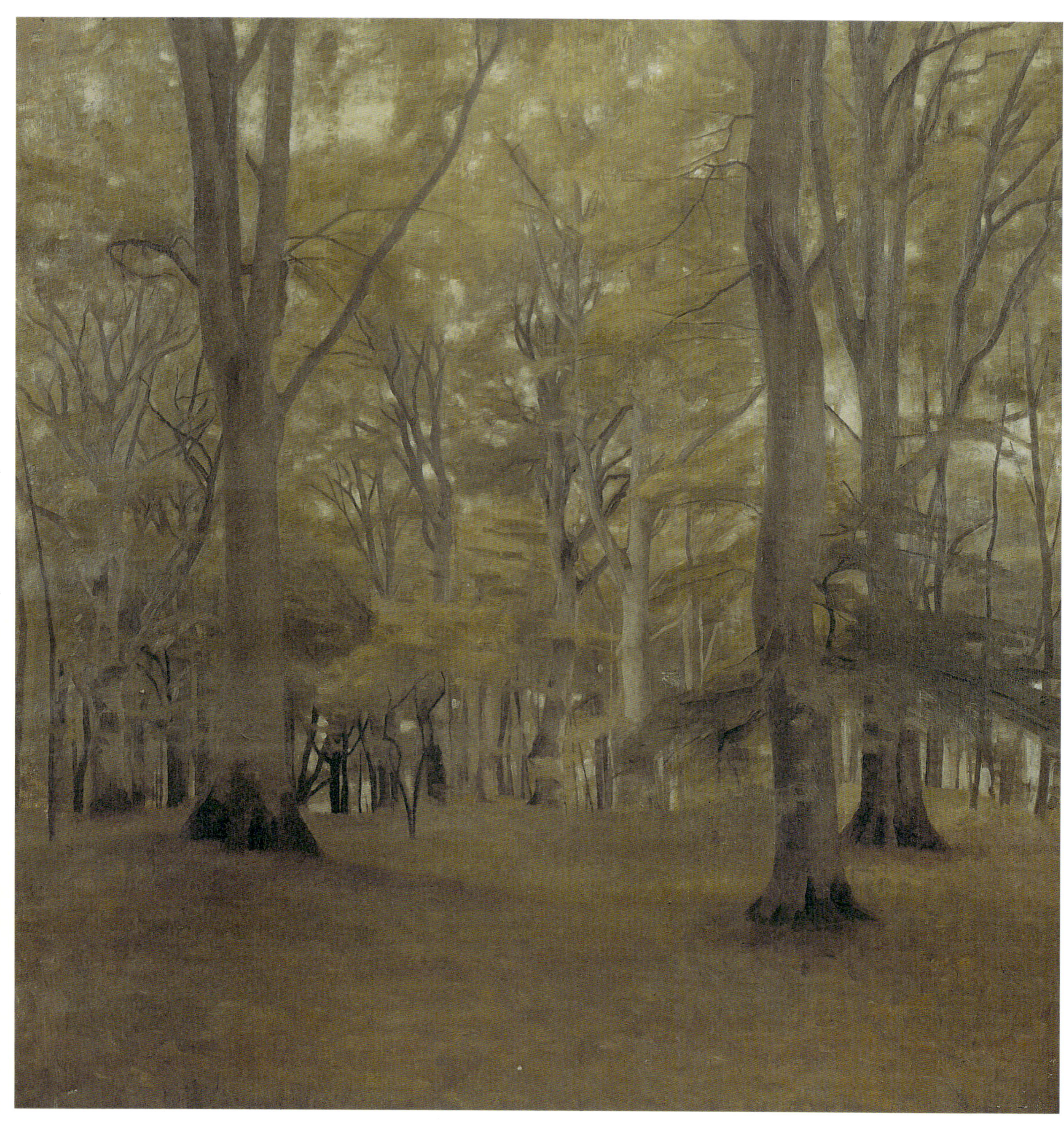

Forest Interior, also called *The Big Trees* [Halskov Vænge, Falster], [1896]
Cat. no. 13

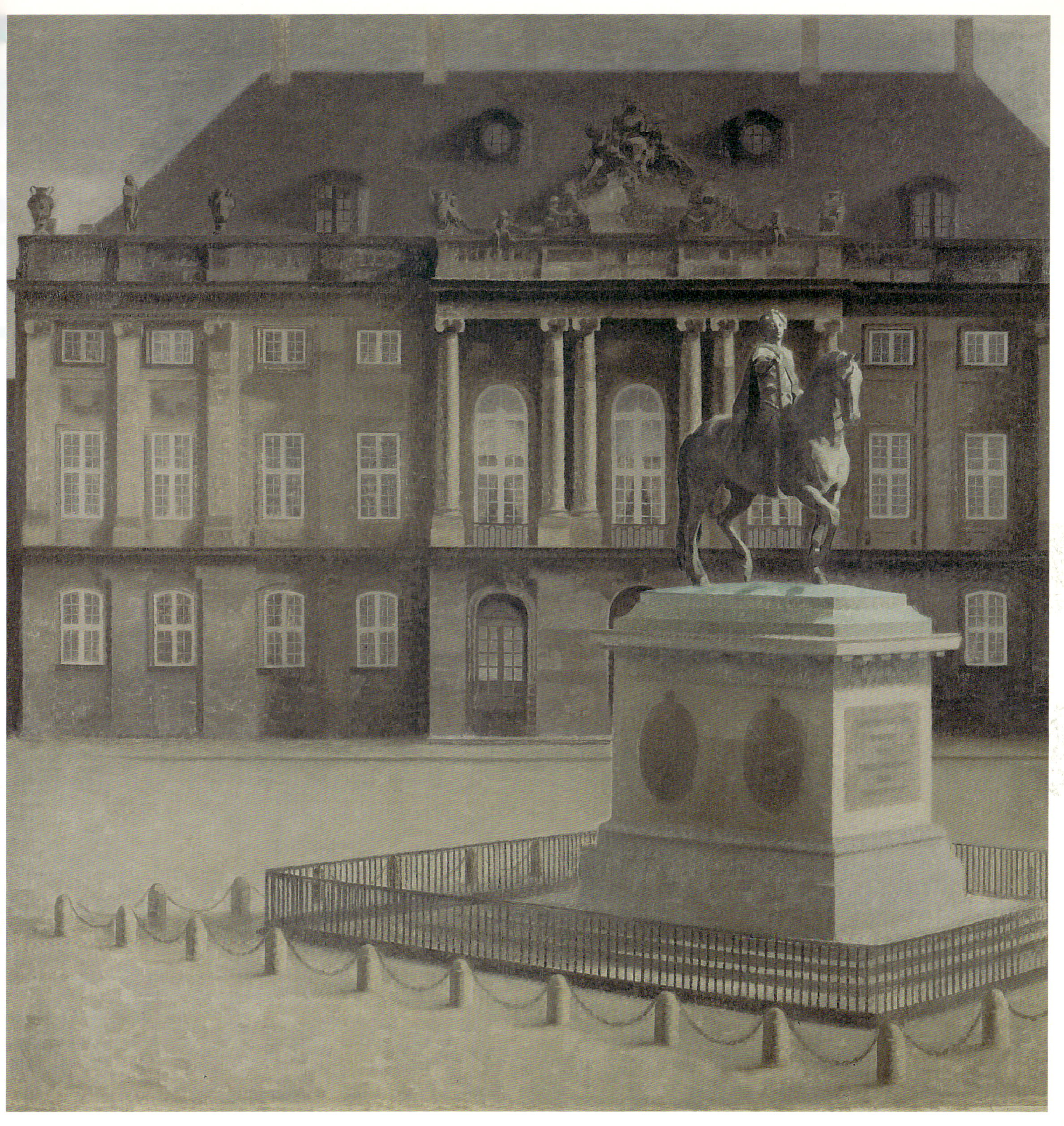

View of Amalienborg Square, [1896]
Cat. no. 12

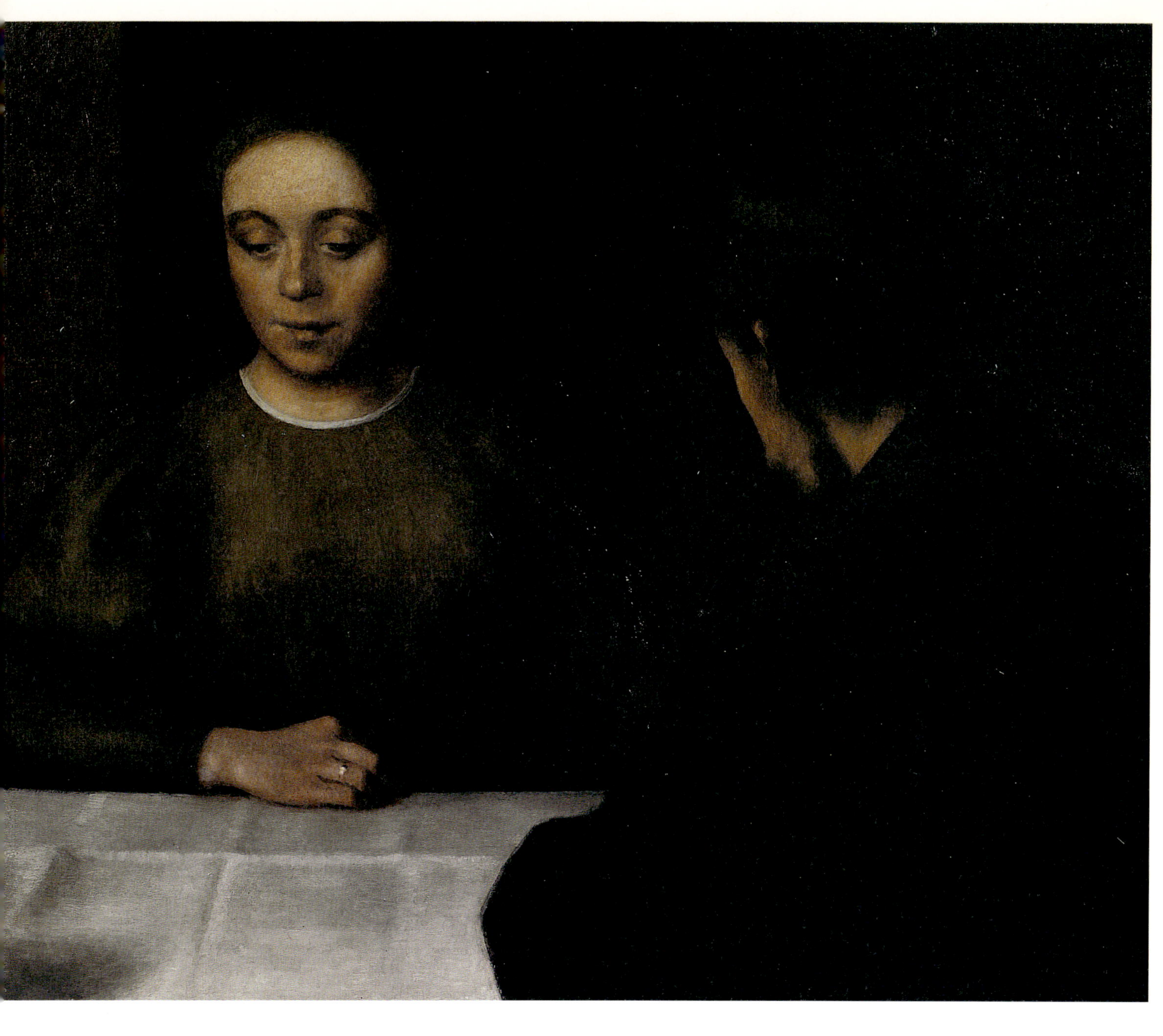

Two Figures (The Artist and His Wife), or *Double Portrait* [London], [1898]
Cat. no. 16

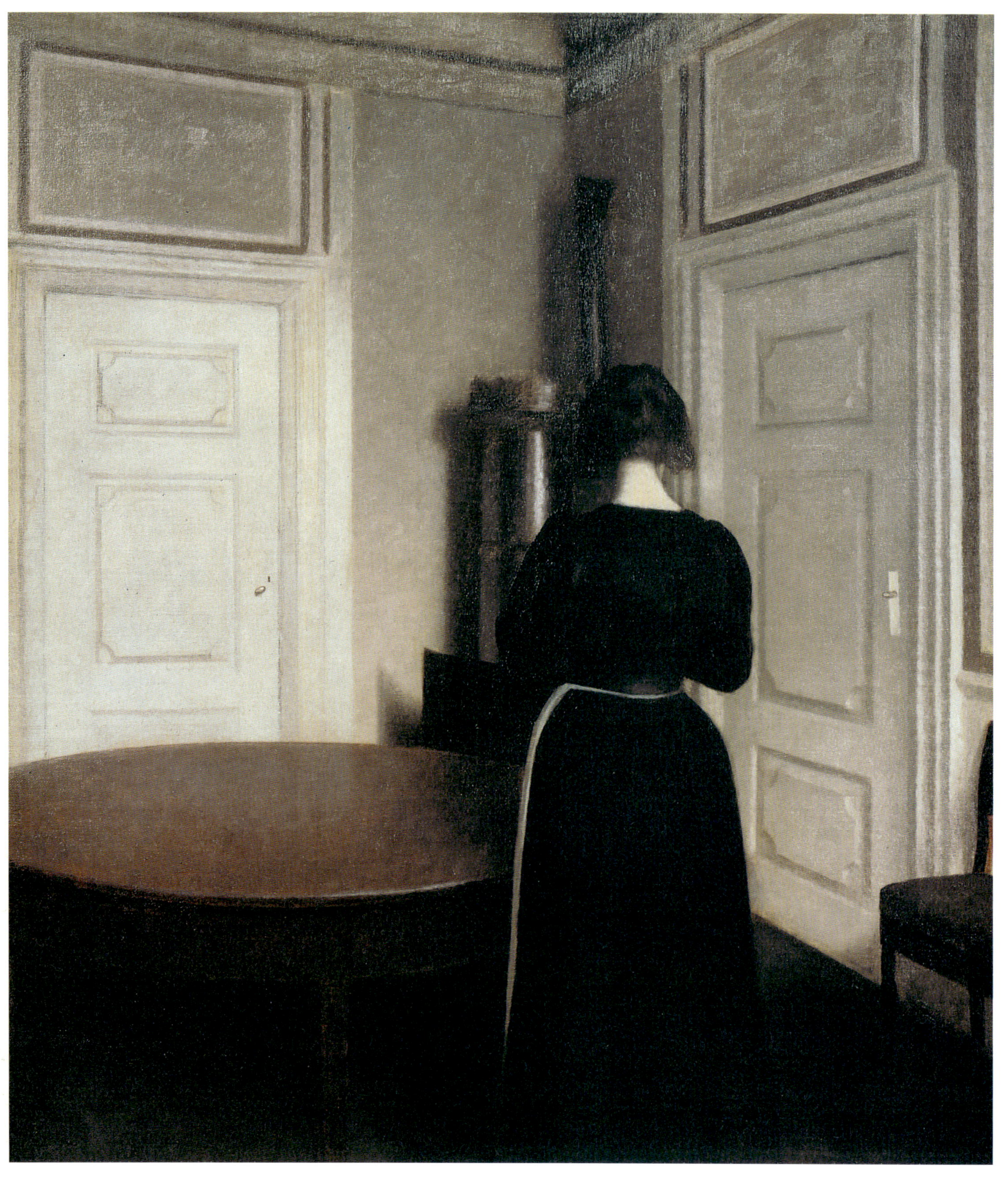

Interior, or *The Corner of a Dining Room* [Strandgade 30], [1899]
Cat. no. 18

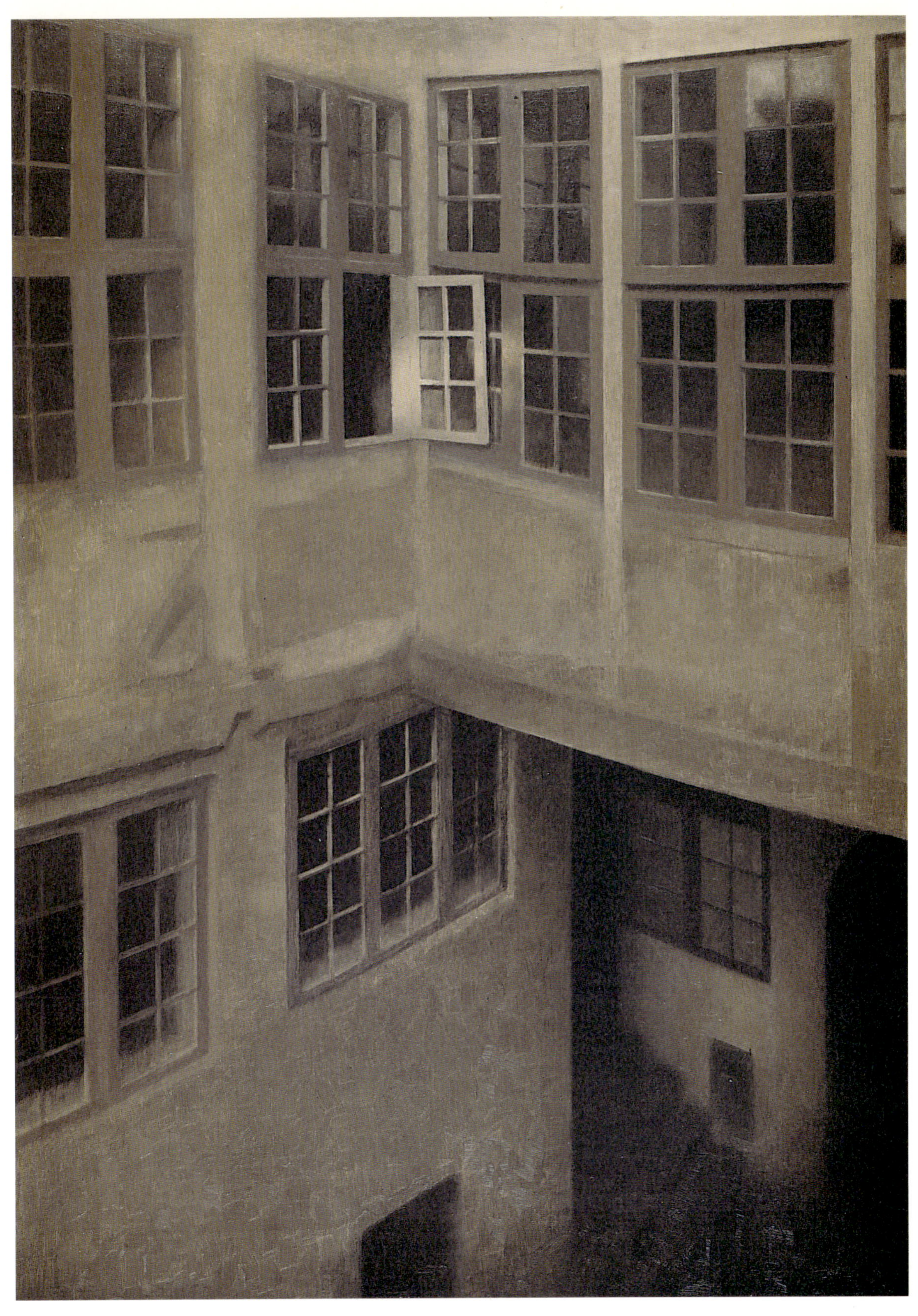

An Old Courtyard in Christianshavn, or *Interior of Courtyard* [Strandgade 30], [1899]. Cat. no. 17

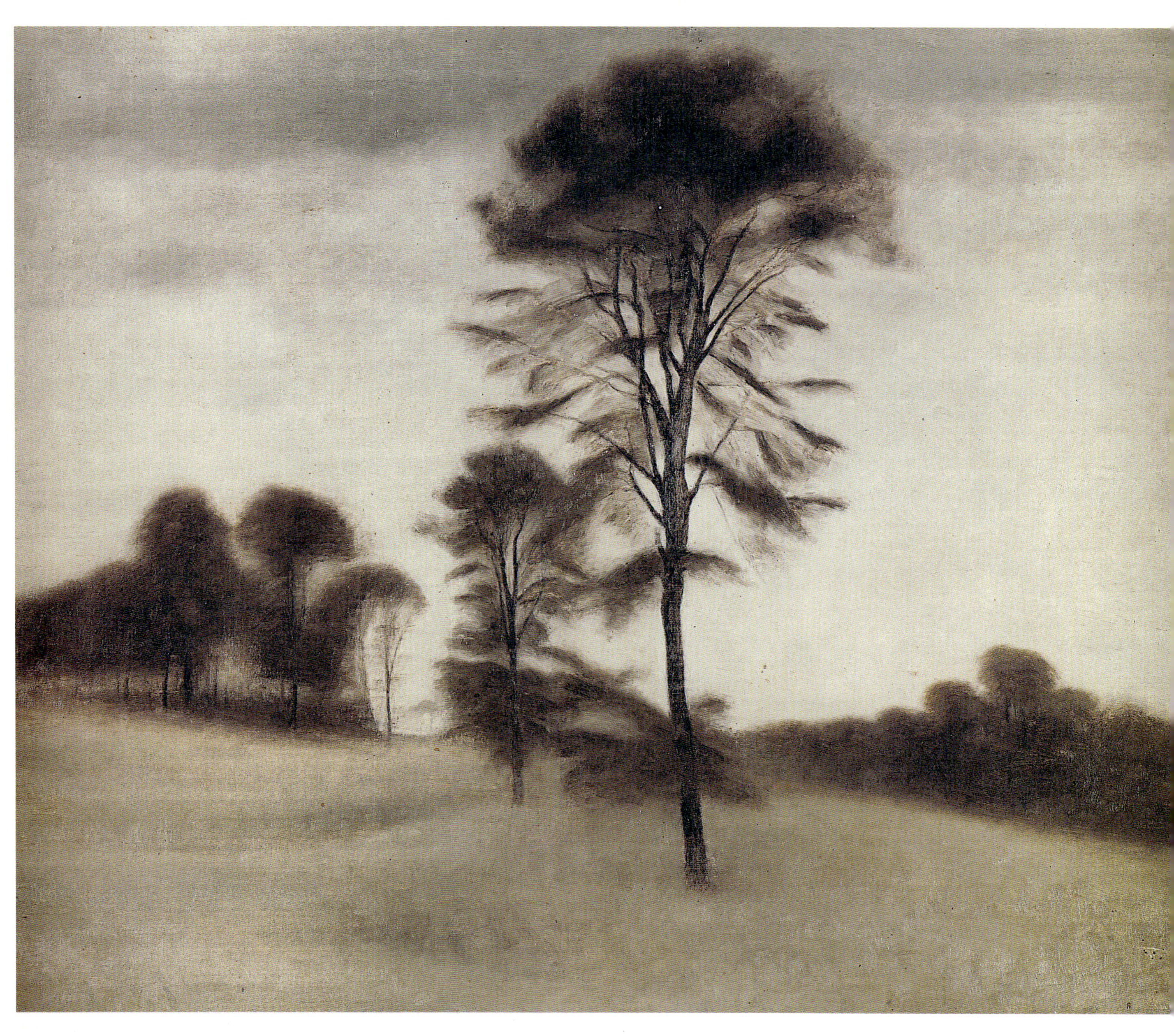

Landscape, Ryet [Farum], [1896]
Cat. no. 14

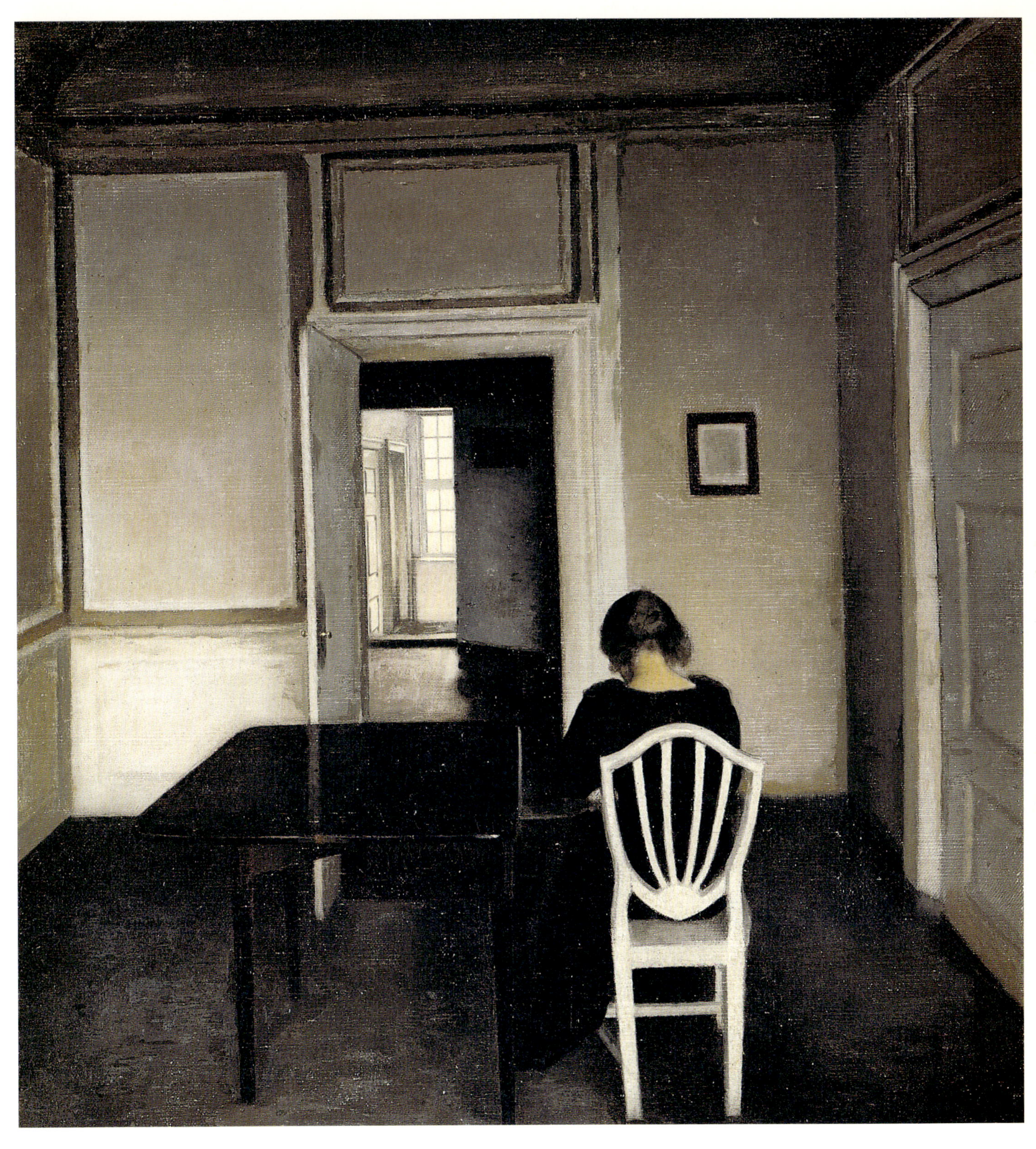

Open Doors [Interior with woman in black on white chair, Strandgade 30], [1900]
Cat. no. 19

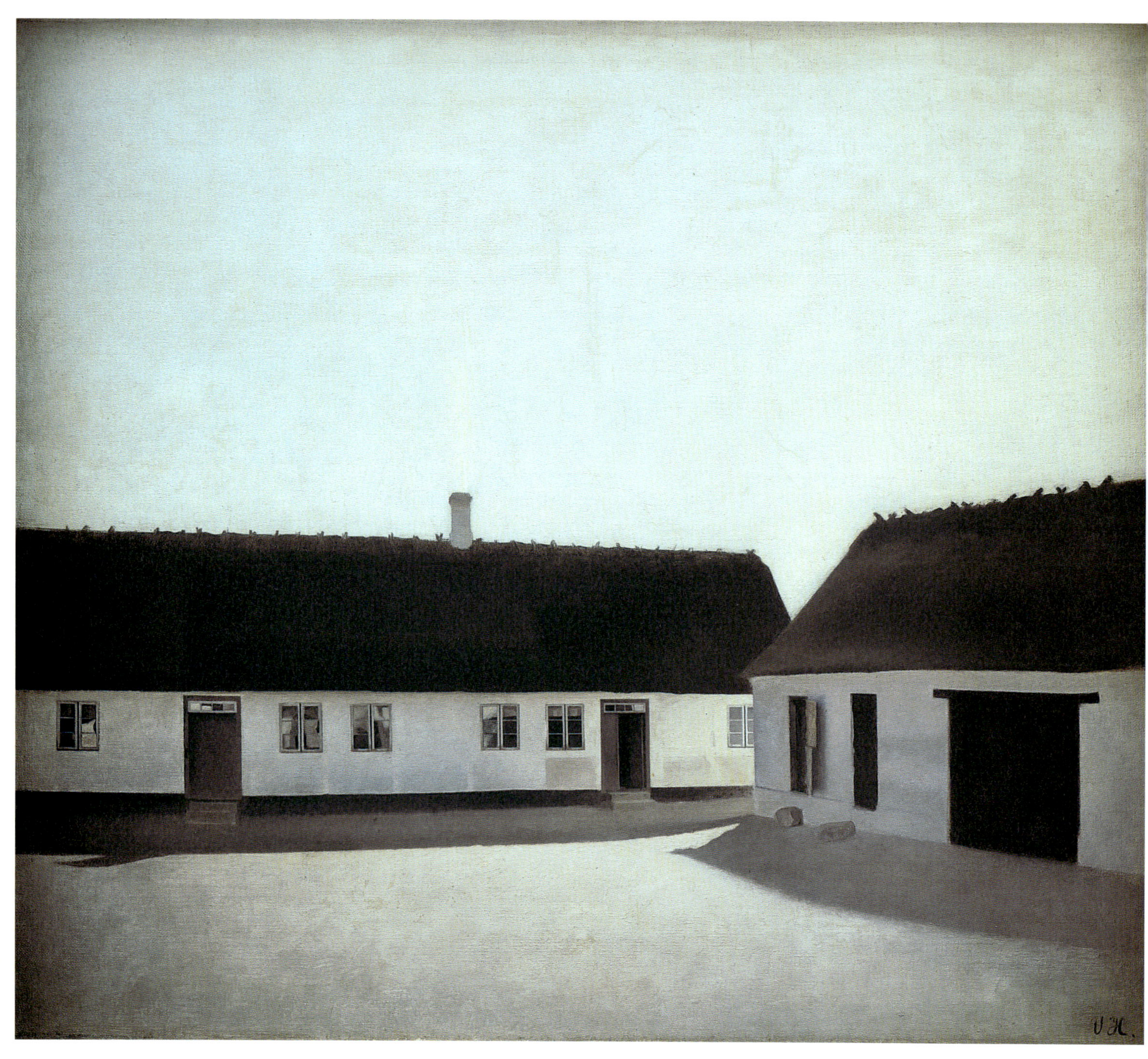

Farm [Refsnæs], [1900]
Cat. no. 21

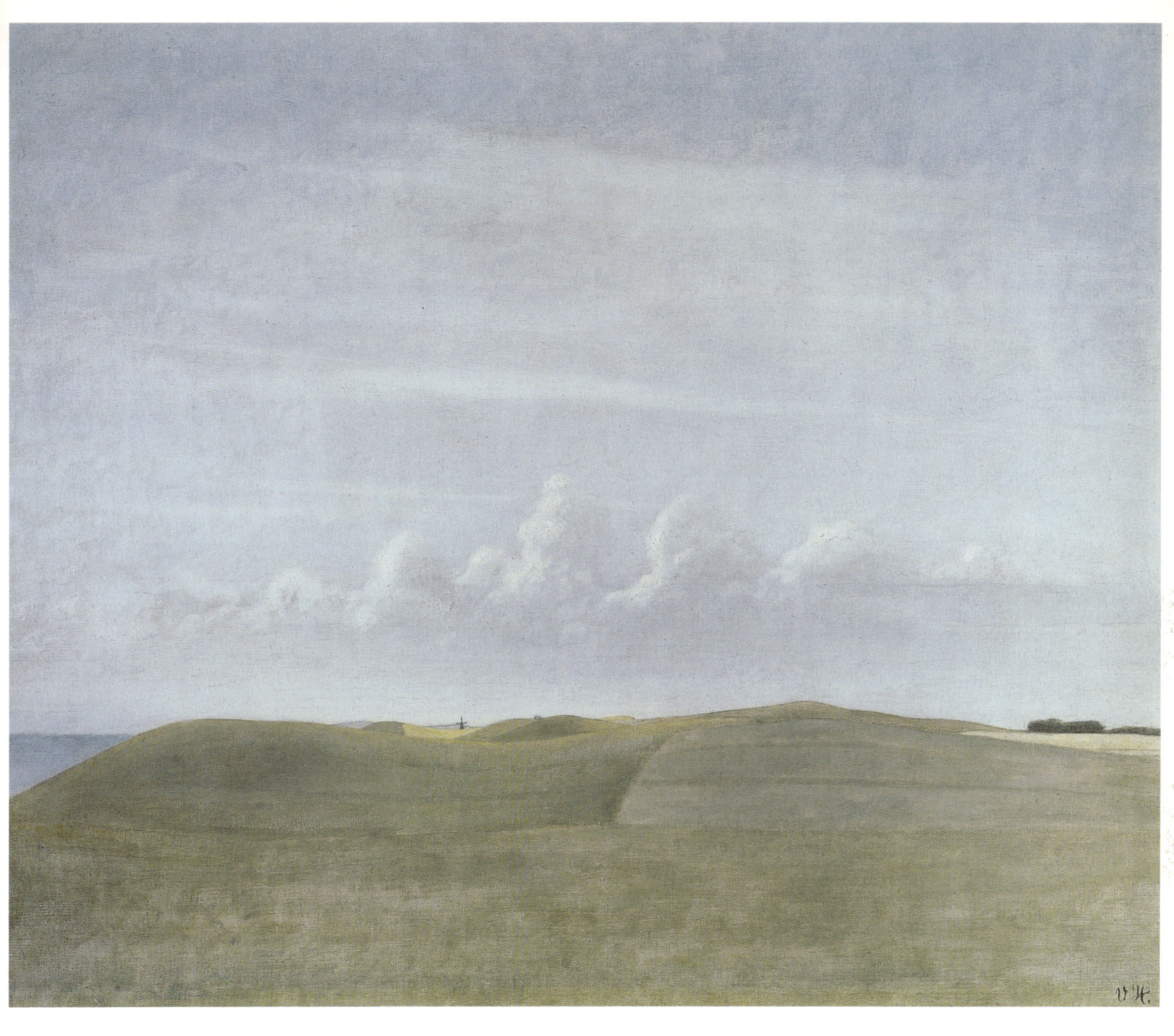

View of Refsnæs, [1900]
Cat. no. 22

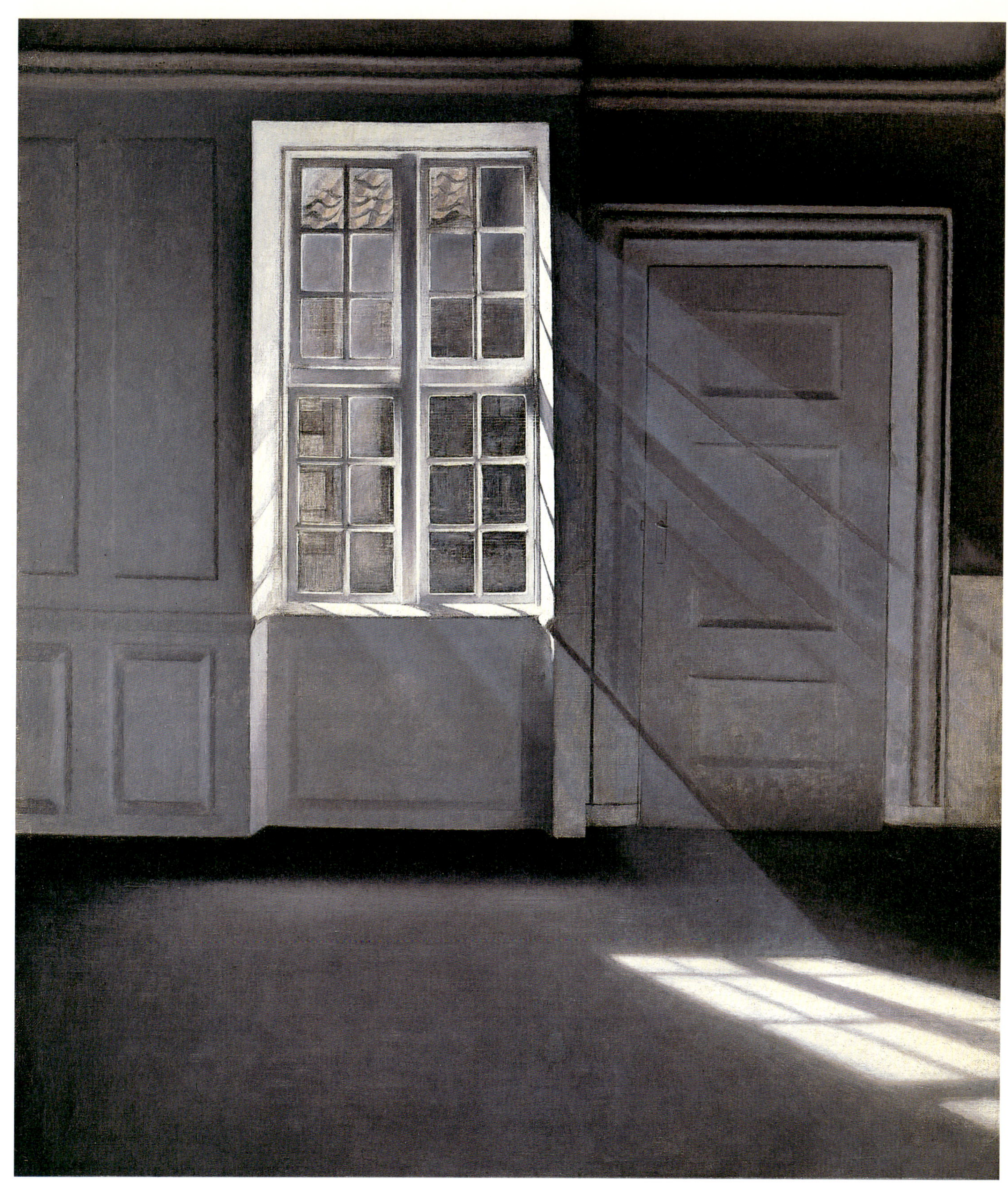

Sunbeams, or *Sunlight*, also called *Dust Motes Dancing in the Sunbeams* [Strandgade 30], [1900]. Cat. no. 20

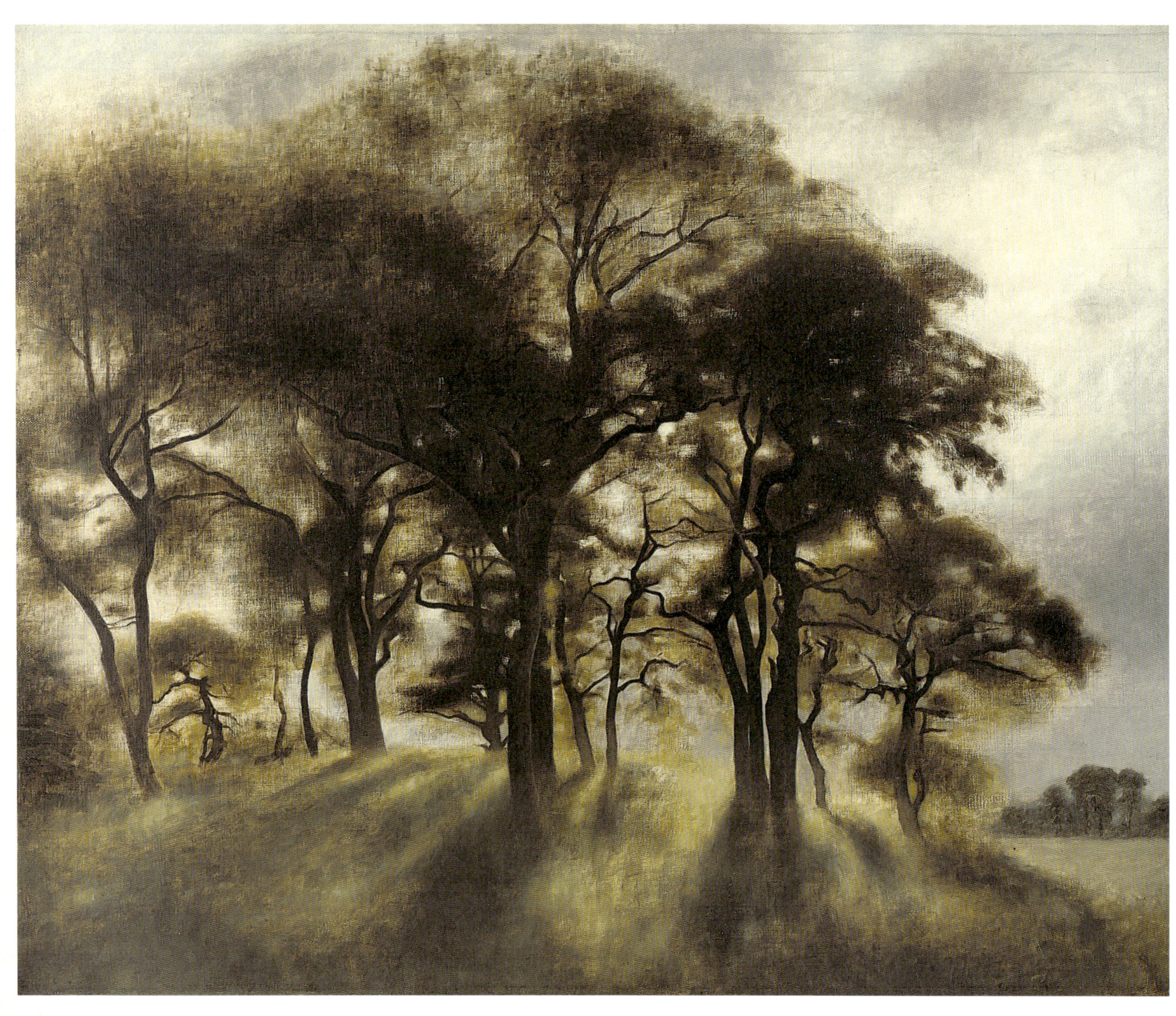

Landscape: View of Fortunen, [1901]
Cat. no. 24

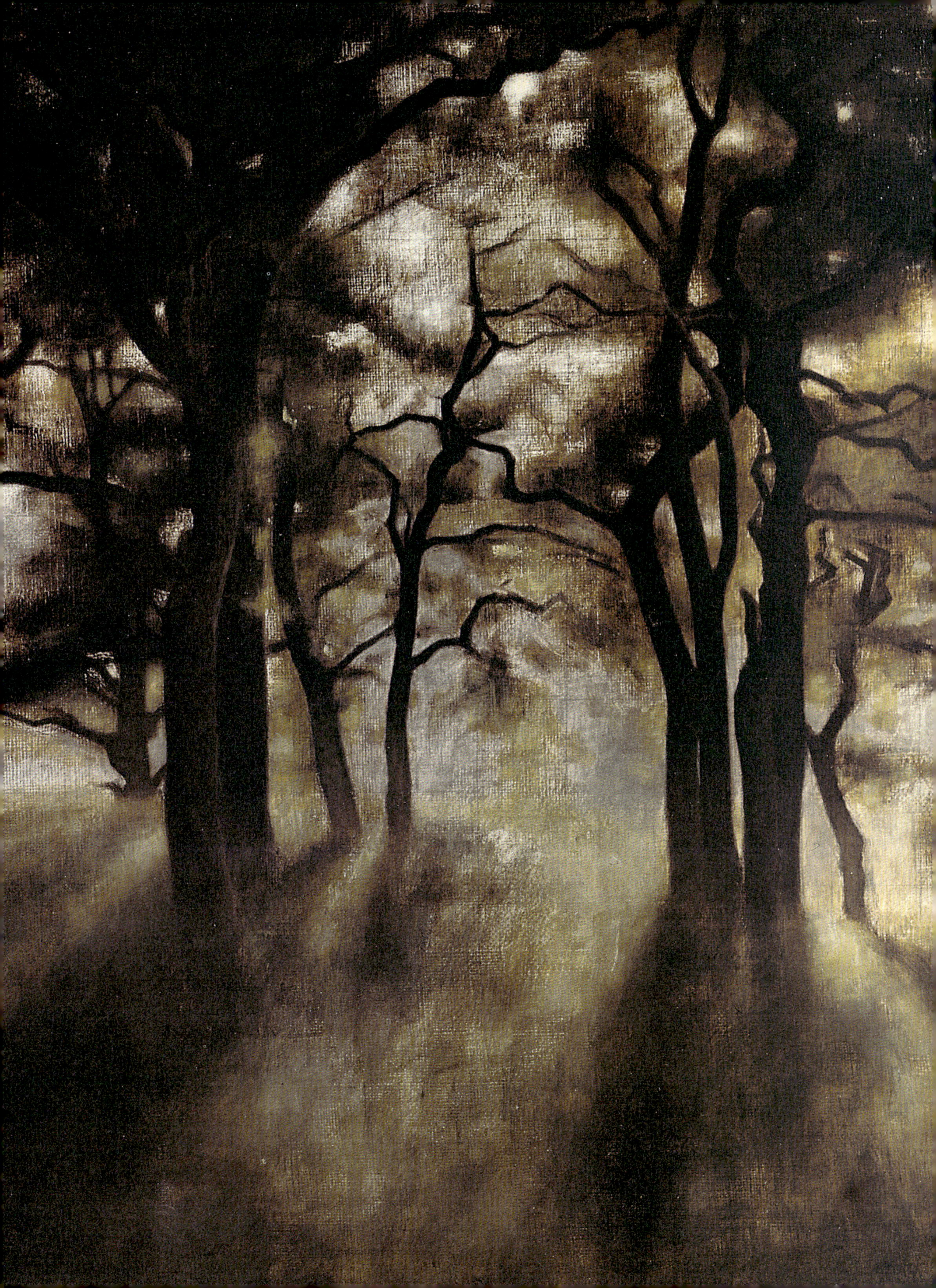

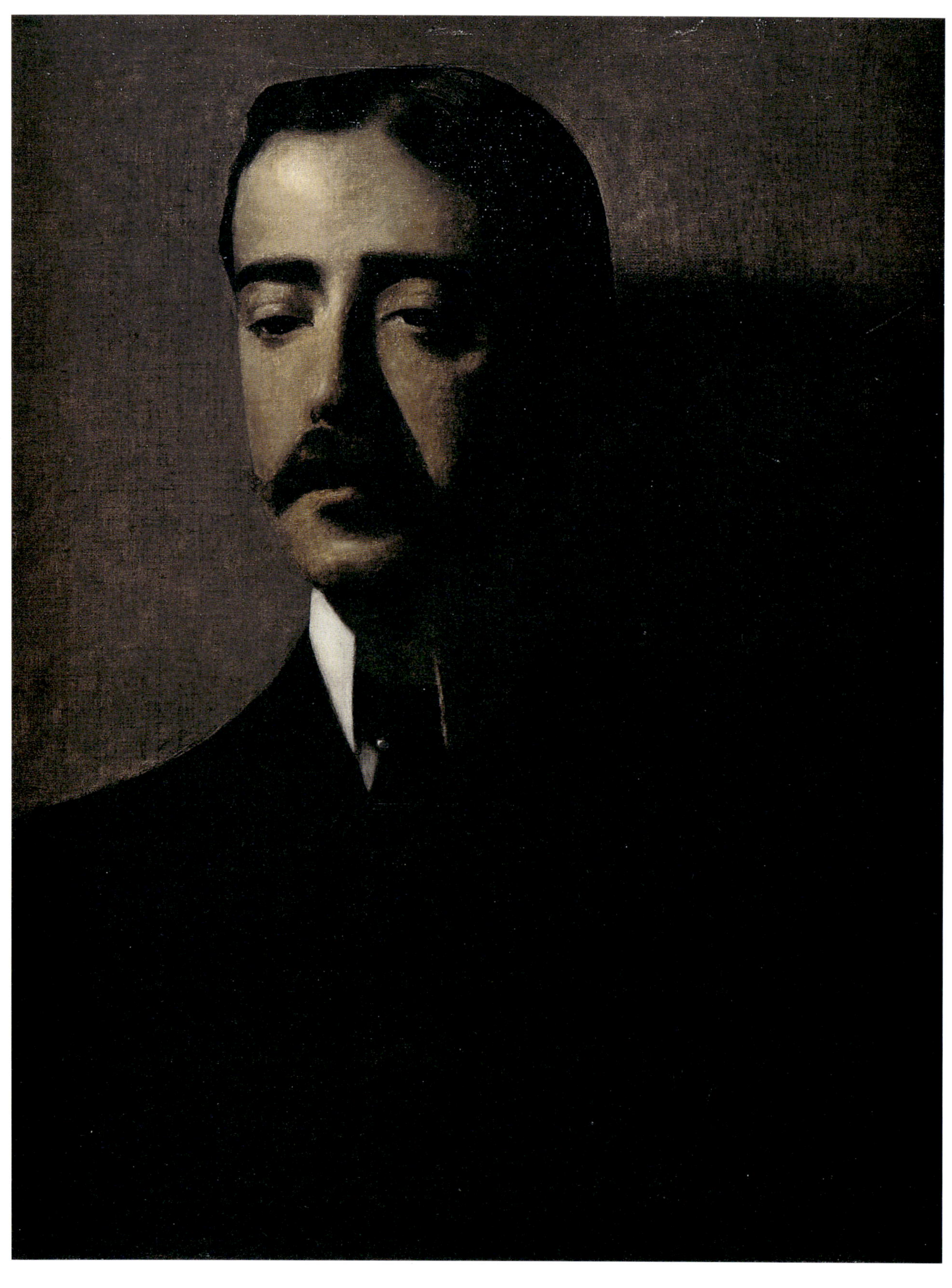

Portrait [Daniel Jacobson Salter], [1901]
Cat. no. 23

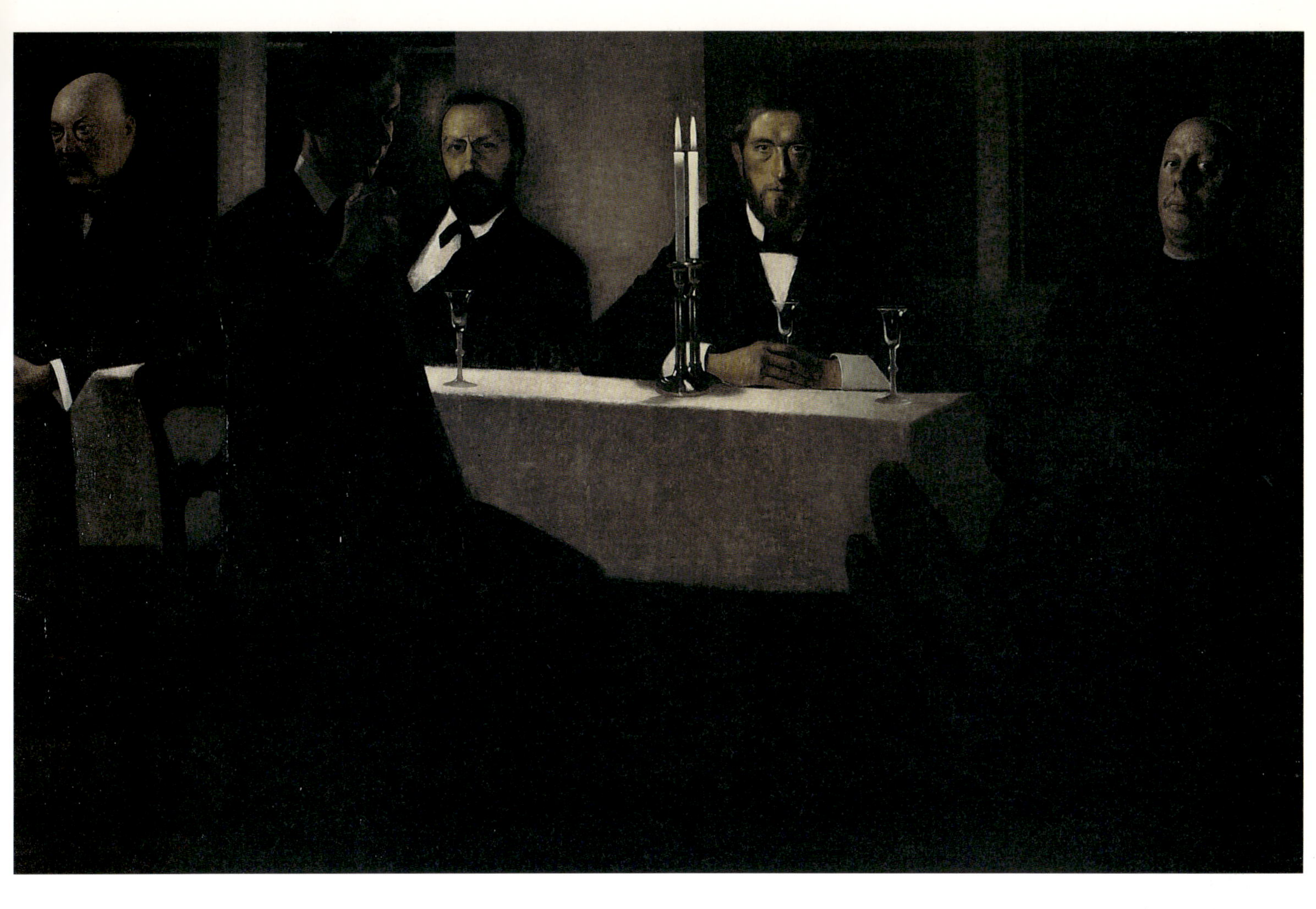

Five Portraits, [1901–02]
Cat. no. 26

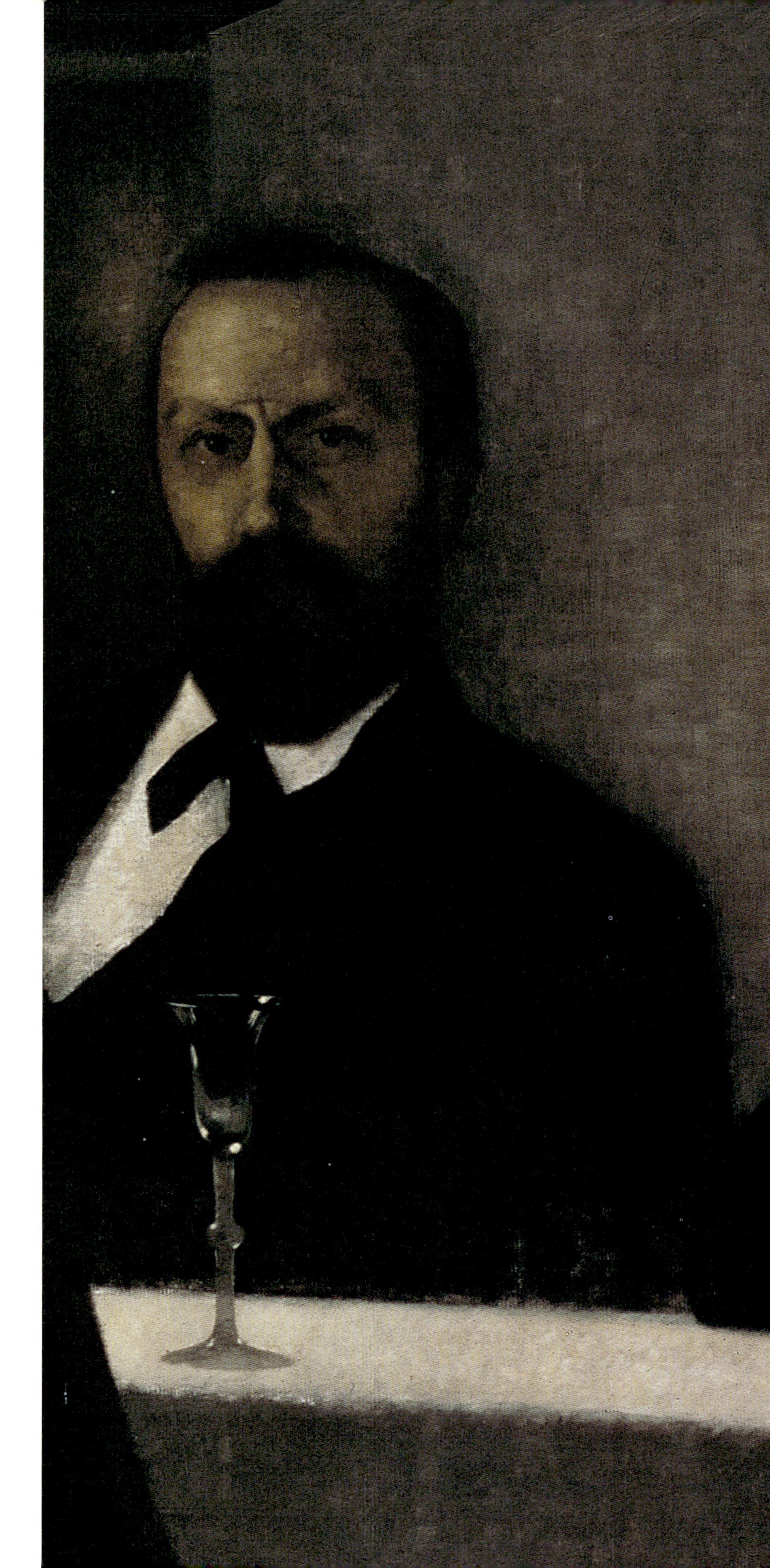

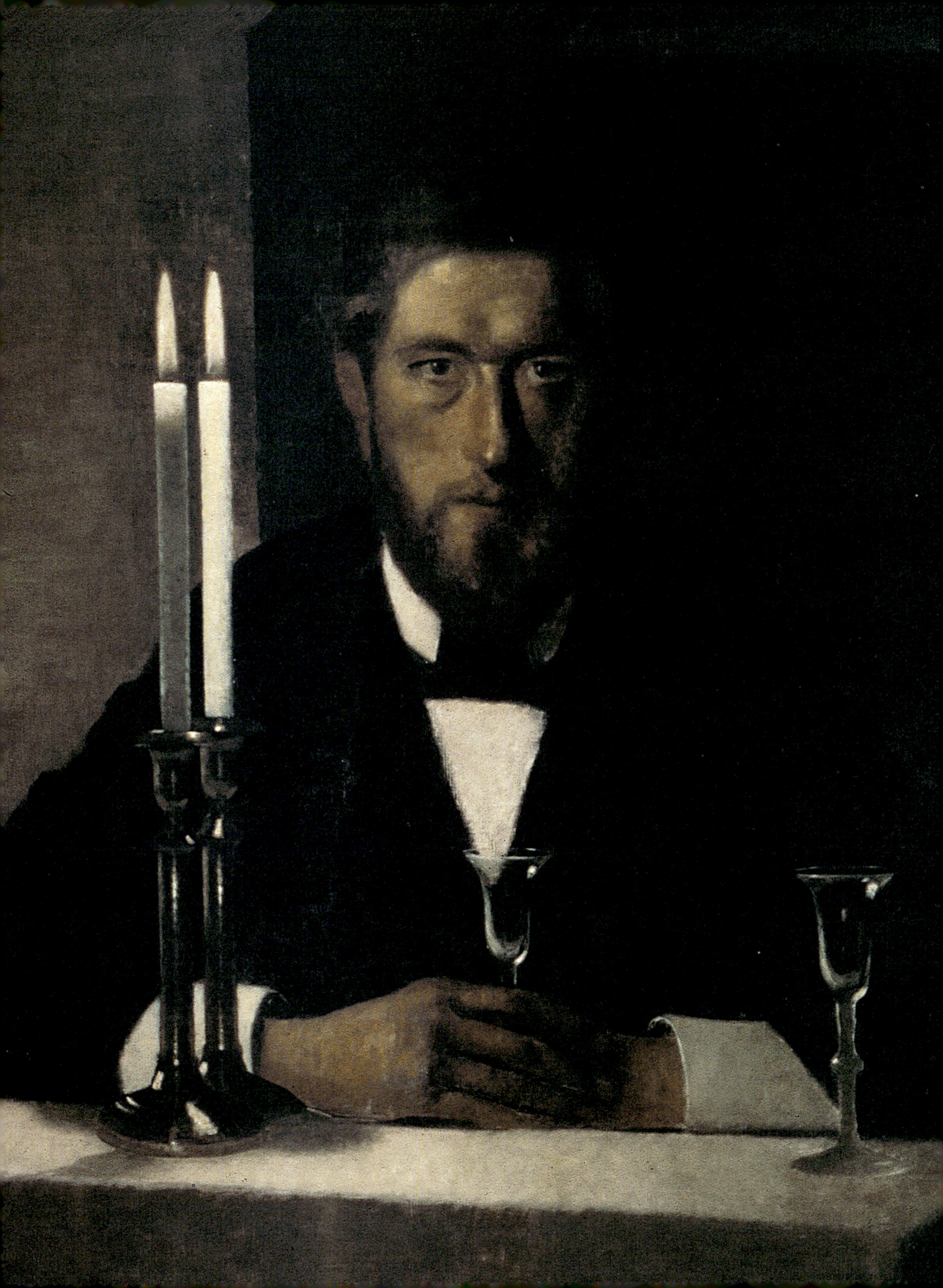

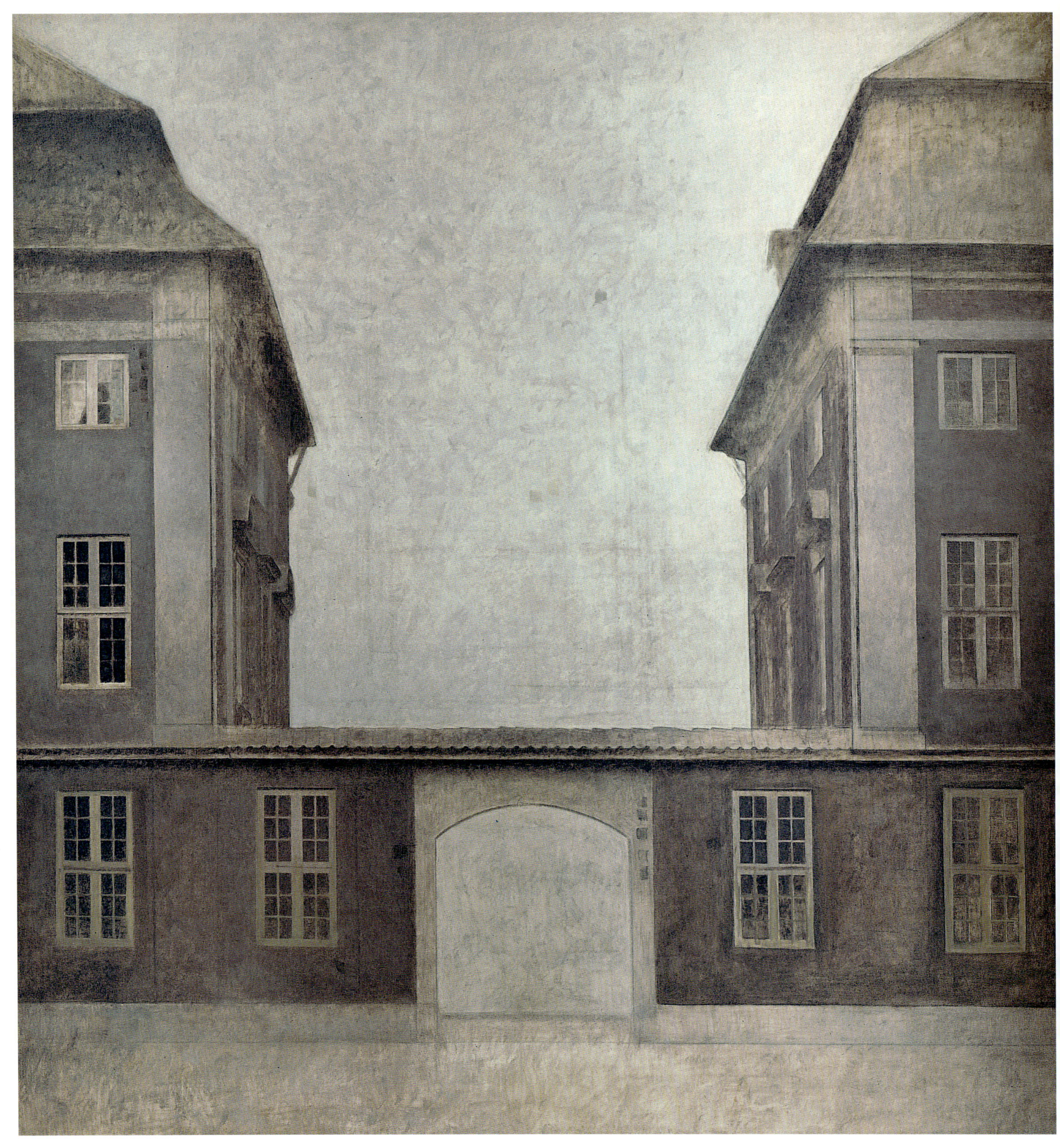

The Asiatic Company Buildings, [1902]
Cat. no. 27

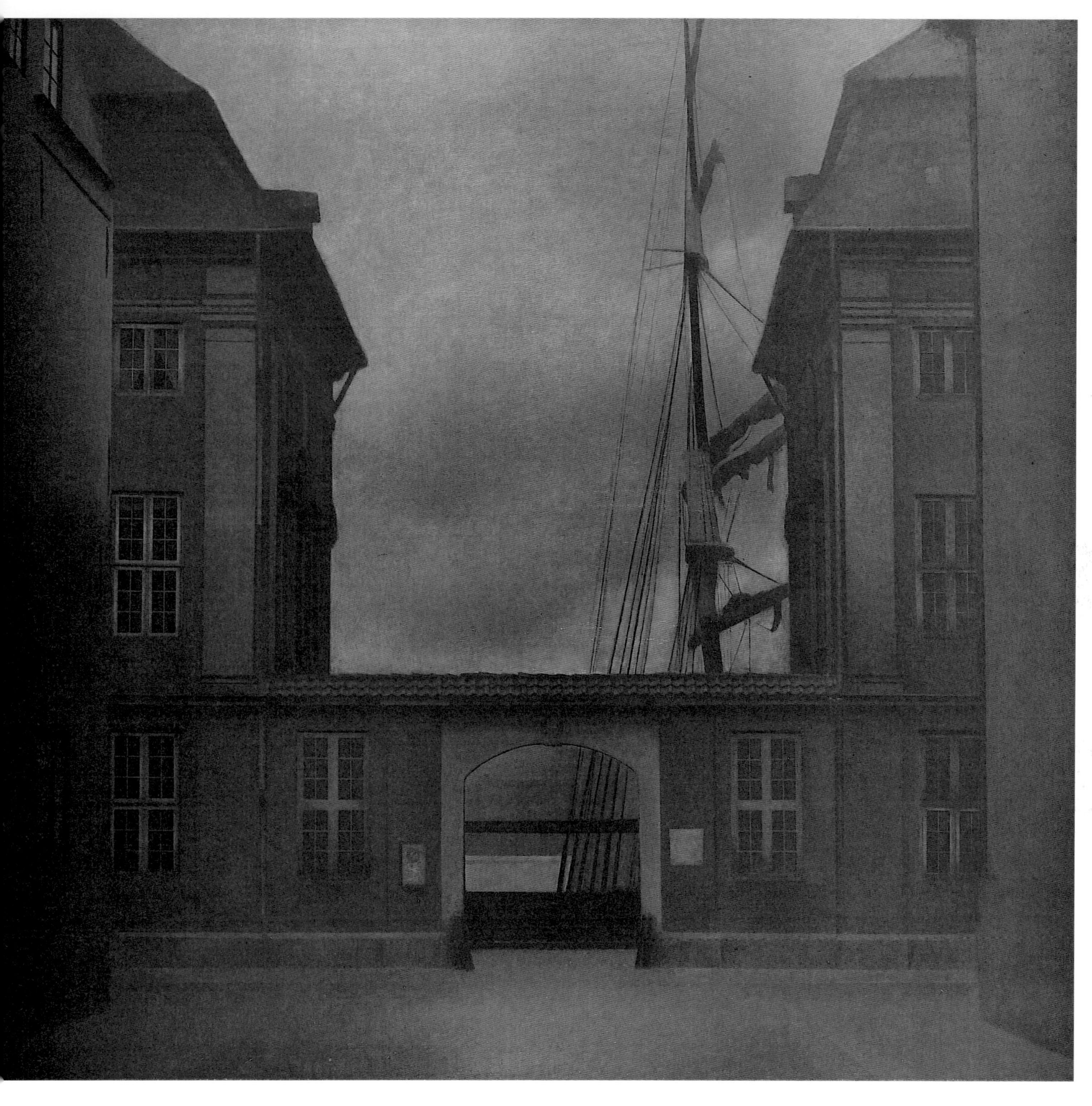

View of the Old Asiatic Company, or *The Asiatic Company Buildings*, [1902]
Cat. no. 28

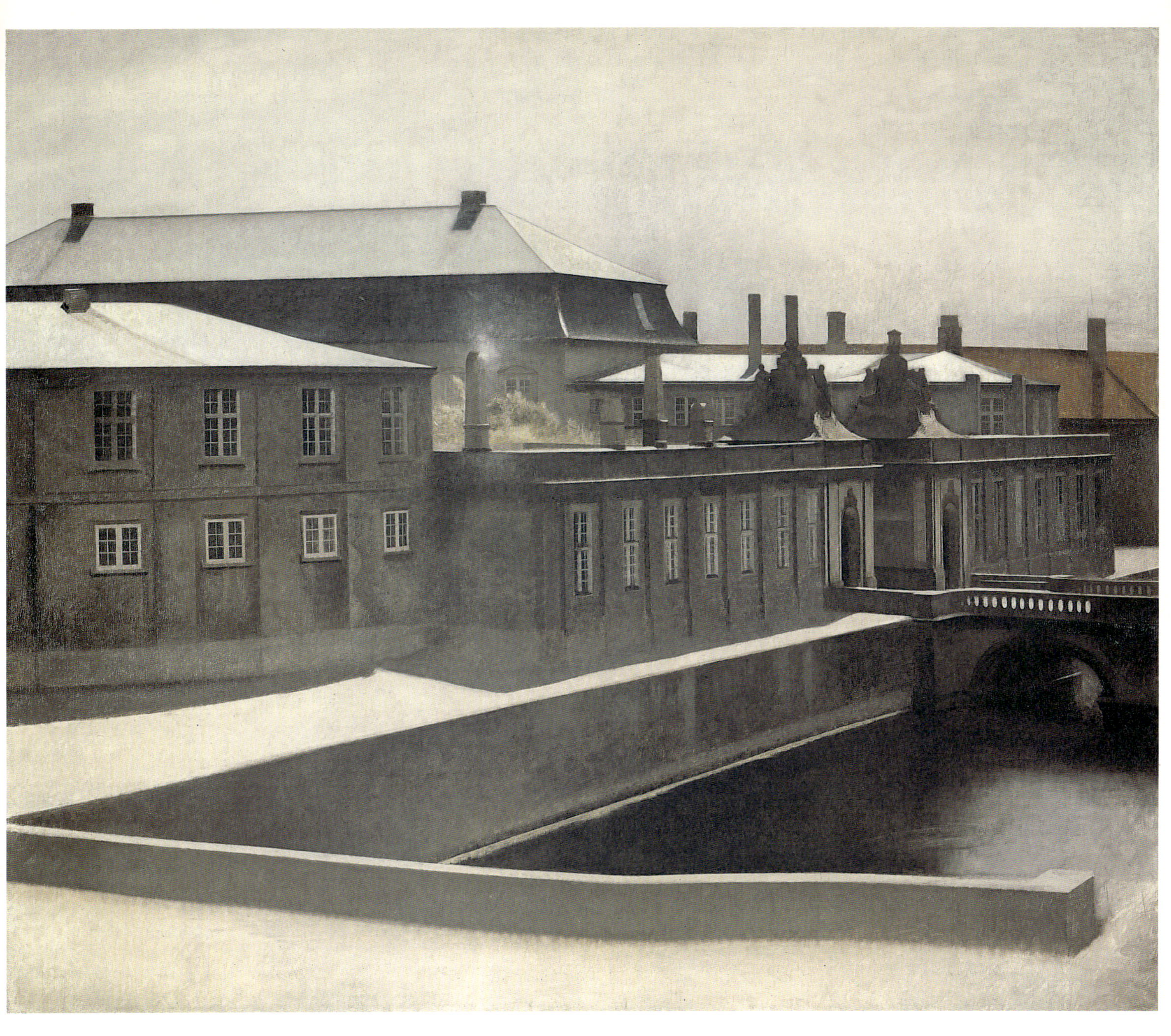

View of Old Christiansborg Palace, [1902]
Cat. no. 29

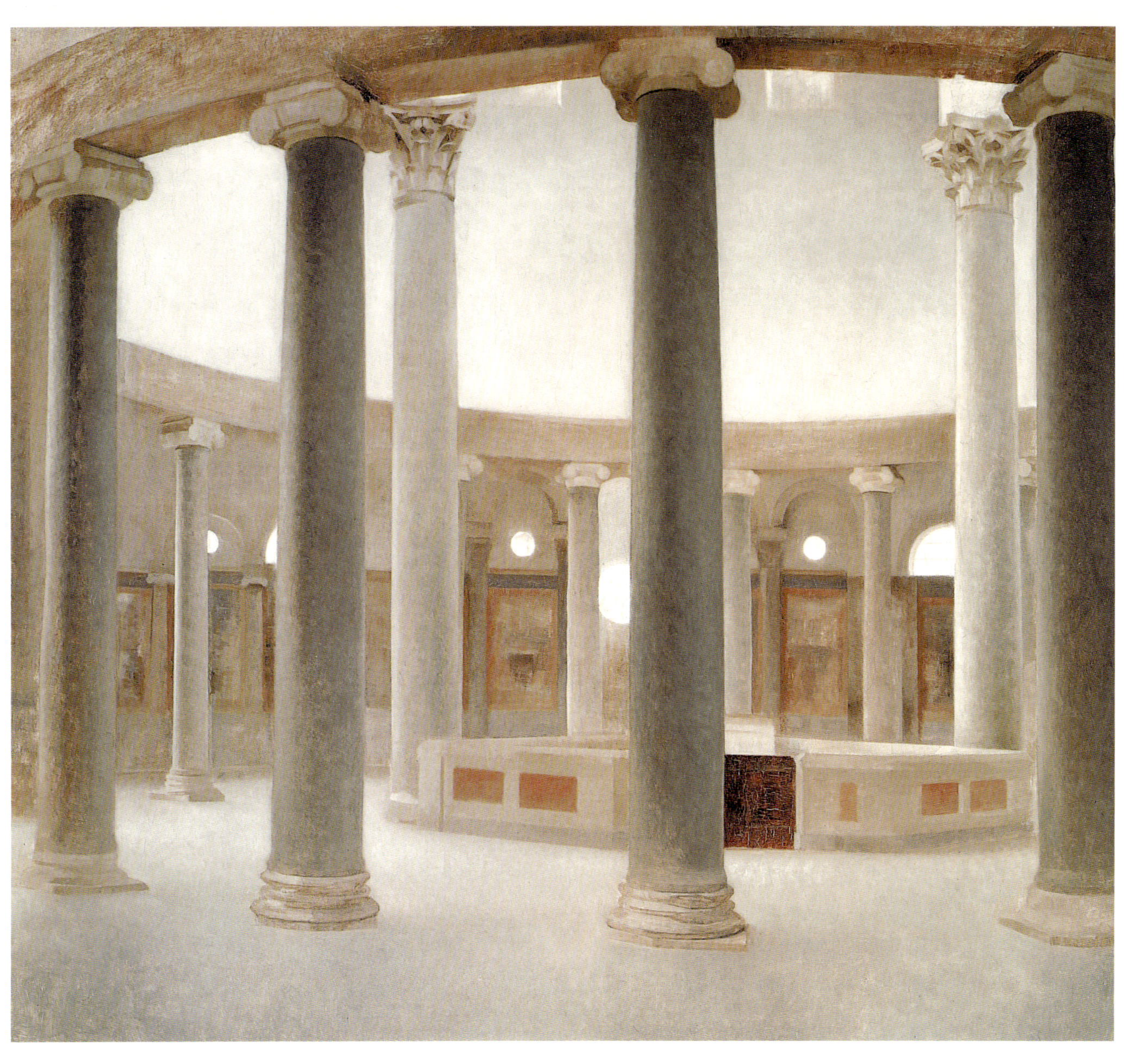

Interior of the Church of San Stefano Rotundo in Rome,
or *Church Interior* [1902–03]. Cat. no. 30

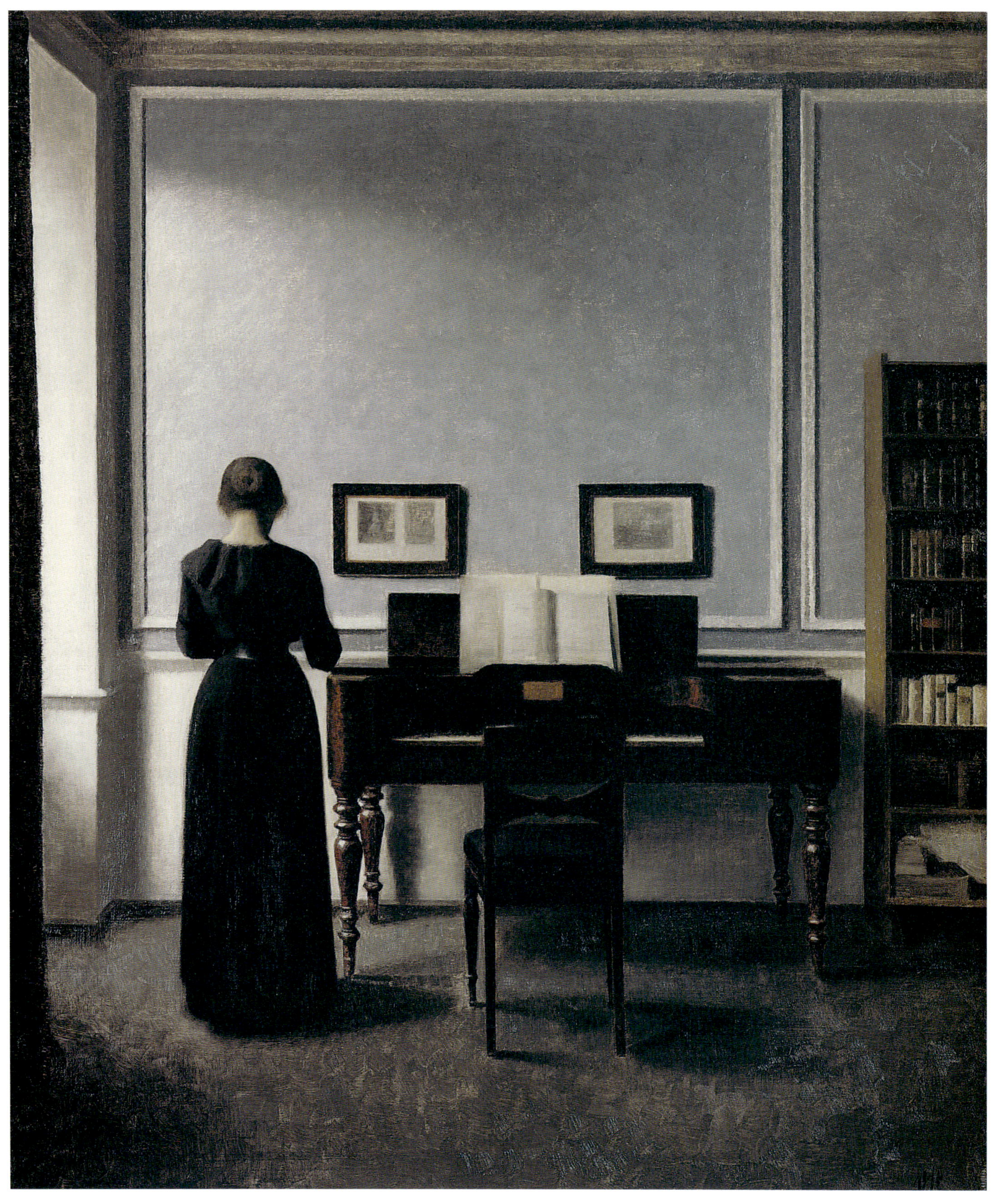

Interior [with piano and woman in black, Strandgade 30], [1901]
Cat. no. 25

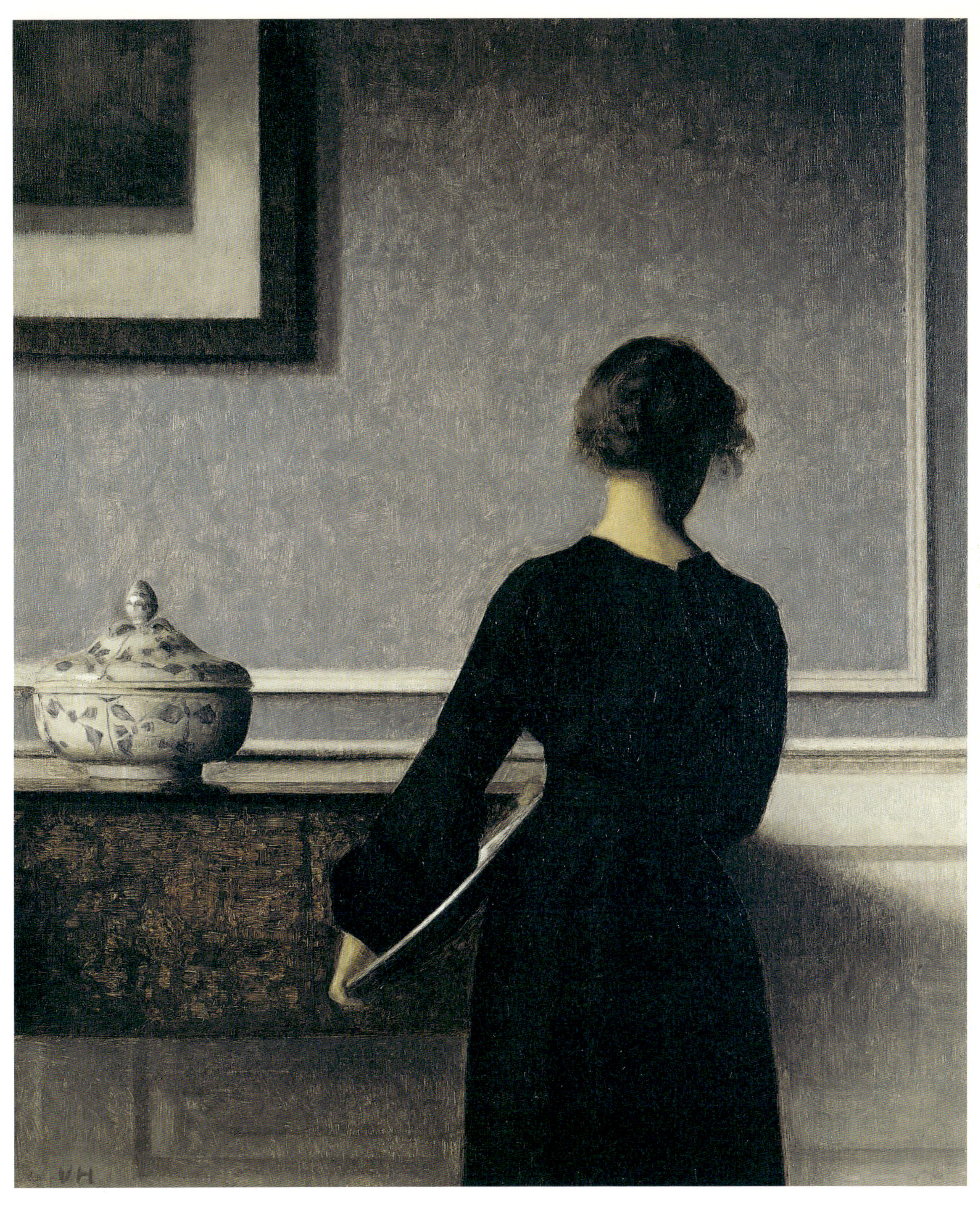

Interior [with young woman seen from behind, Strandgade 30], [ca. 1903–04]
Cat. no. 32

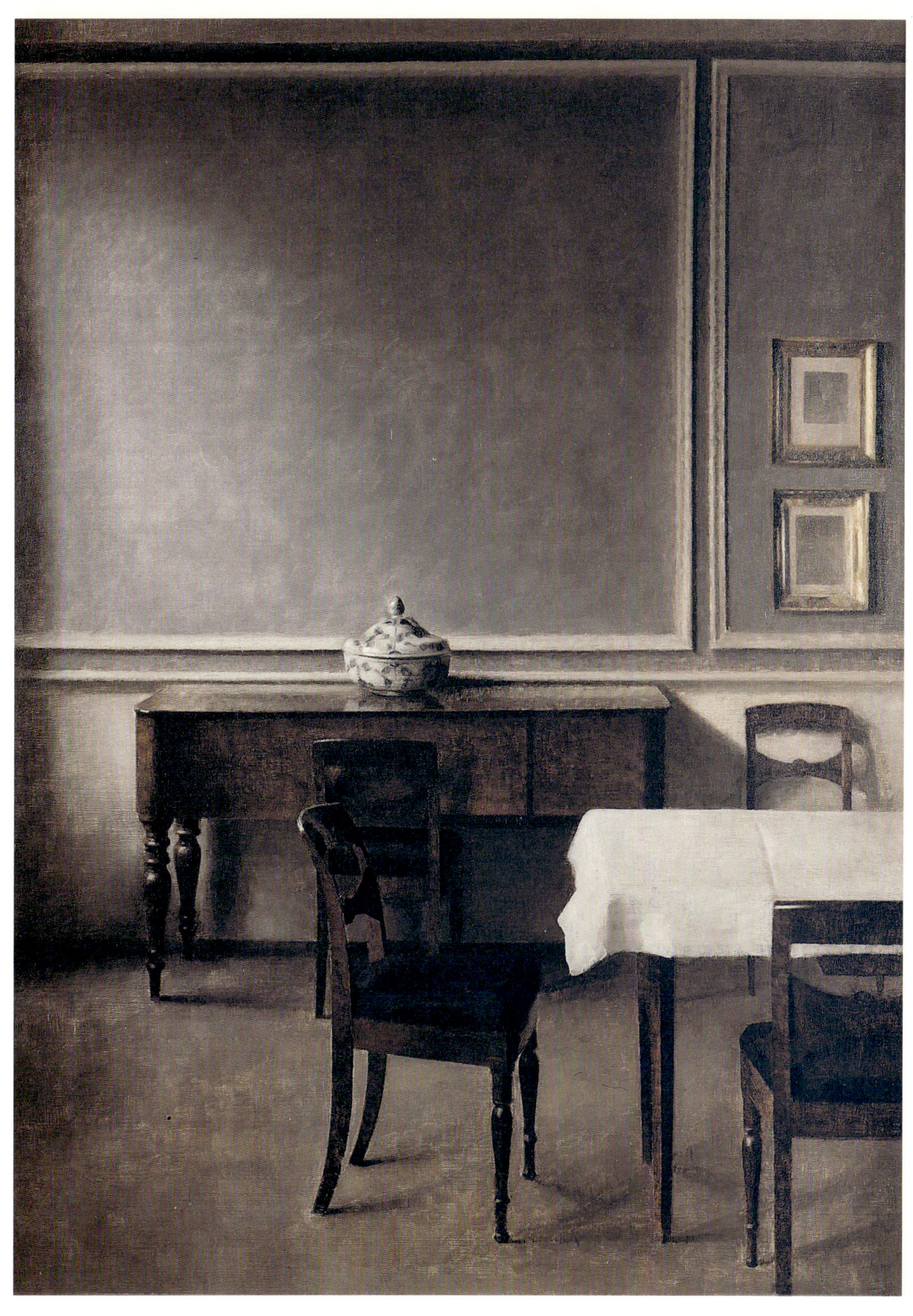

Interior with Punch Bowl [Strandgade 30], [1904]
Cat. no. 33

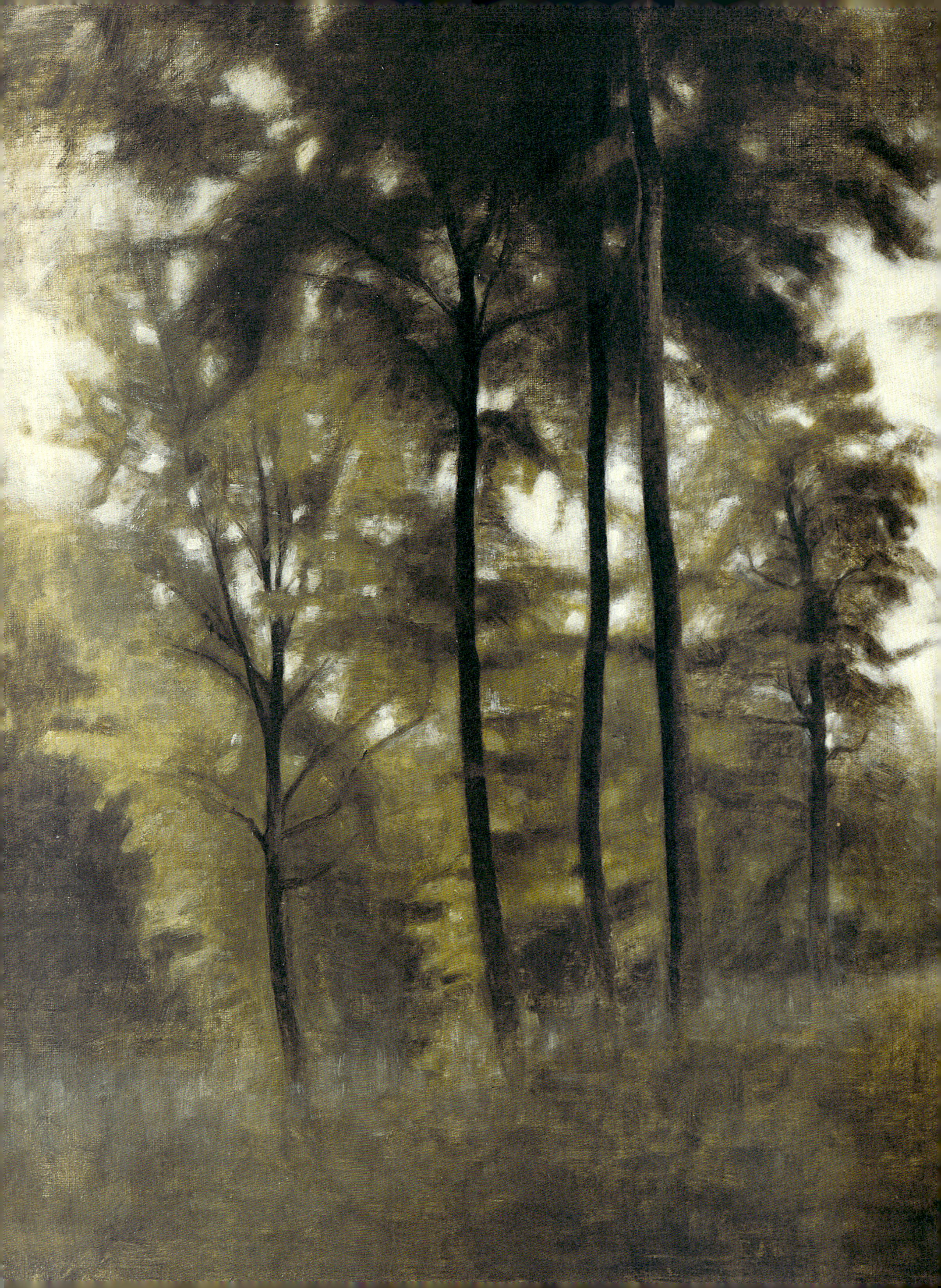

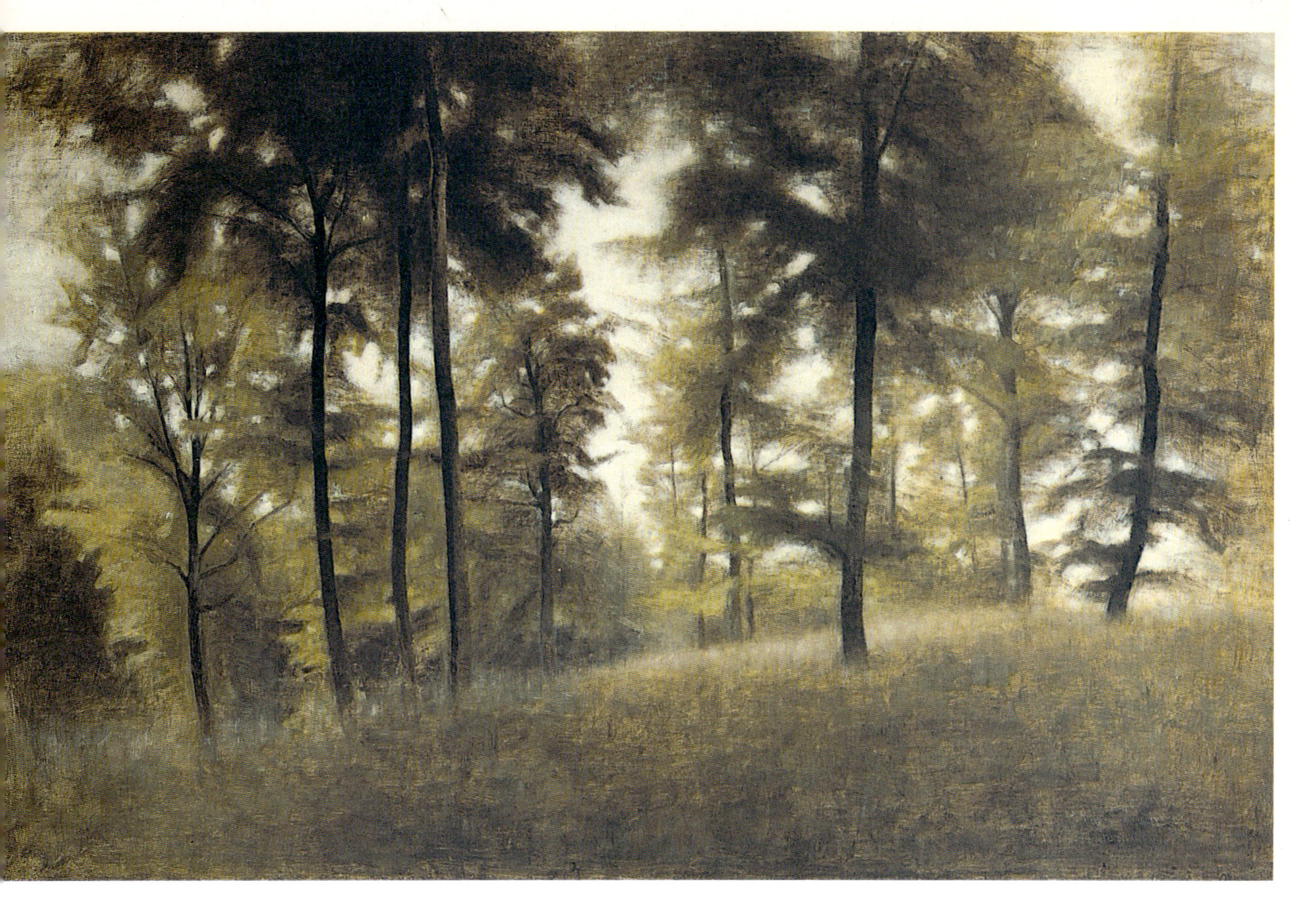

Young Beech Forest [Arresødal, Frederiksværk], [1904]
Cat. no. 35

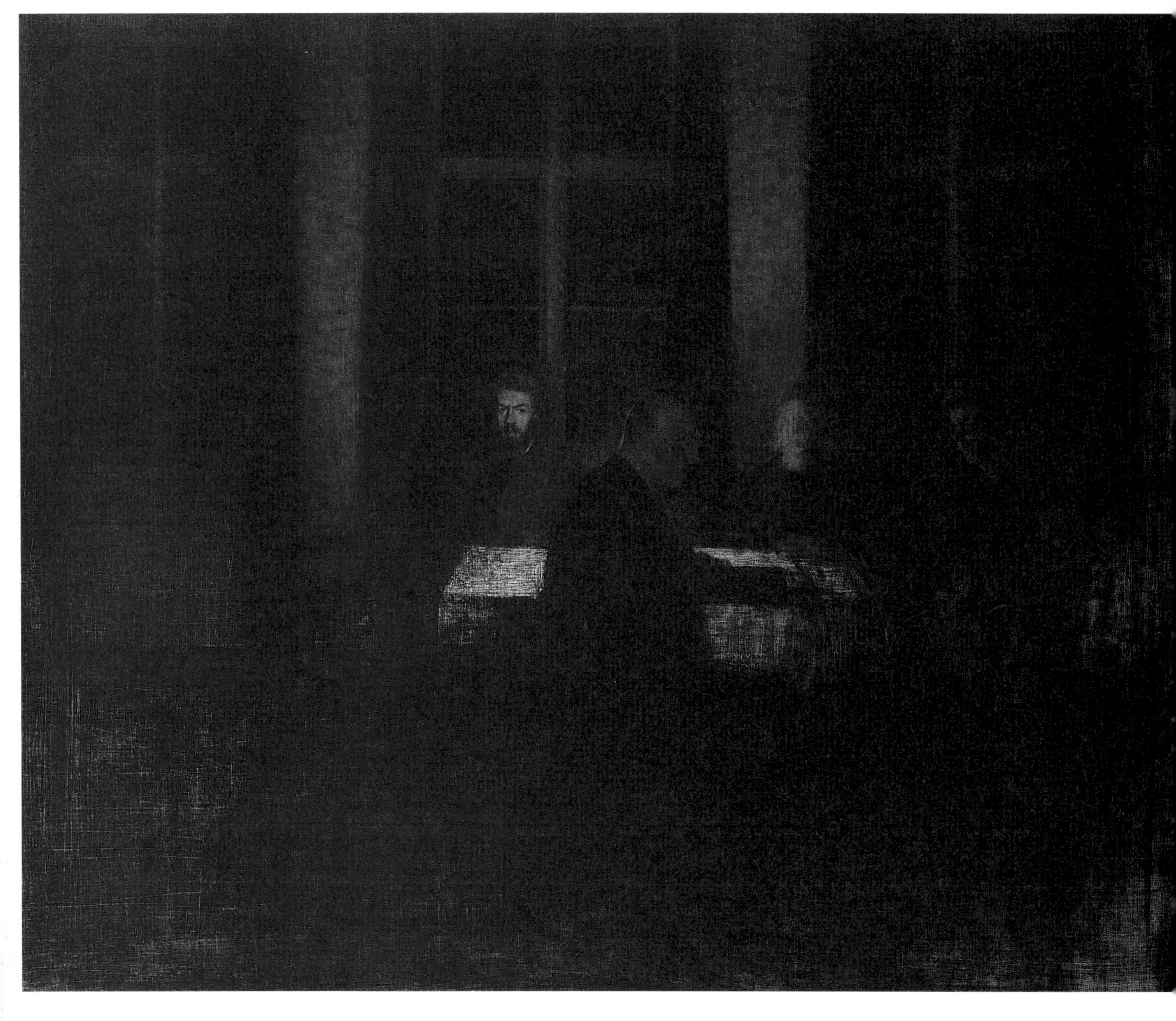

Soirée in the Living Room, [1904]
Cat. no. 36

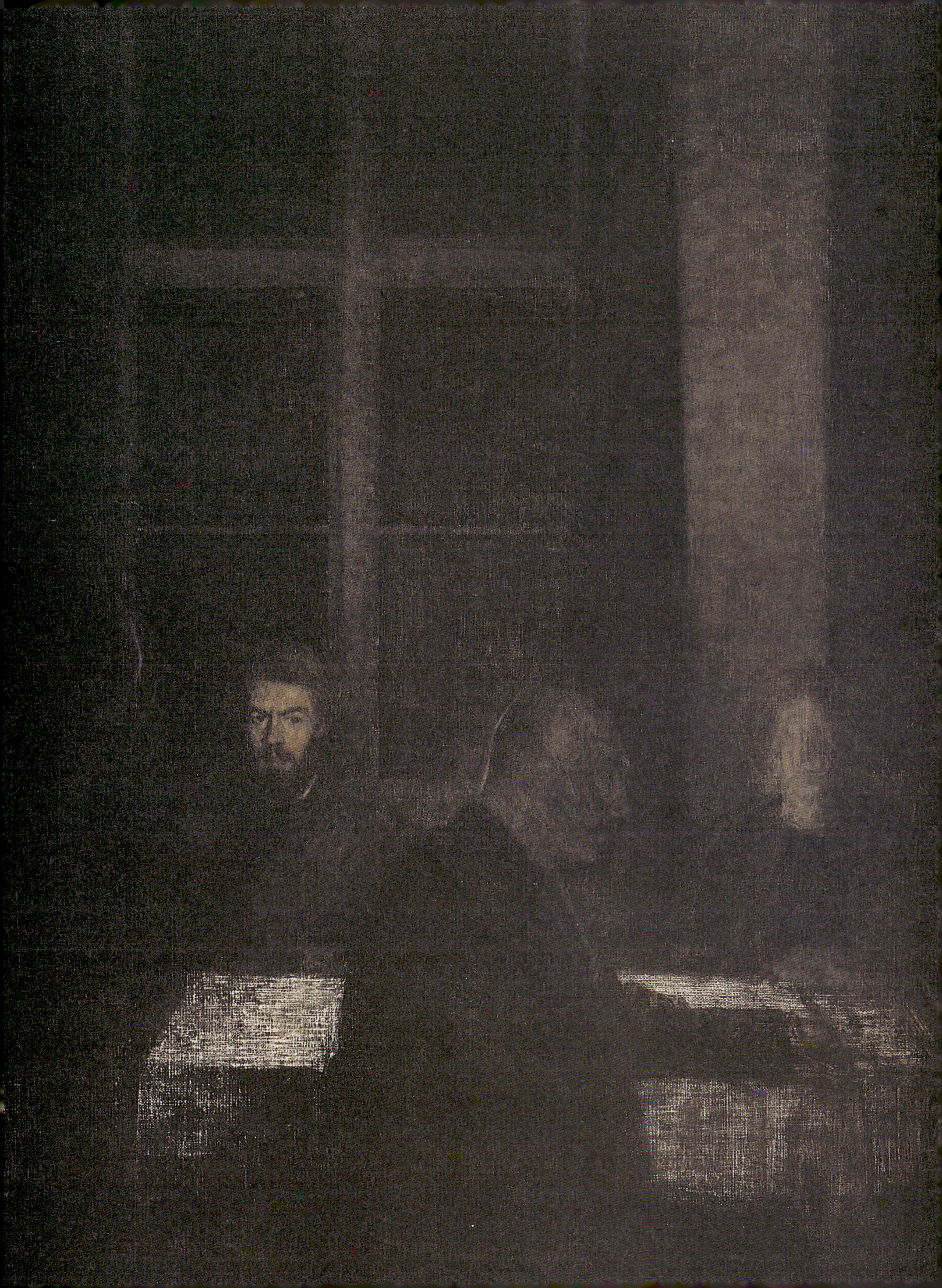

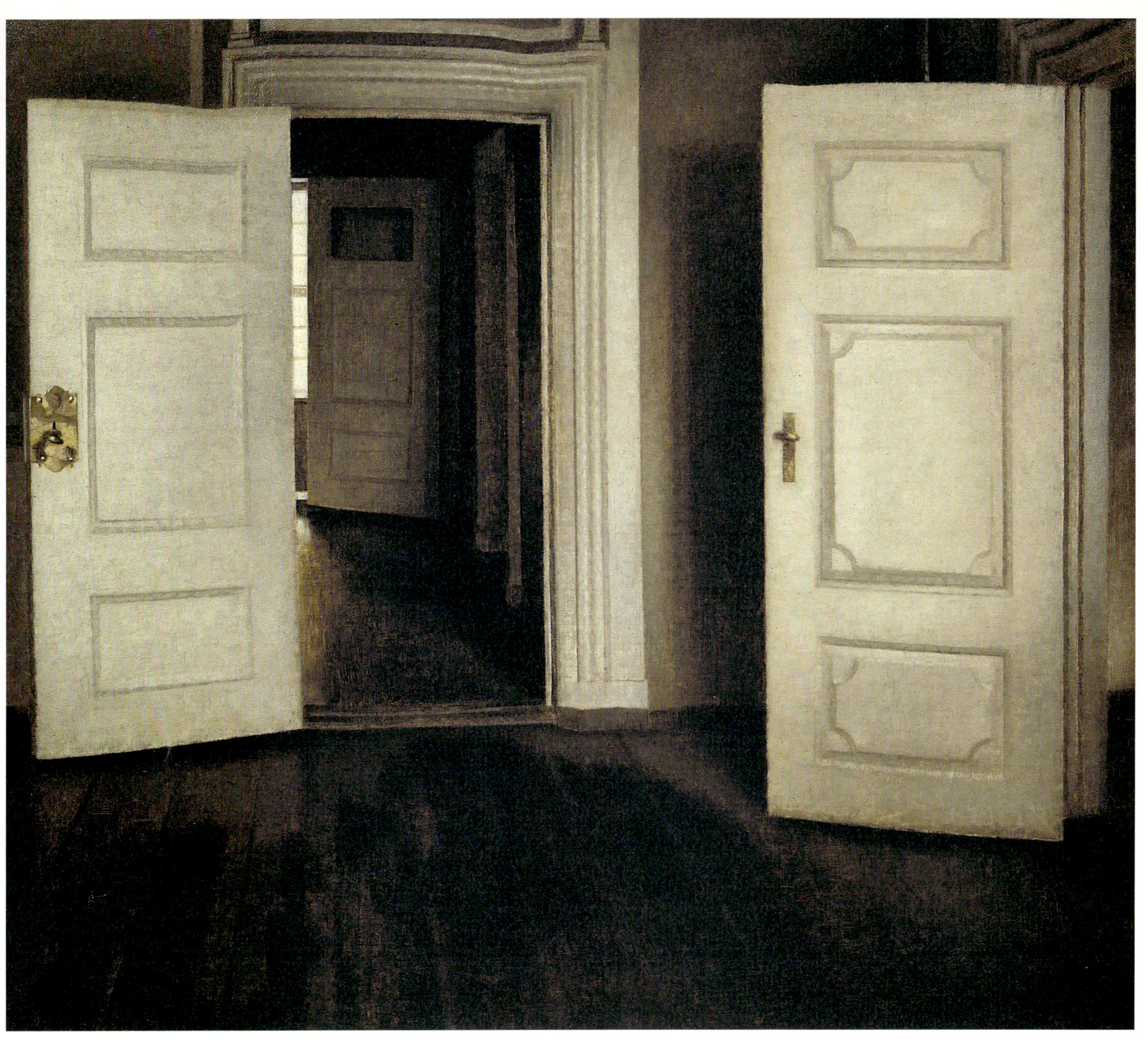

White Doors, or *Open Doors* [Strandgade 30], [1905]
Cat. no. 38

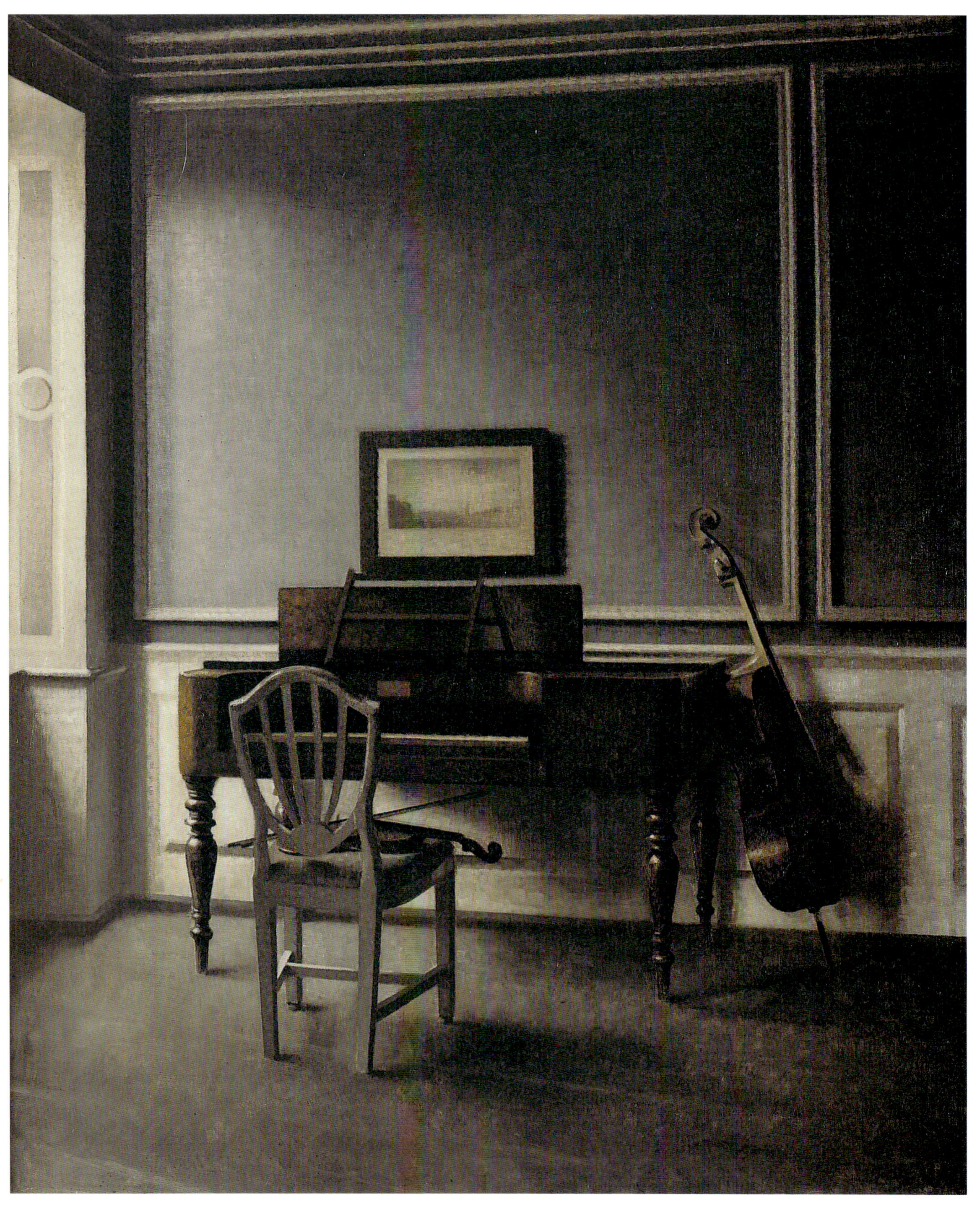

Music Room [Strandgade 30], [1907]
Cat. no. 50

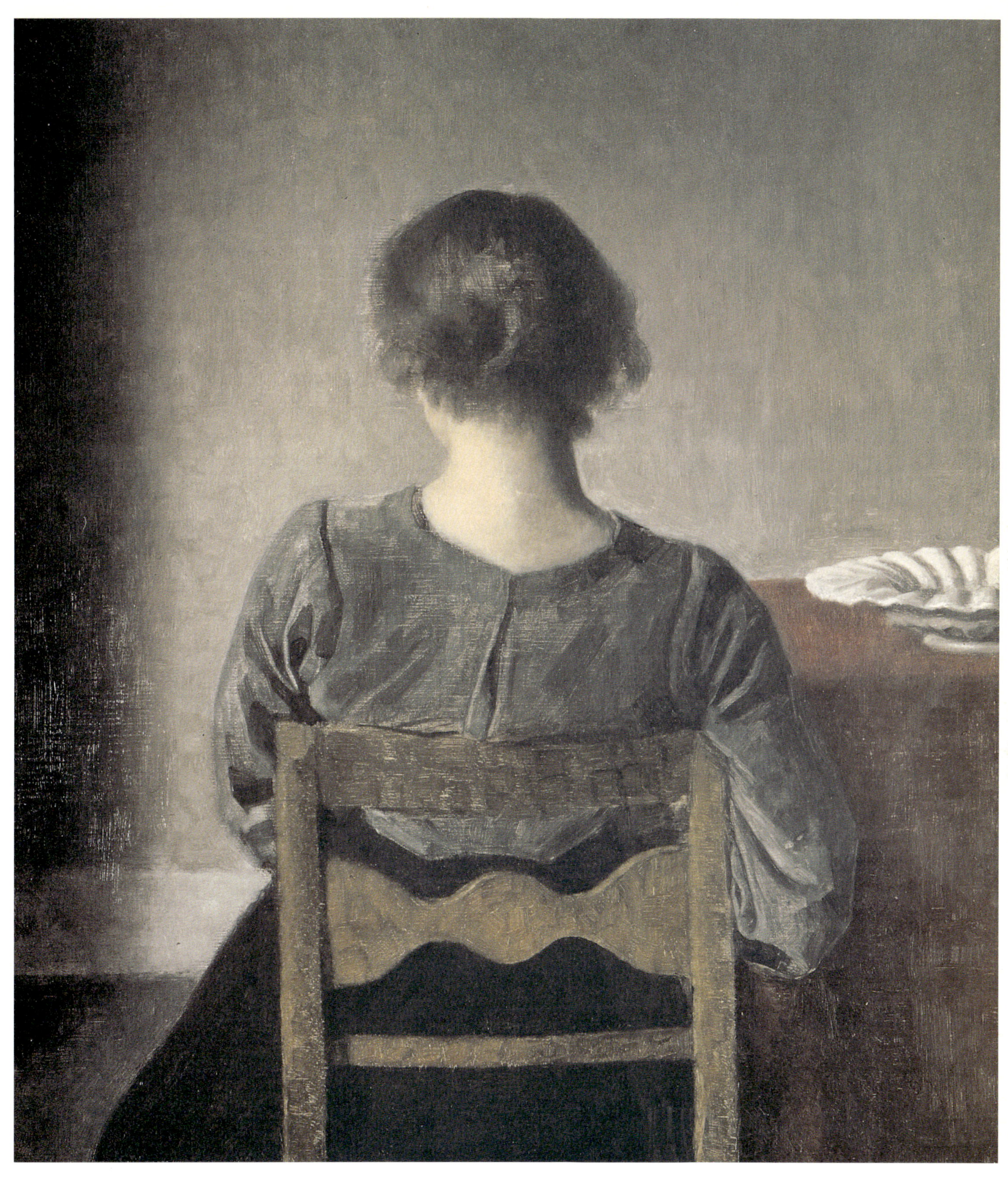

Young Lady, also called *Resting* [Strandgade 30], [1905]
Cat. no. 39

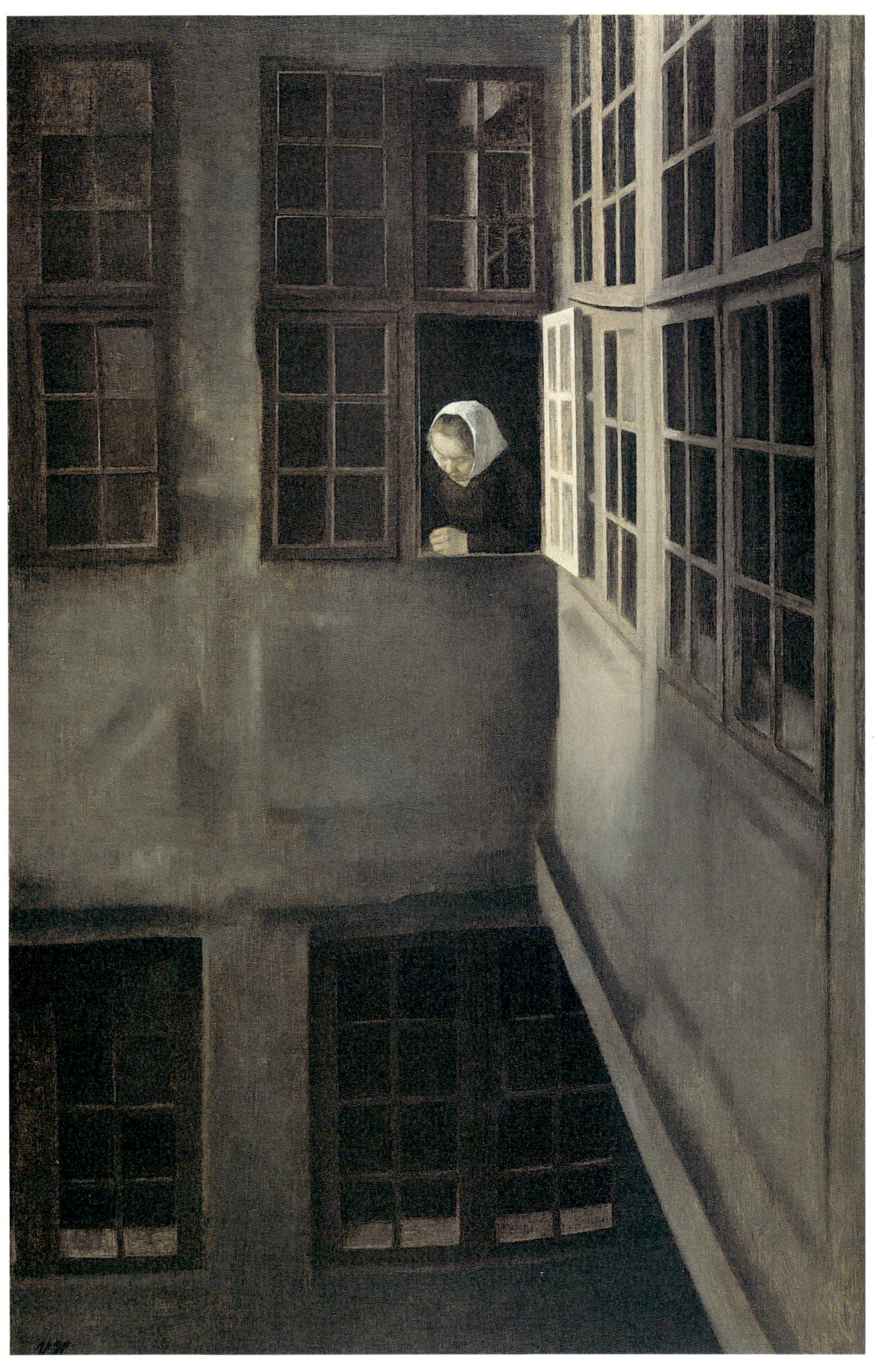

Interior of Courtyard [Strandgade 30], [1905]
Cat. no. 41

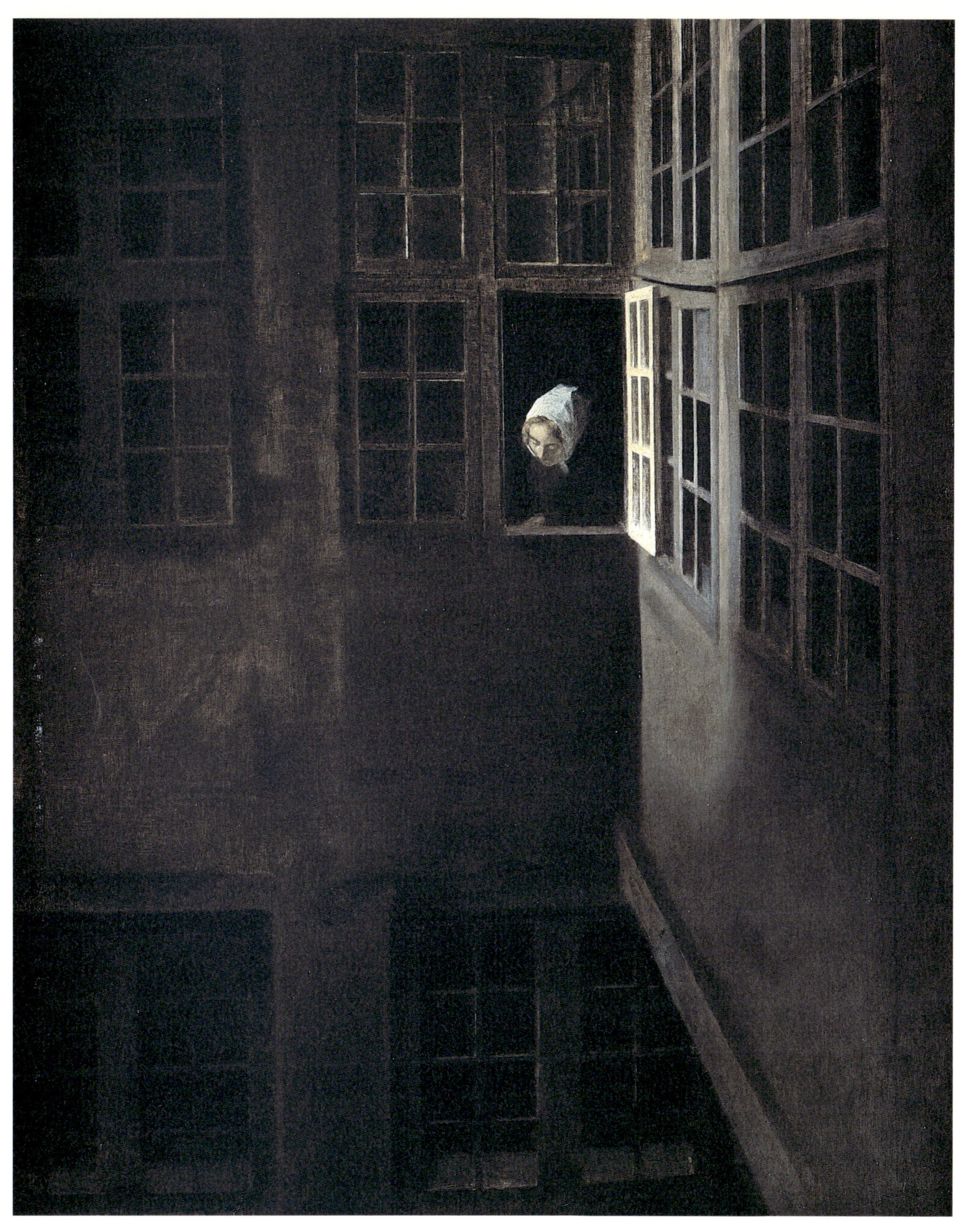

Interior of Courtyard [Strandgade 30], [1905]
Cat. no. 40

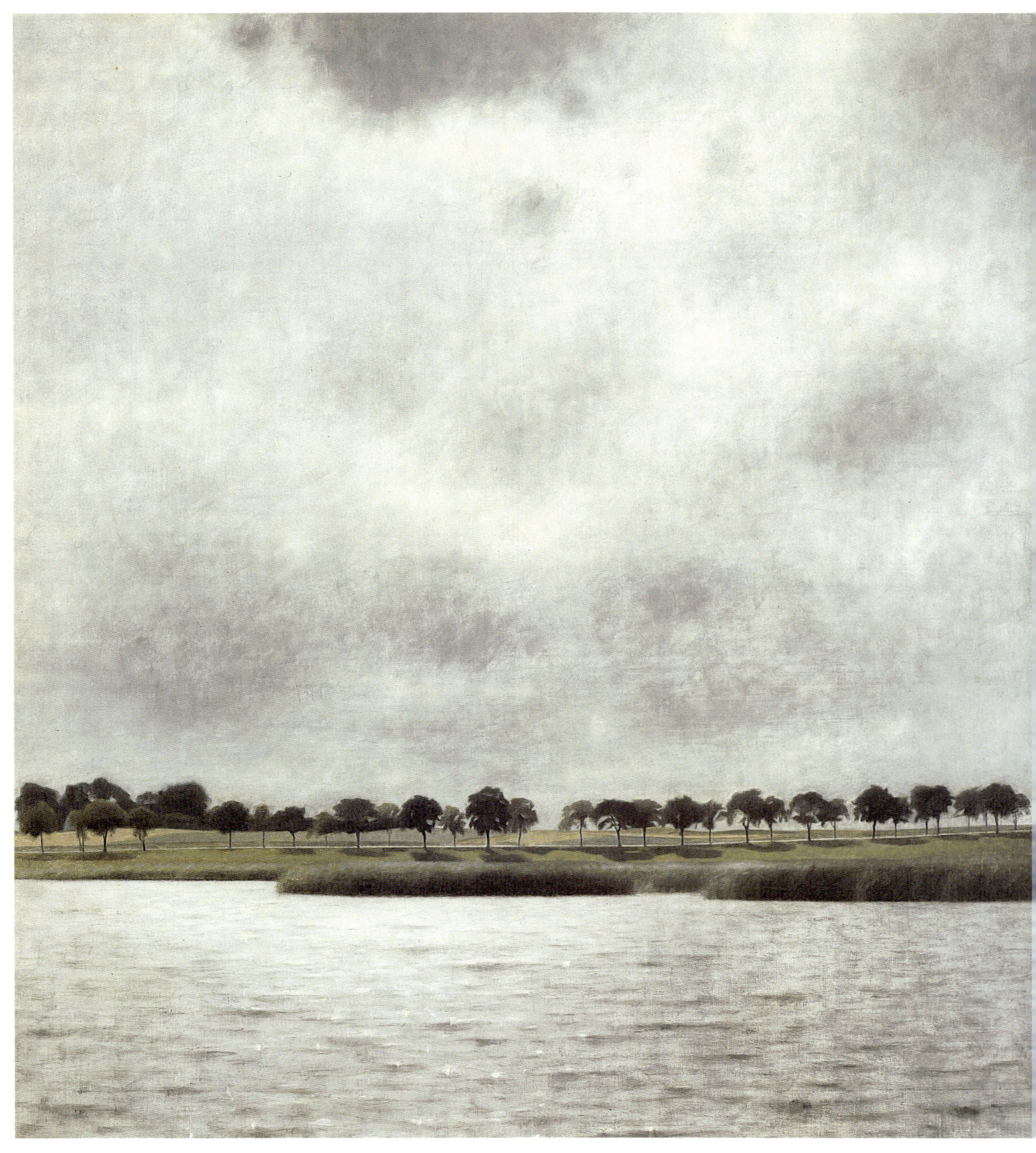

View of Gentofte Lake, also called *Sunshower*, [1903]
Cat. no. 31

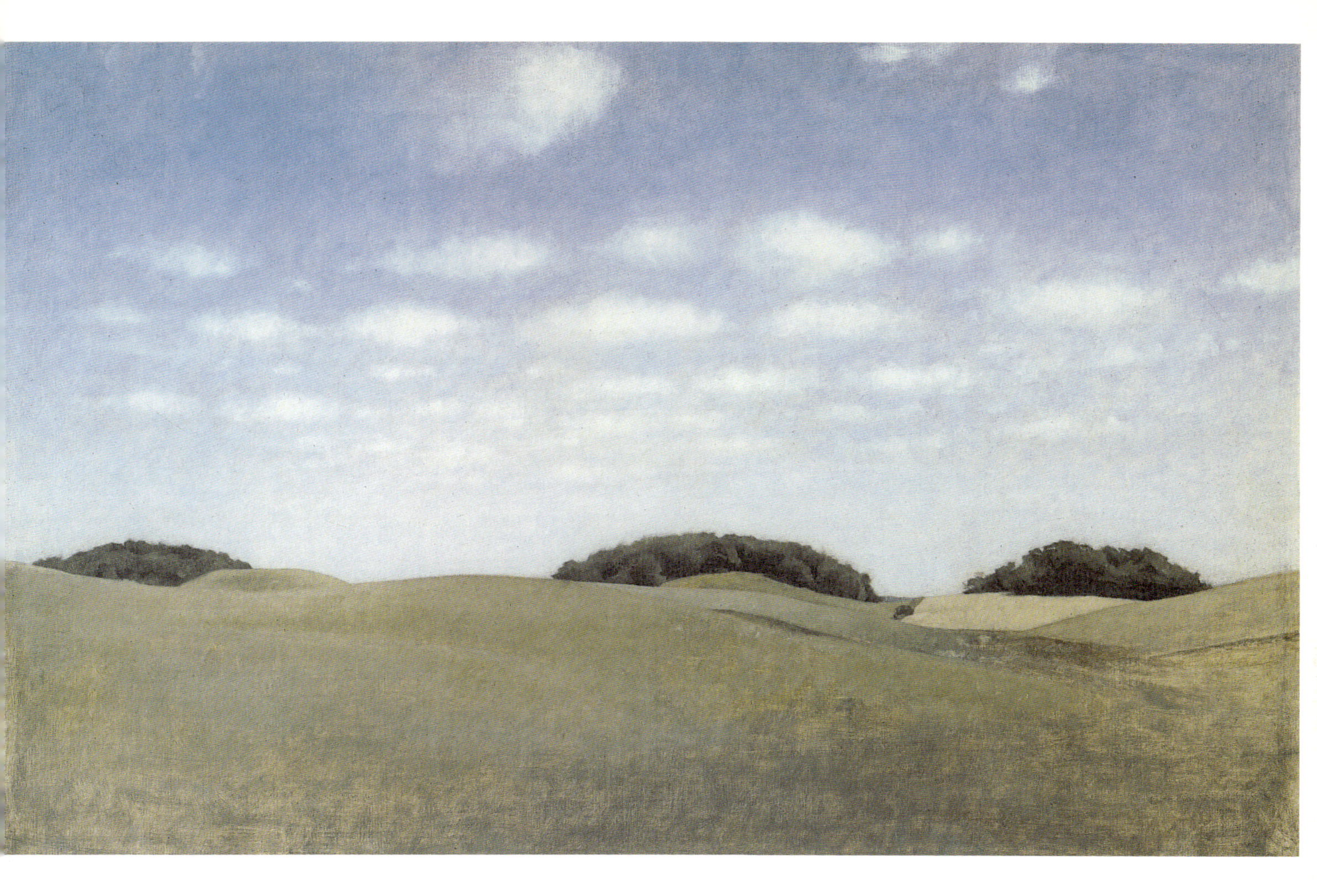

Landscape: View of Lejre, [1905]
Cat. no. 42

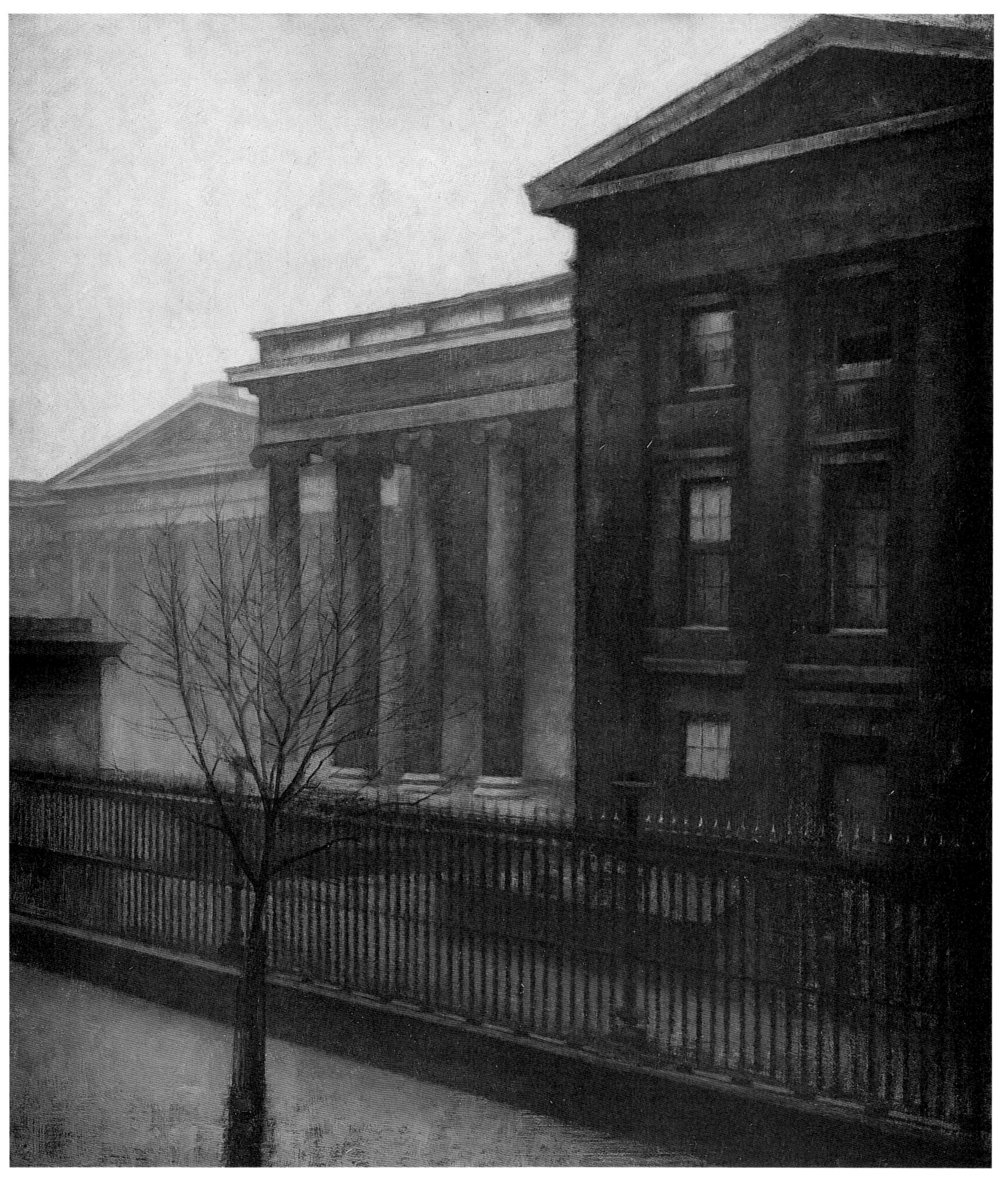

View of the British Museum [London], [1905–06]
Cat. no. 44

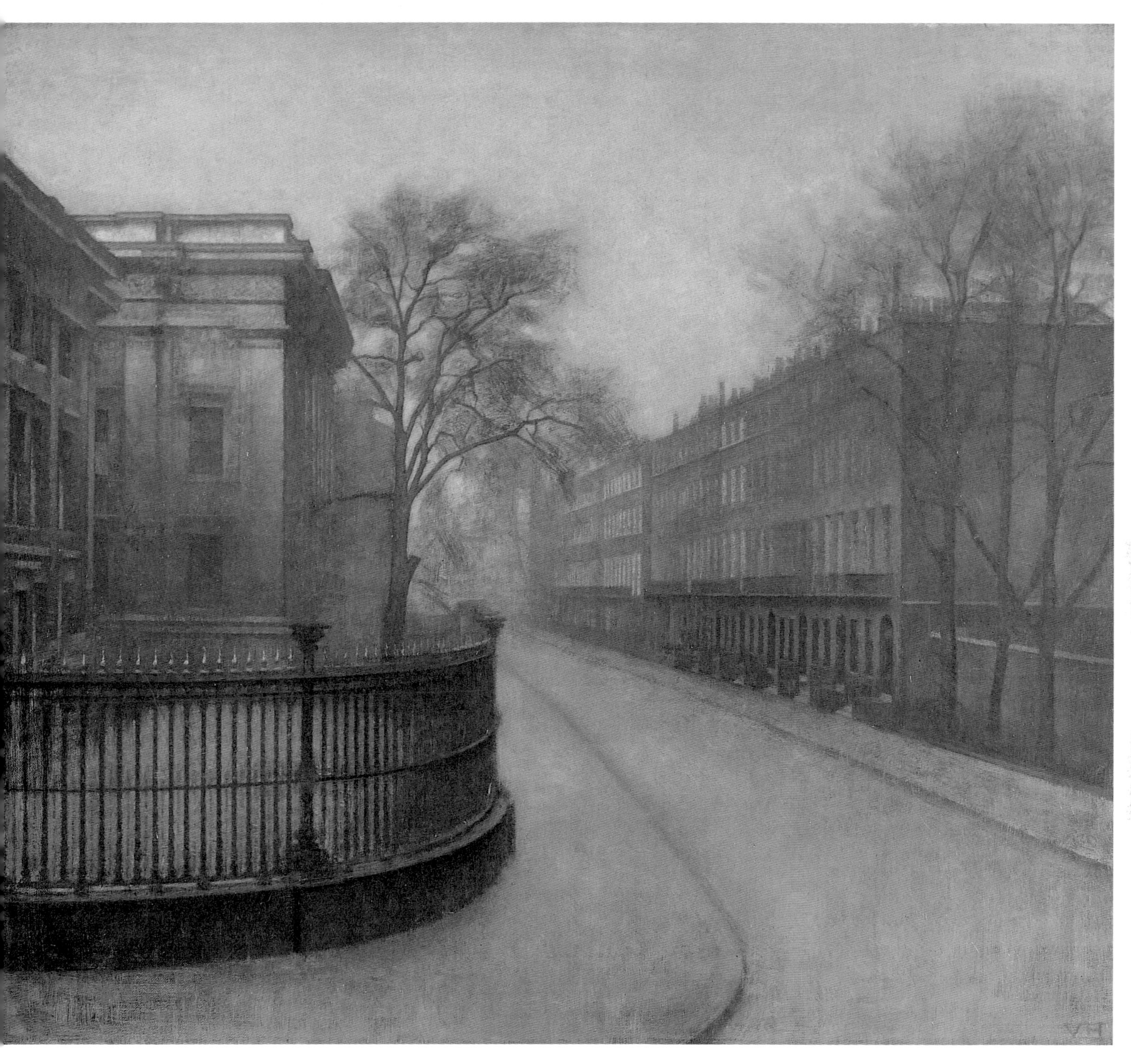

Montague Street in London, or *Side View of the British Museum. Corner of Montague Street*, [1905–06]. Cat. no. 43

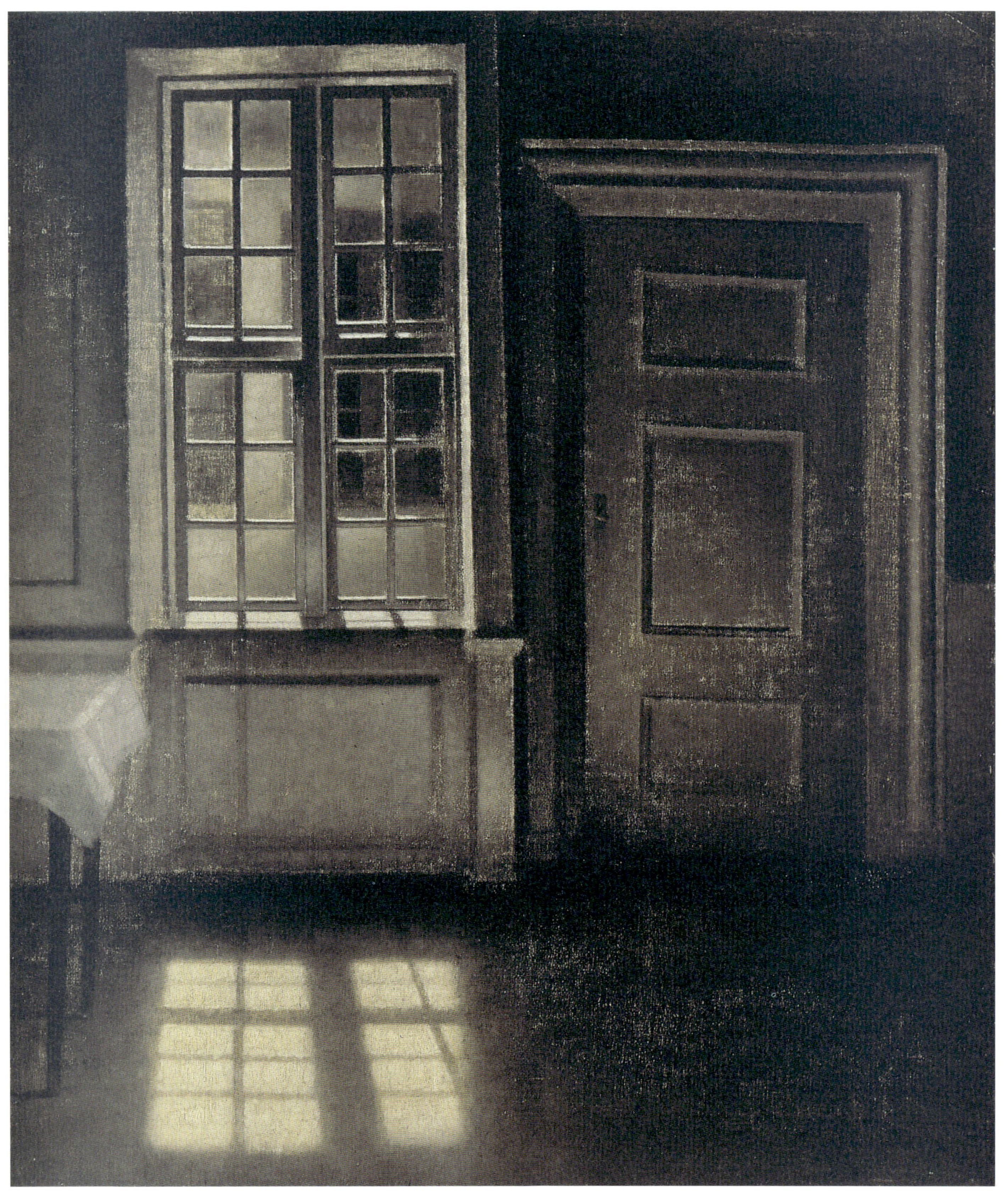

Interior, also called *The Quiet Room* [Strandgade 30], [1906]
Cat. no. 46

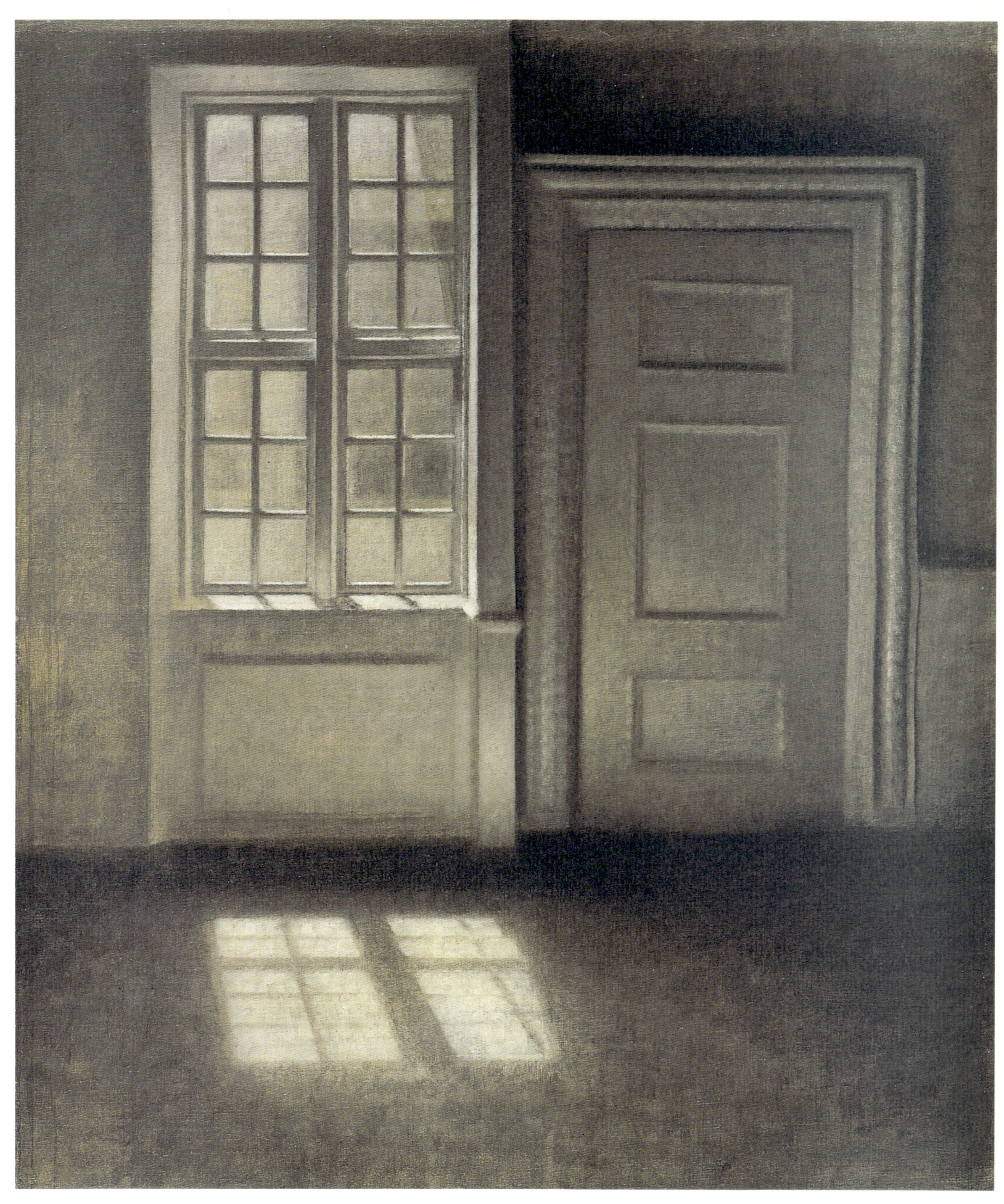

Study in Sunlight [Strandgade 30], [1906]
Cat. no. 45

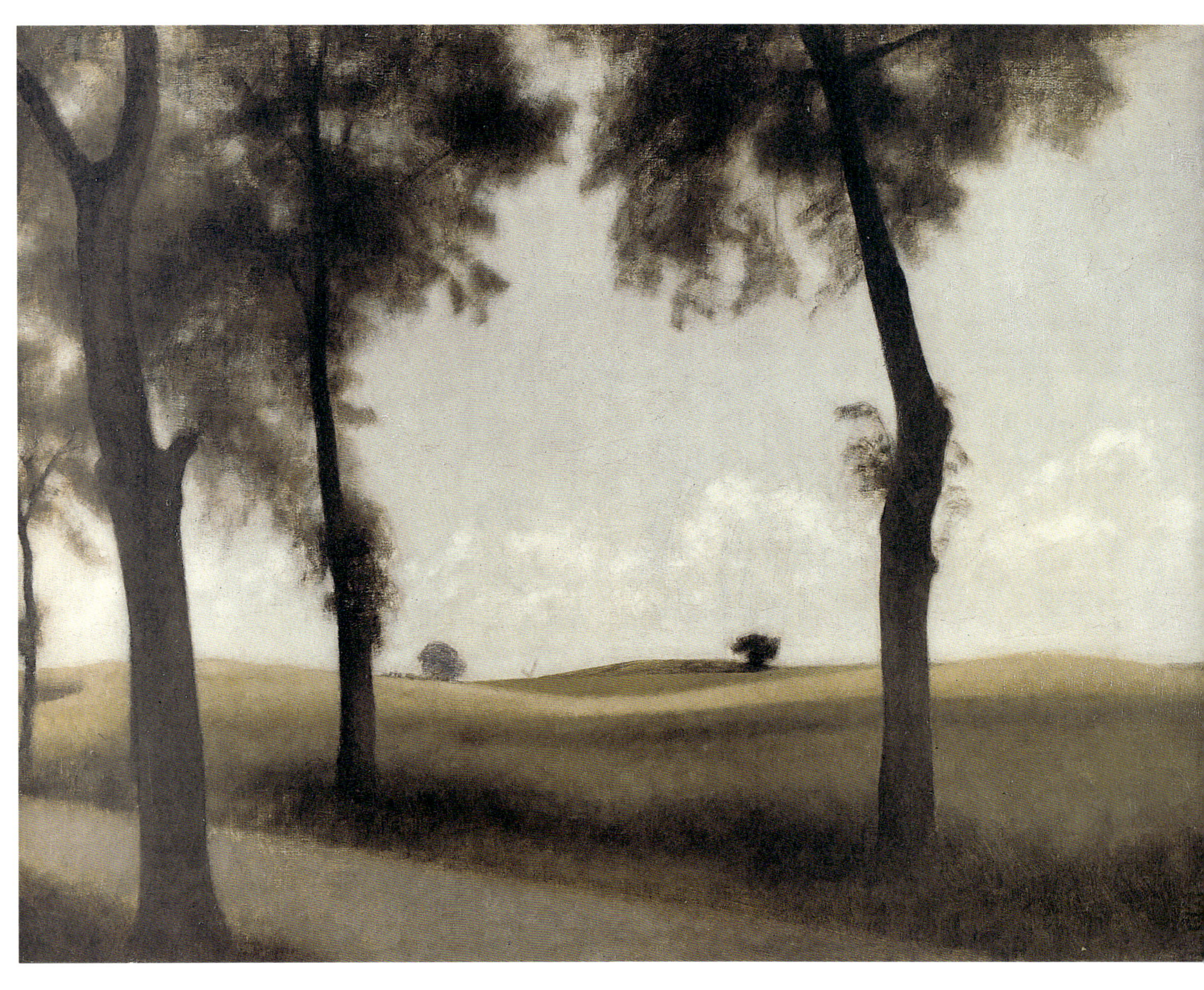

Avenue of Rowan Trees near Snekkersten, [1906]
Cat. no. 47

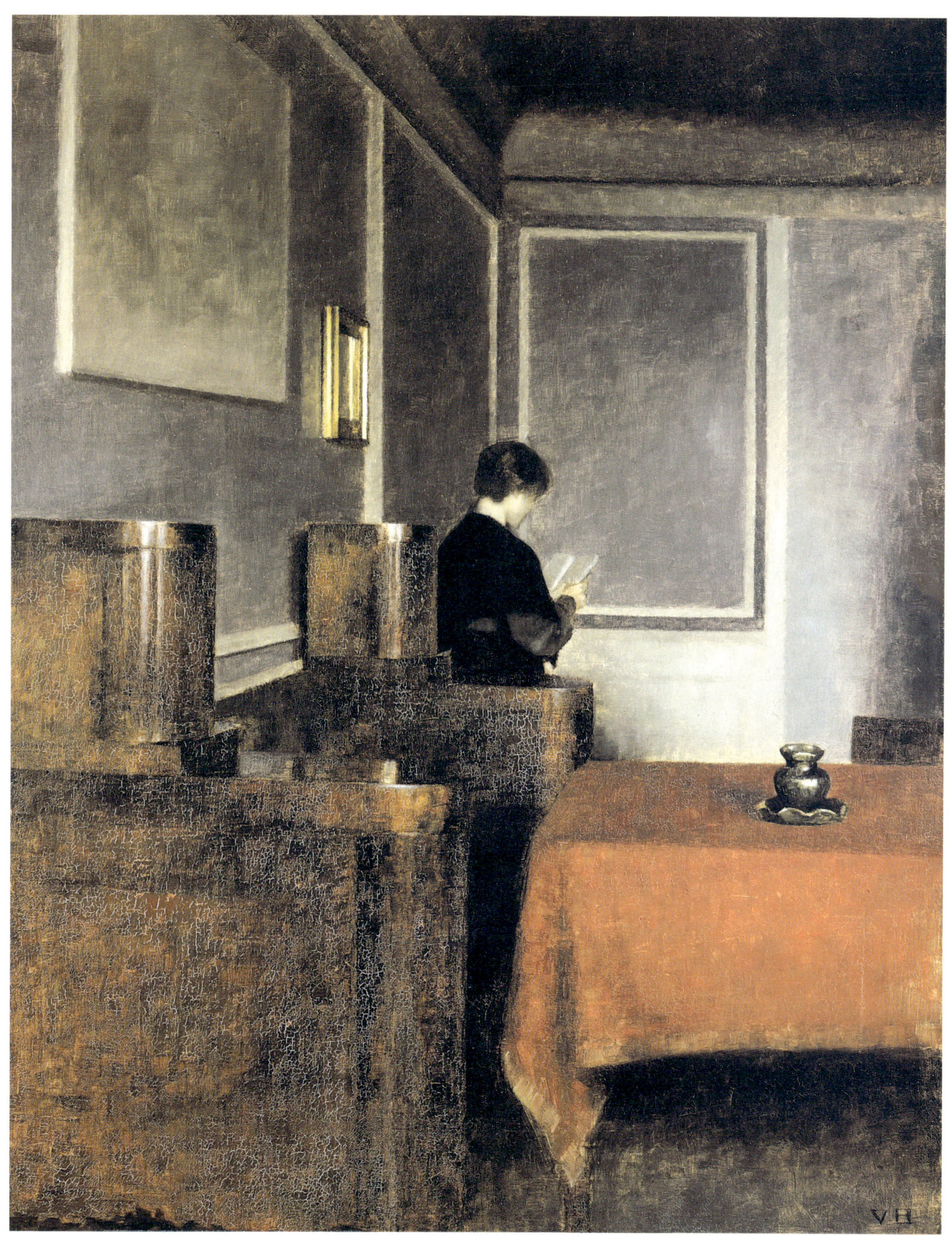

The Cabinet Sofa [Strandgade 30], [1904]
Cat. no. 34

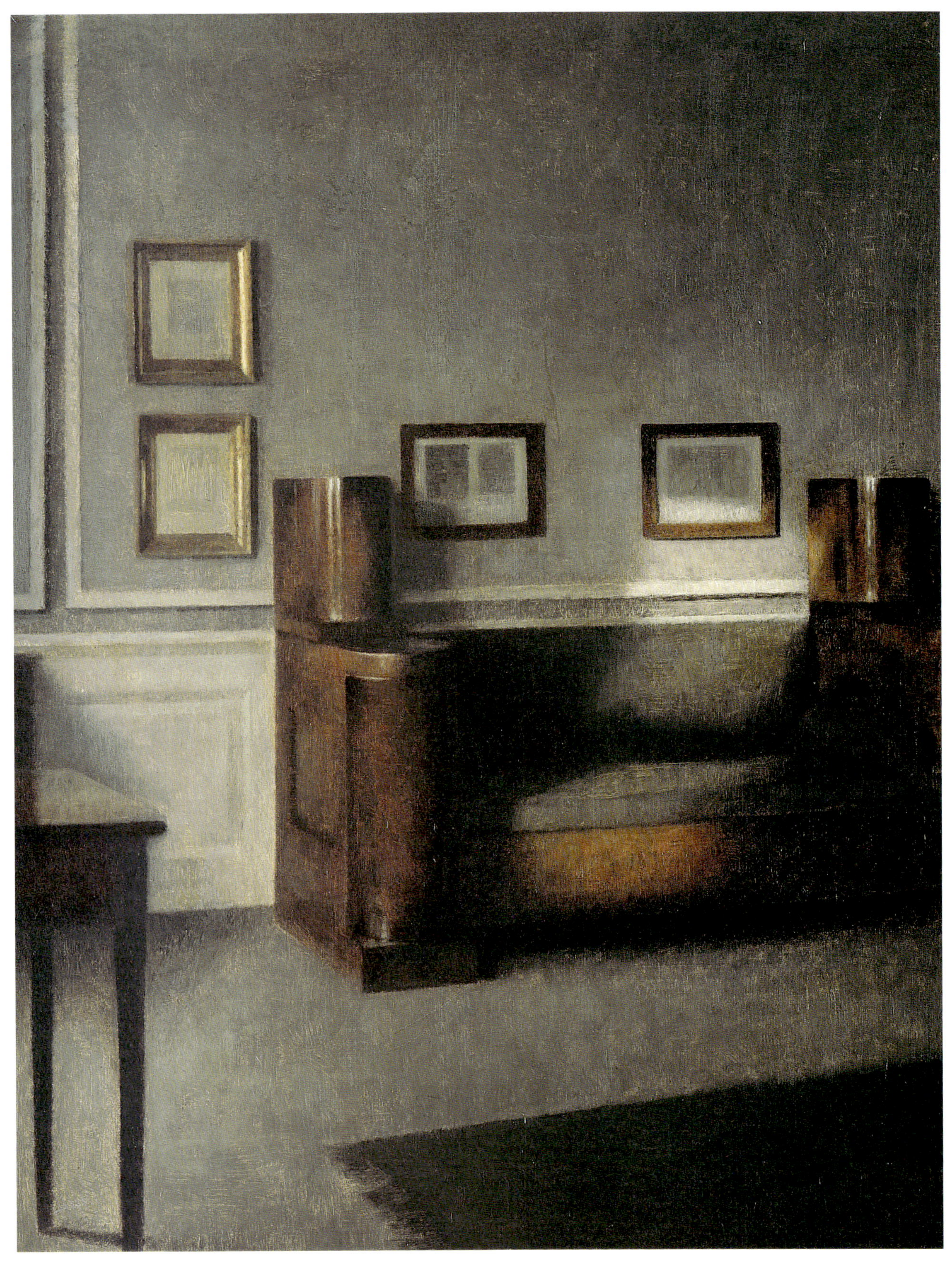

Interior, also called *The Old Cabinet Sofa* [Strandgade 30], [1905]
Cat. no. 37

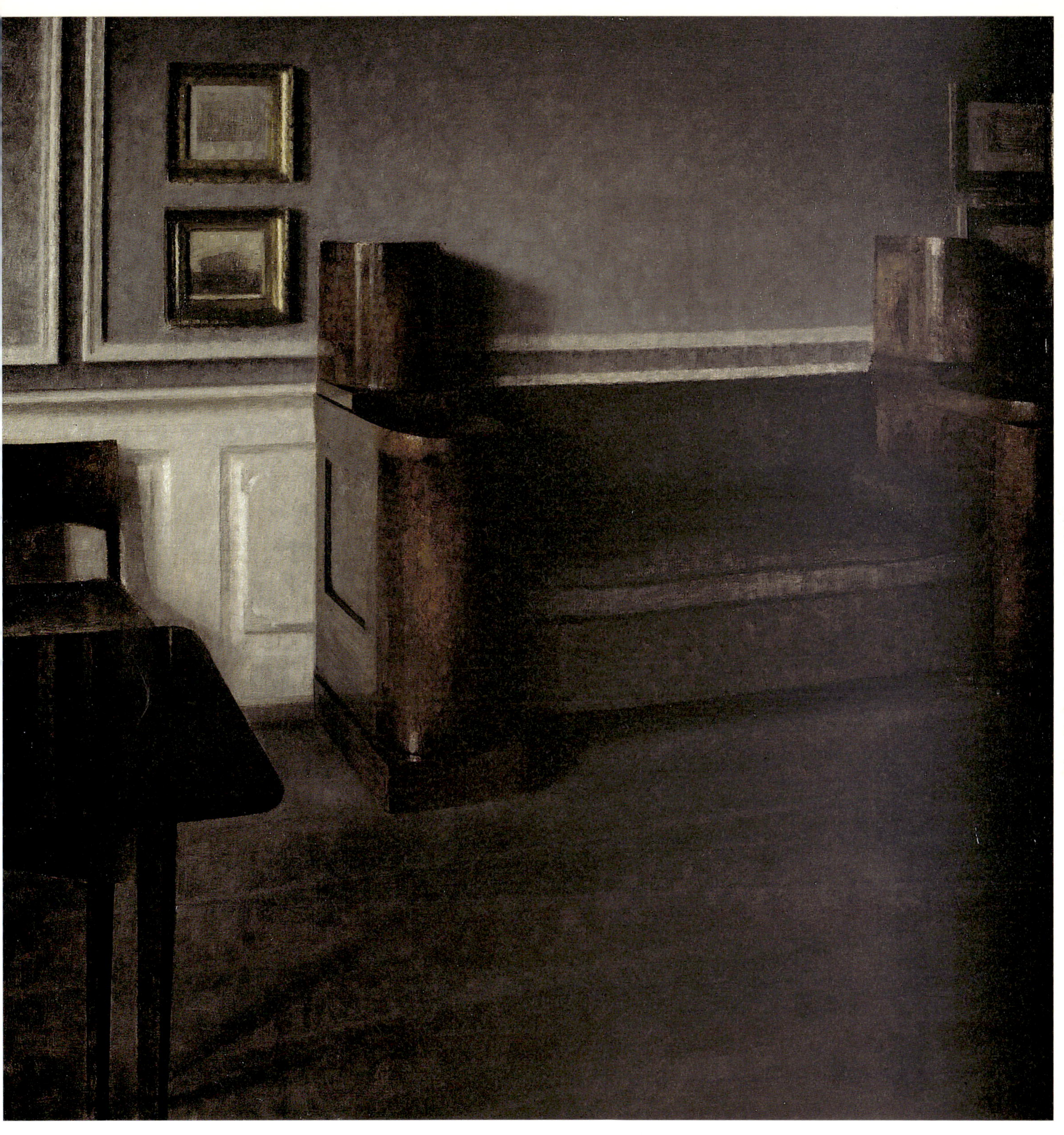

Interior with Cabinet Sofa [Strandgade 30], [1907]
Cat. no. 48

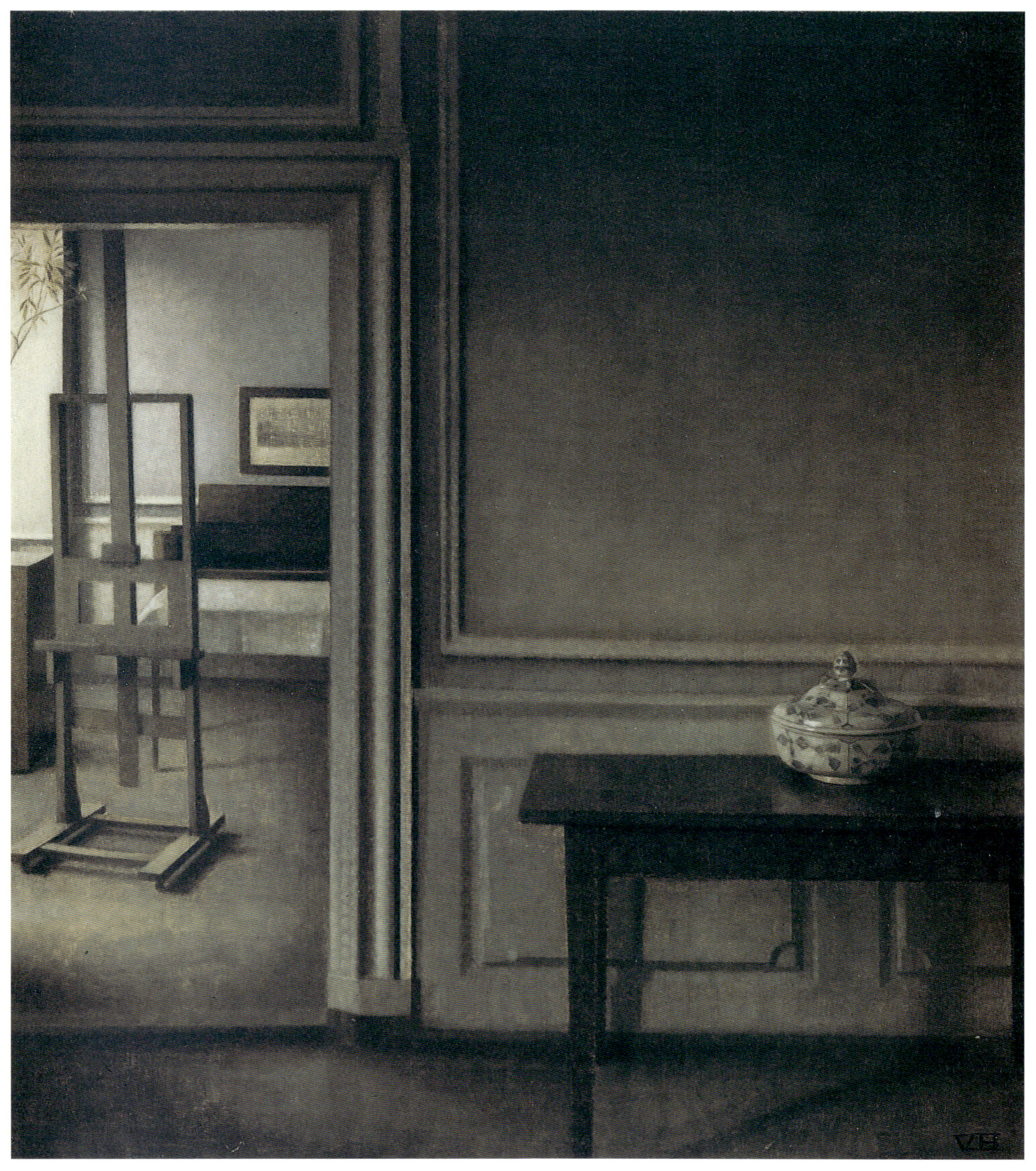

Interior [with easel and punch bowl, Strandgade 30], [1907]
Cat. no. 49

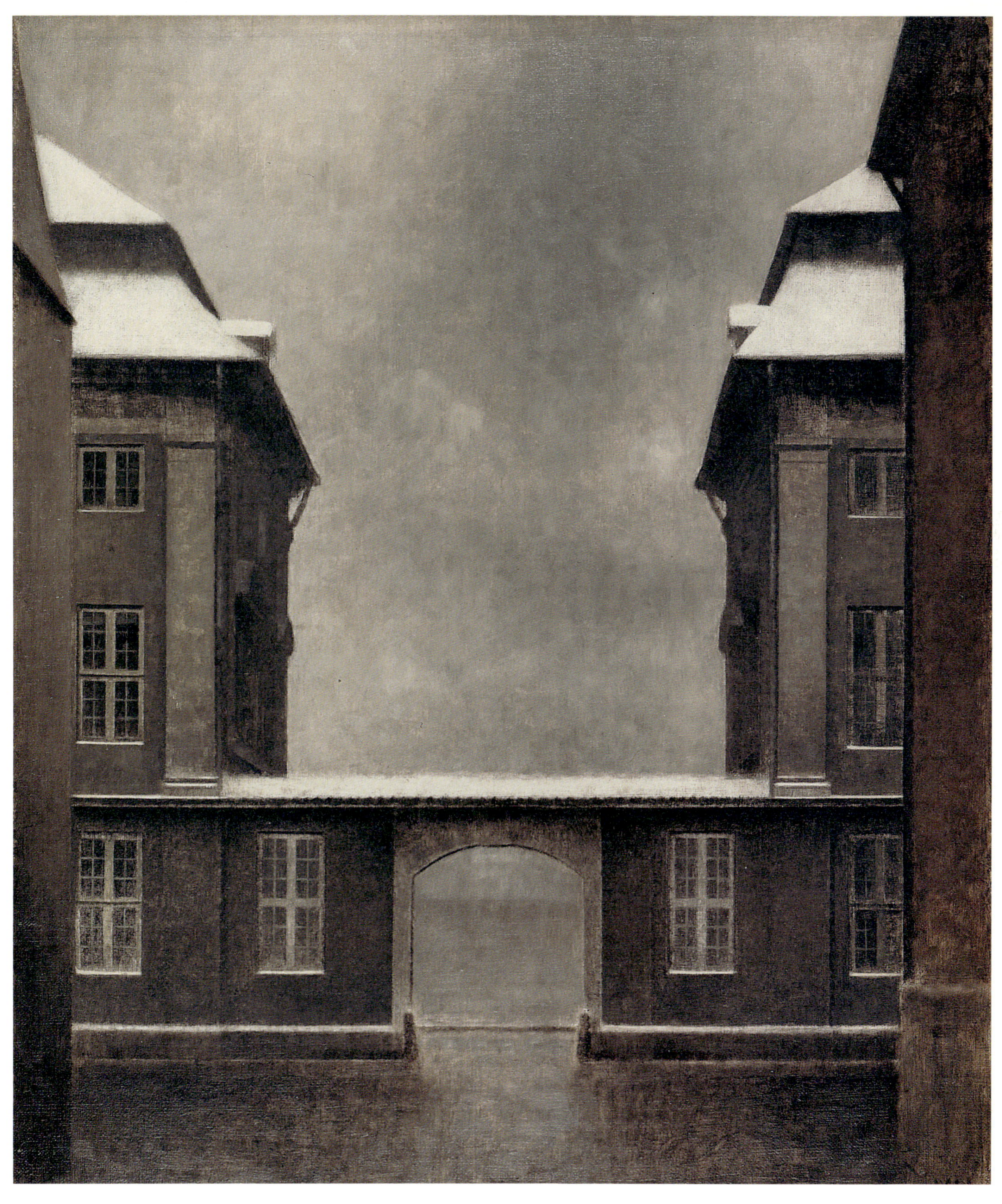

View of the Asiatic Company, or *Entryway to the Asiatic Company Dock*, [1907]
Cat. no. 51

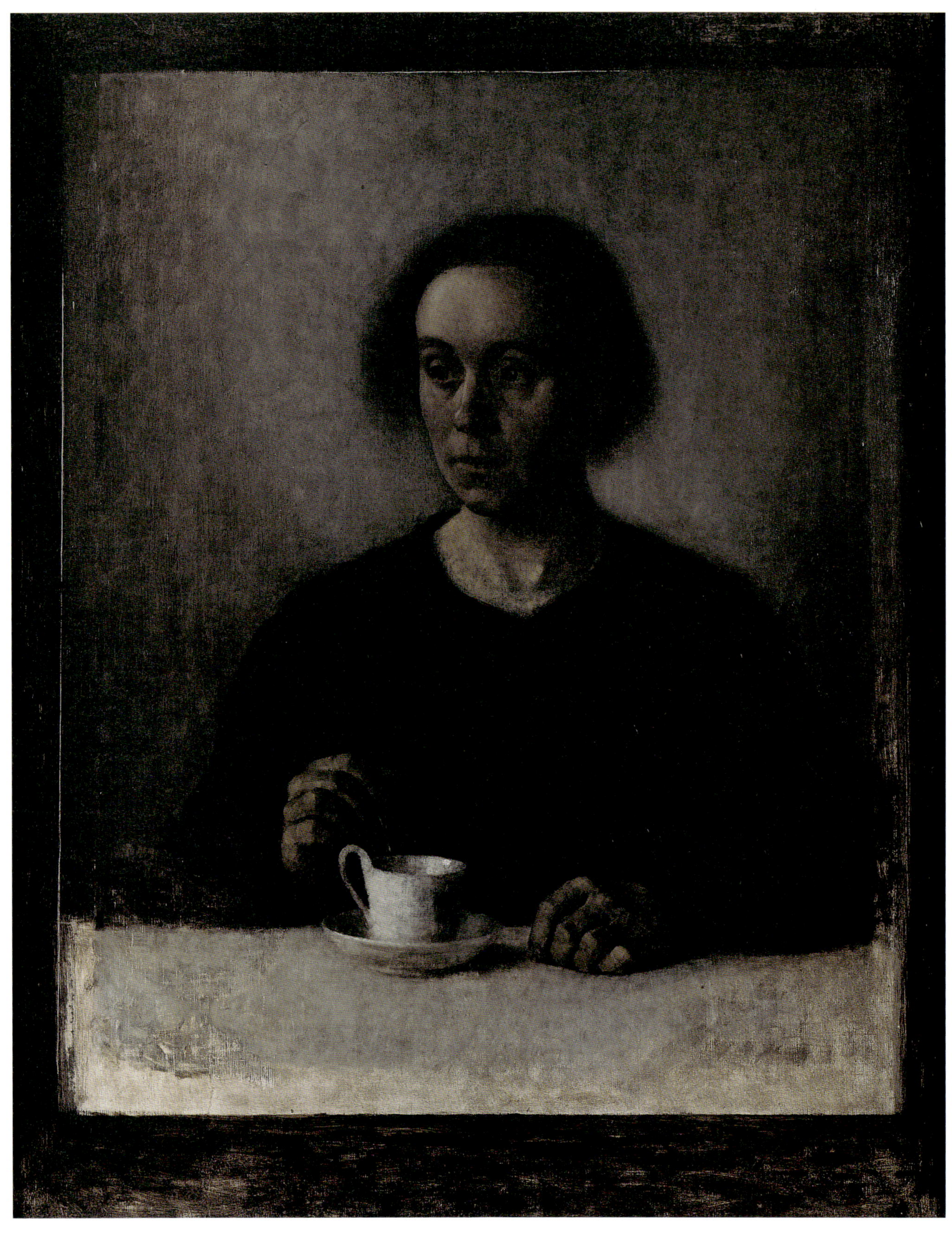

Portrait [Ida Hammershøi], [1907]
Cat. no. 52

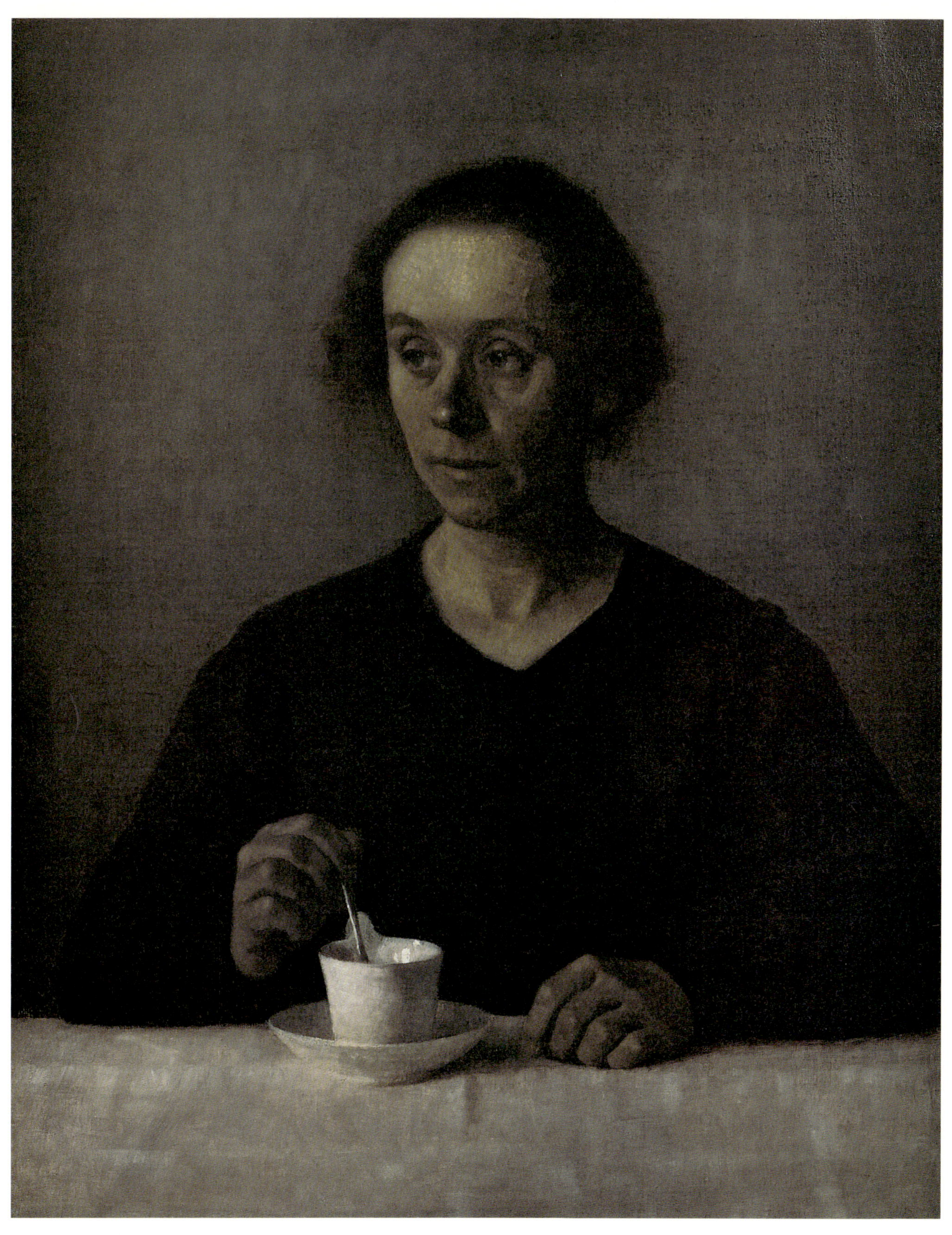

Portrait [Ida Hammershøi], [1907]
Cat. no. 53

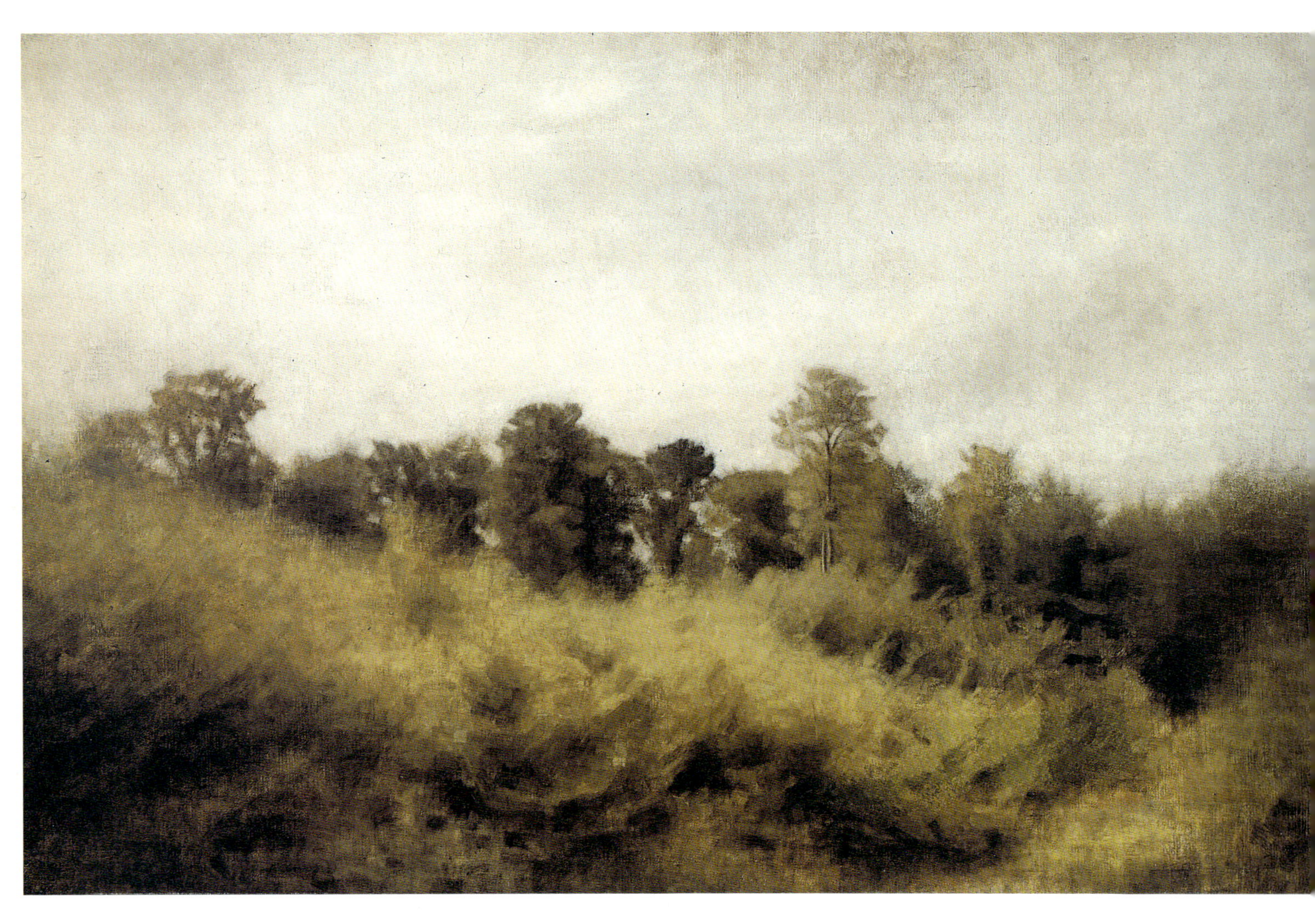

Trørød Forest, also called *Young Forest*, [1907]
Cat. no. 55

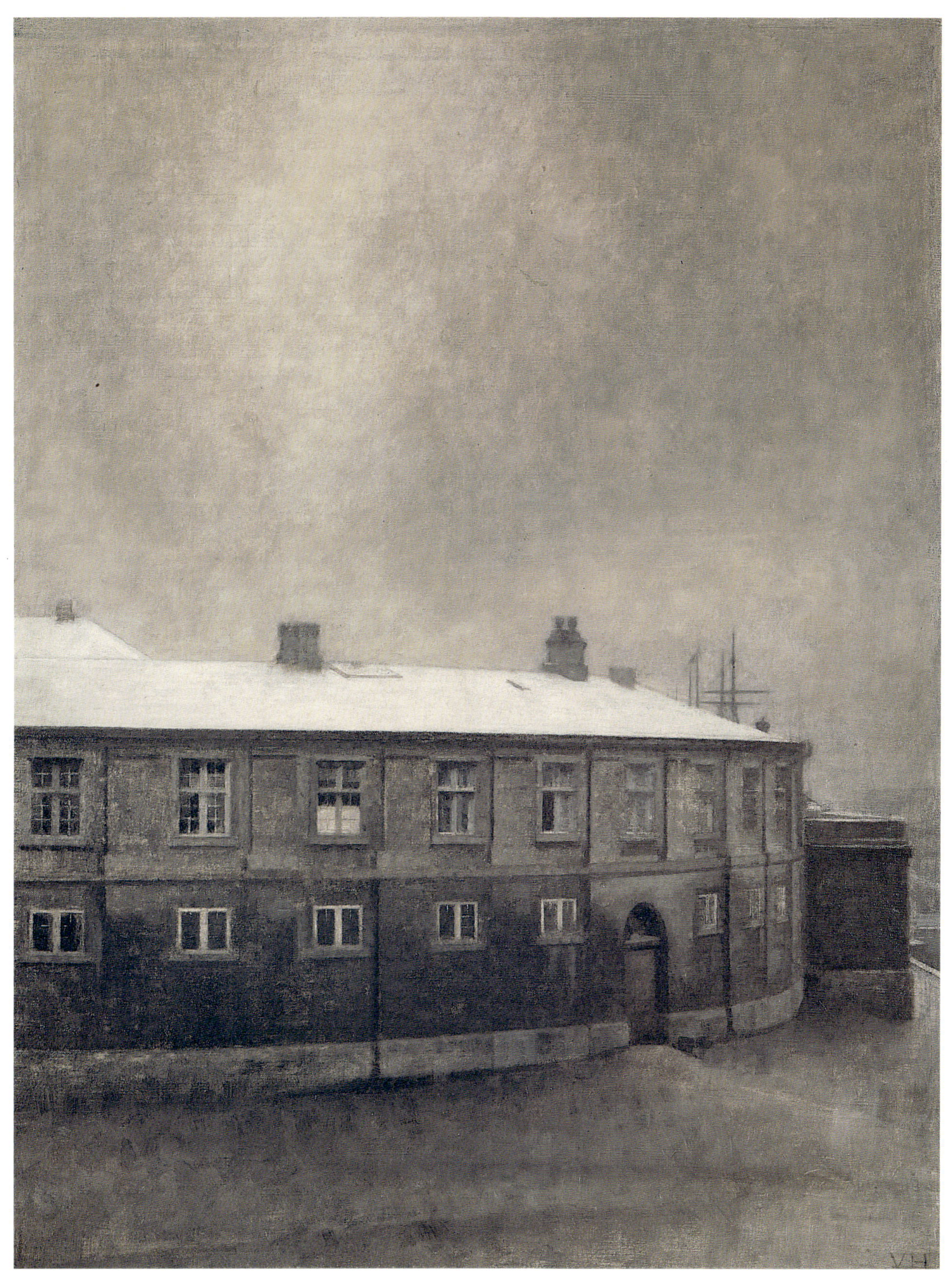

View of Old Christiansborg Palace, [1907]
Cat. no. 56

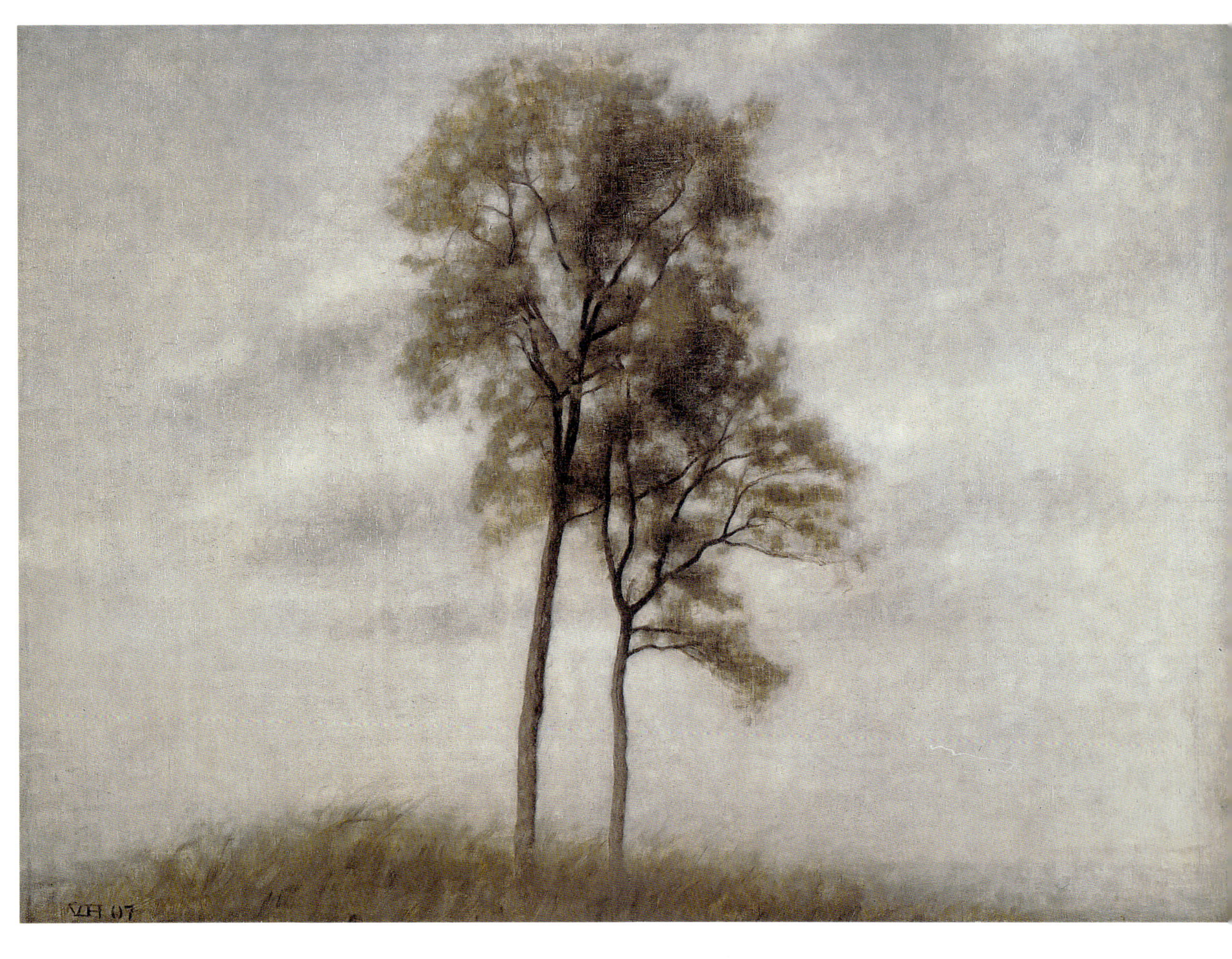

Two Oak Trees, or *Young Oak Trees*, 1907
Cat no. 54

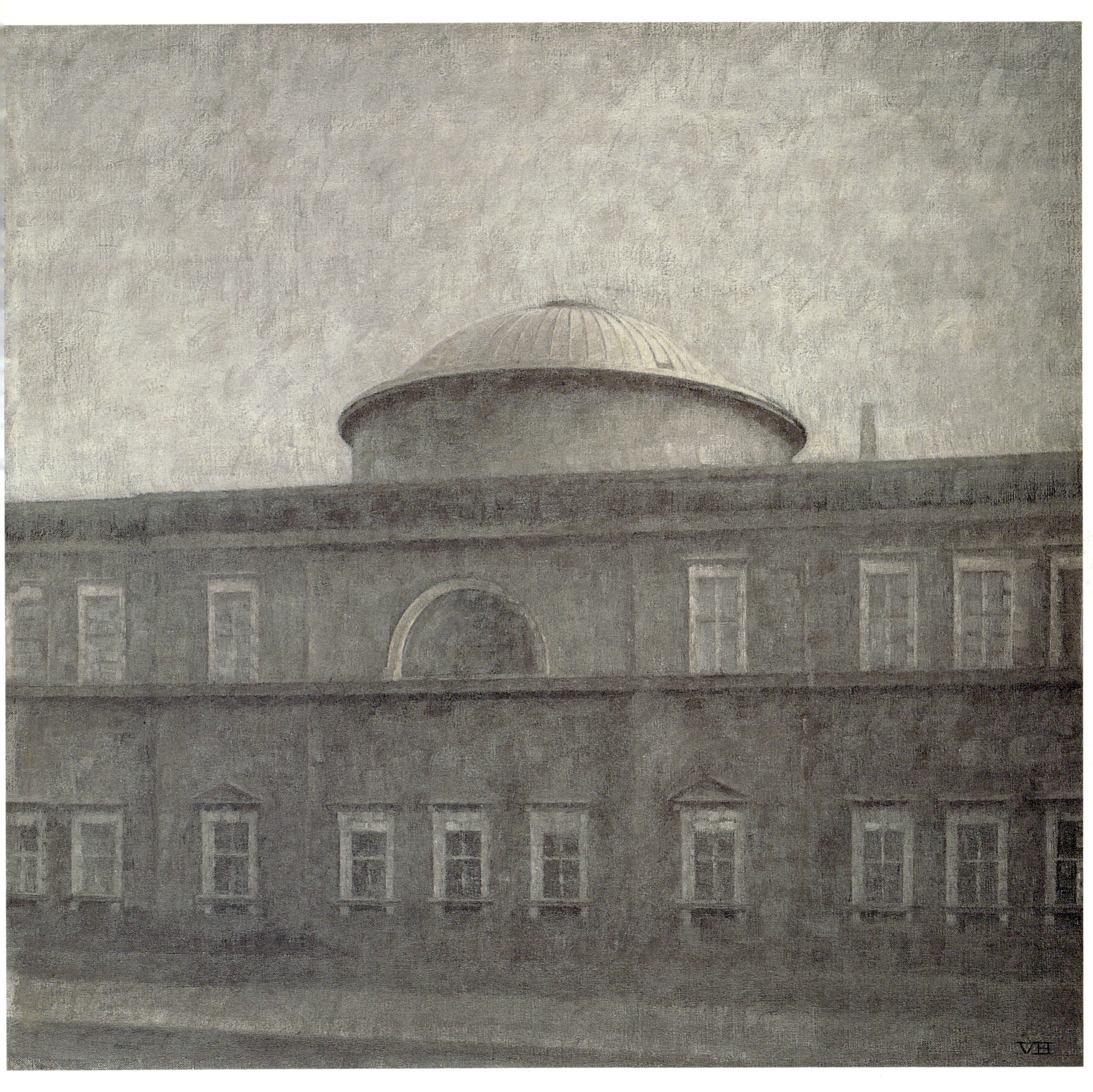

Christiansborg Palace Chapel, Copenhagen, [1910]
Cat. no. 66

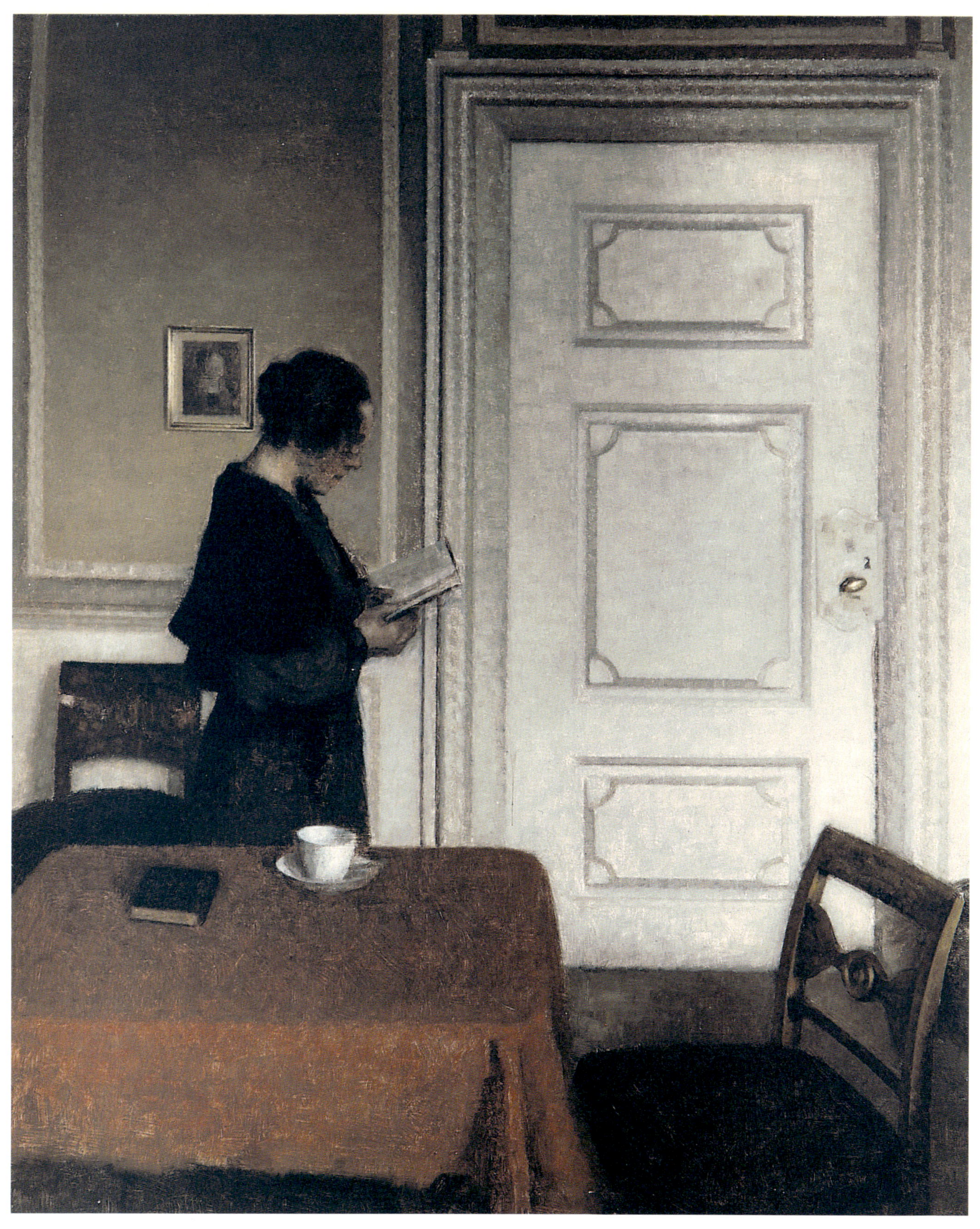

Woman Reading [Strandgade 30], [1908]
Cat. no. 58

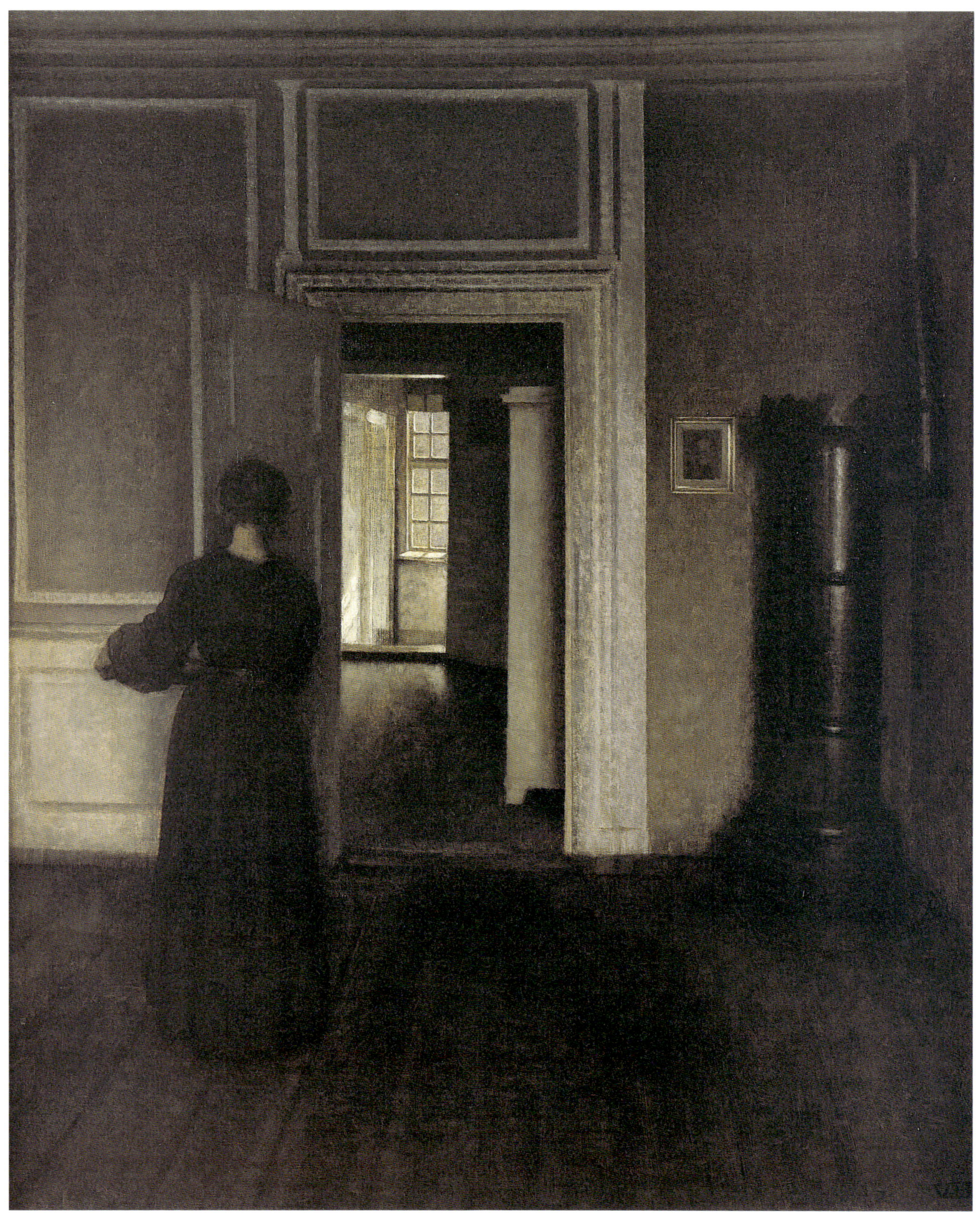

Interior [with stove and standing woman dressed in black, Strandgade 30], [1909]
Cat. no. 60

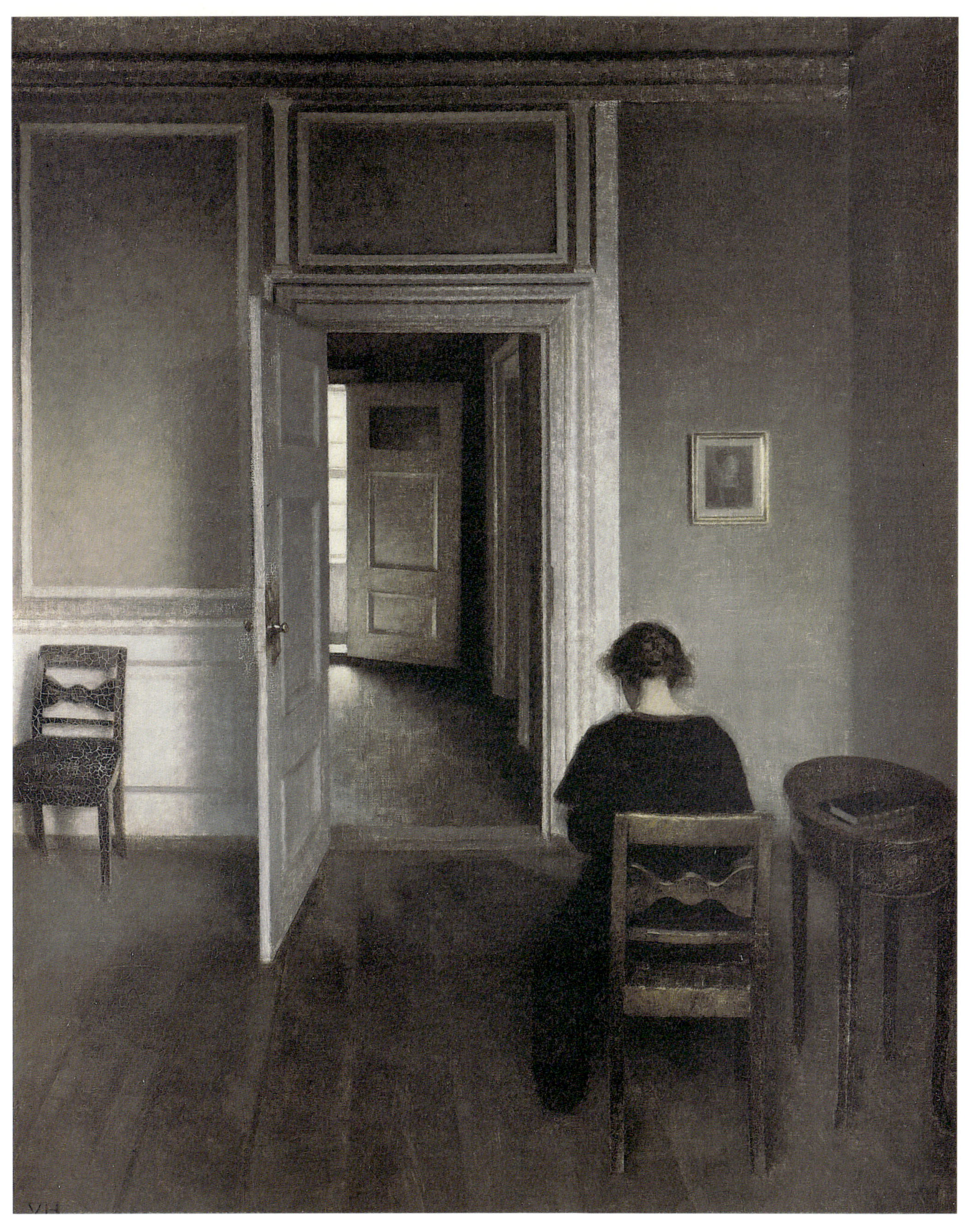

Interior [with woman dressed in black sitting on yellow-brown chair, Strandgade 30], [1908]. Cat. no. 57

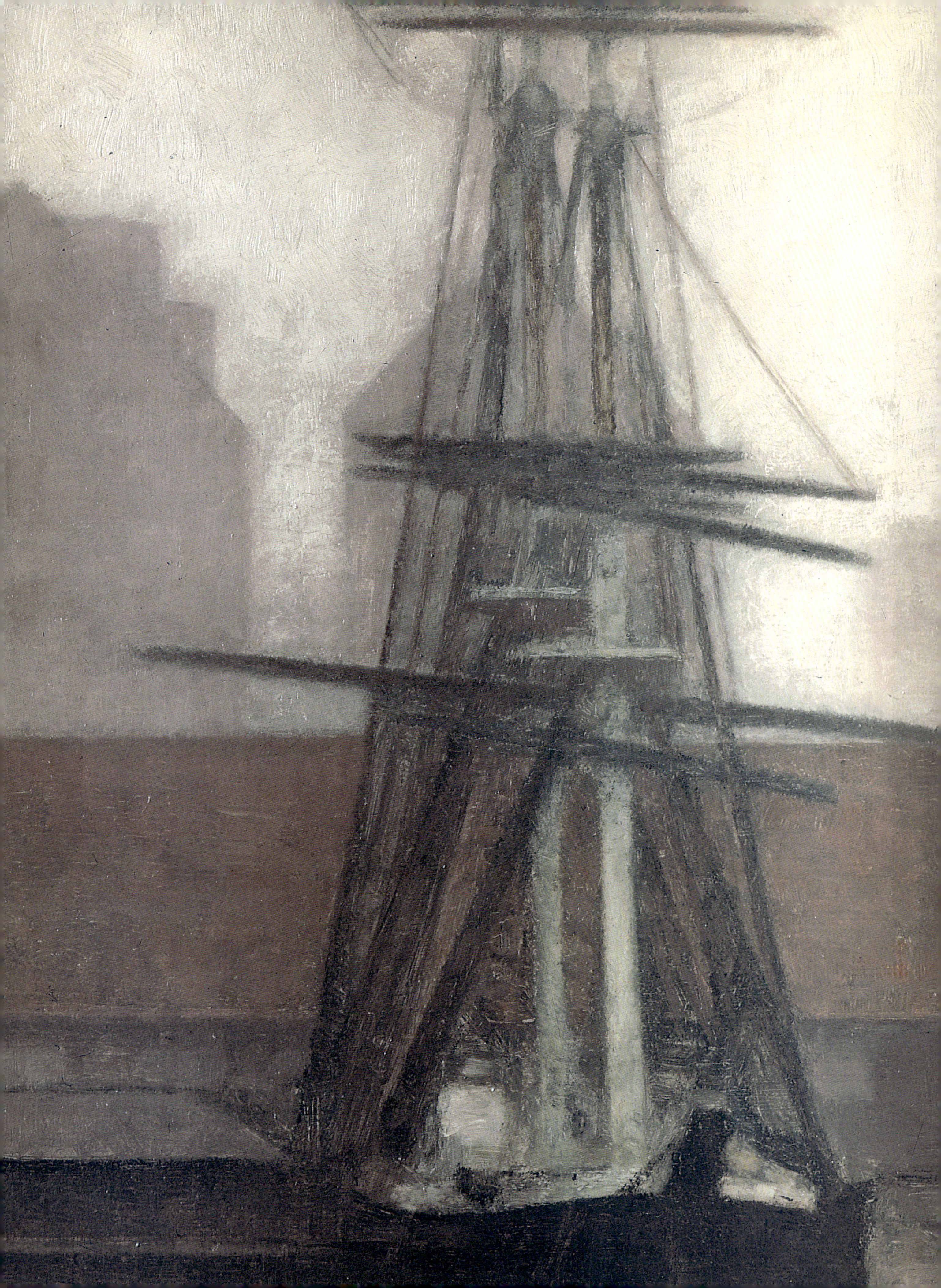

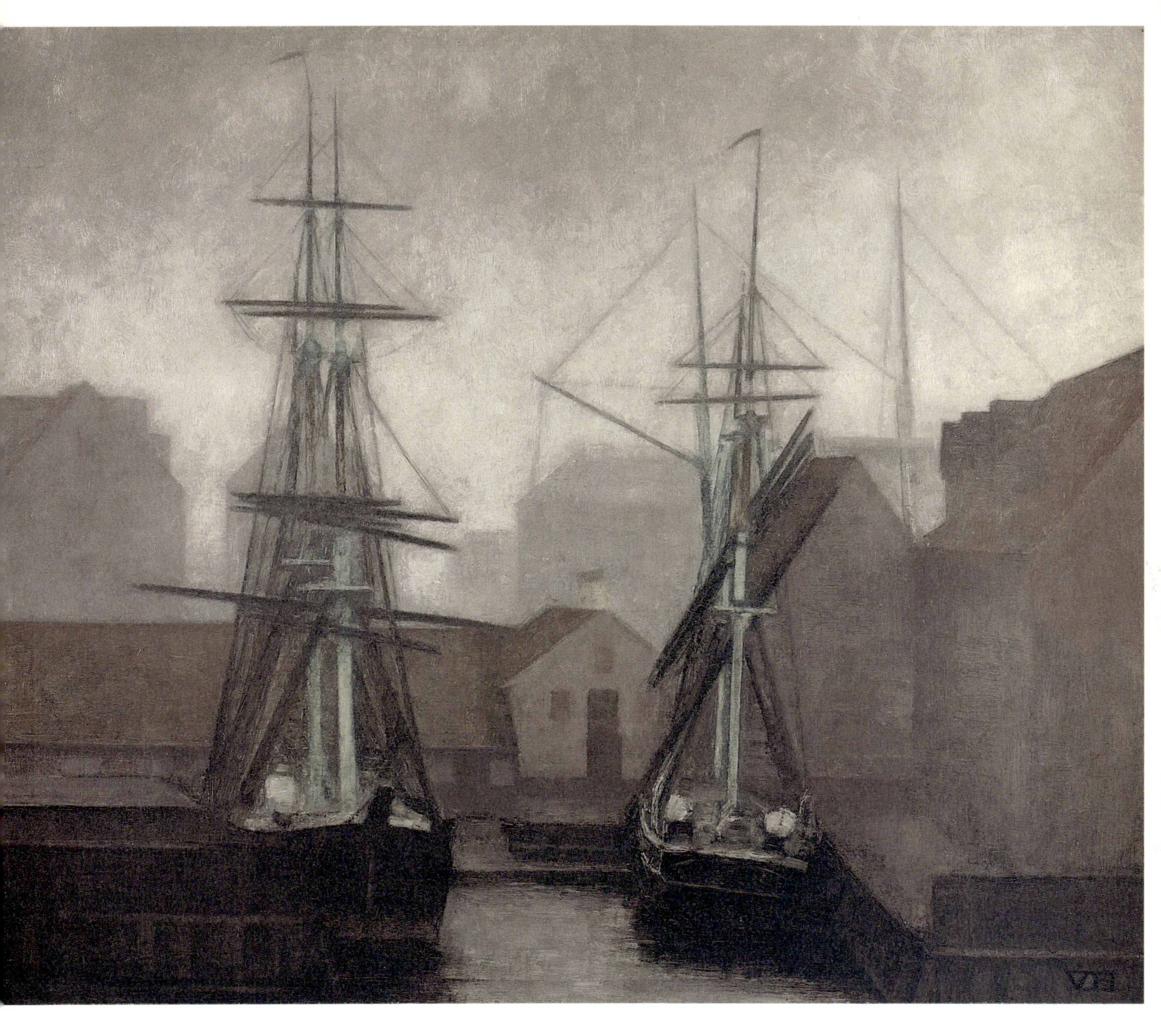

View of the Greenland Trading Company Dock, [1908]
Cat. no. 59

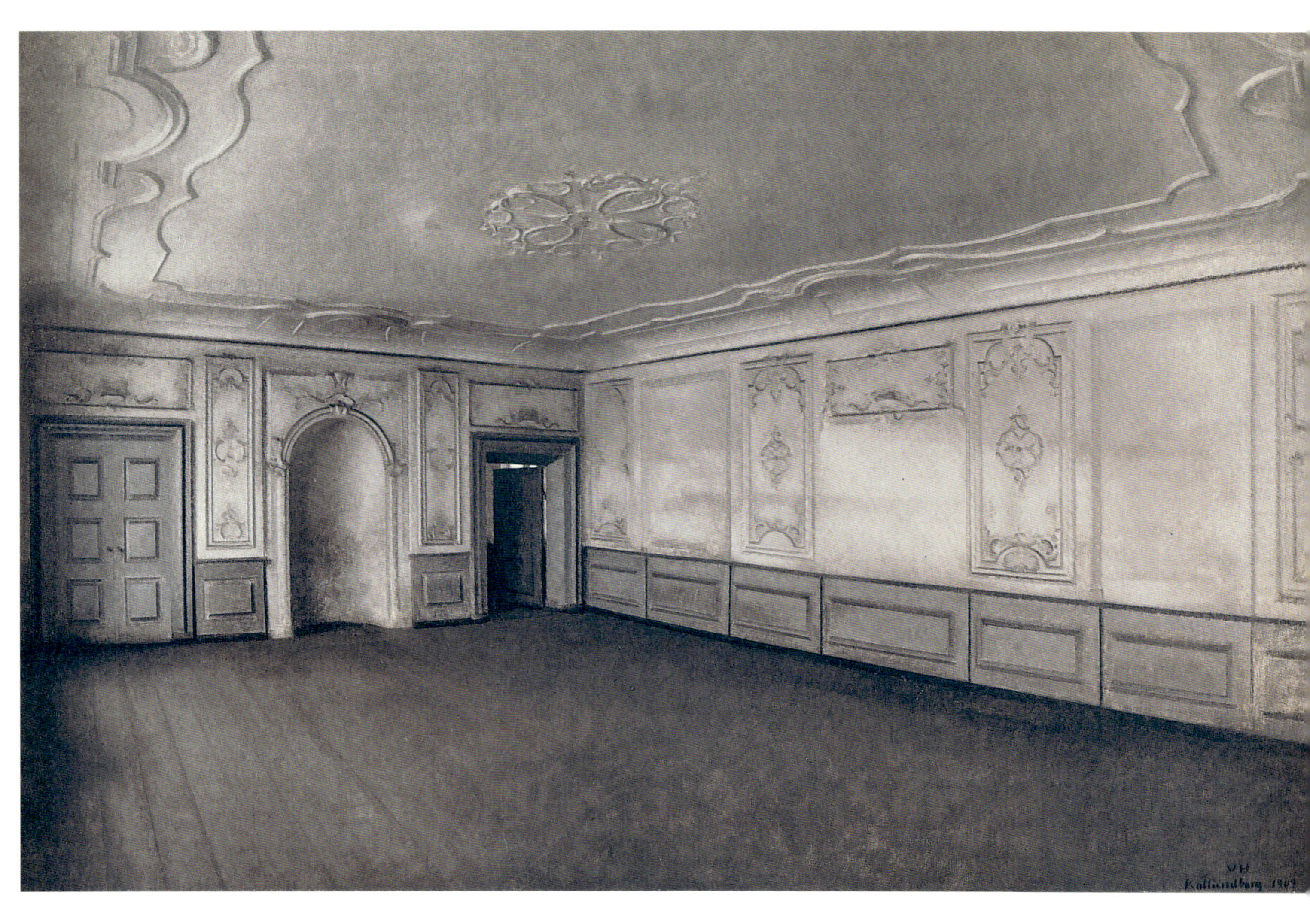

Interior of the Great Hall in Lindegården [Kalundborg], 1909
Cat. no. 61

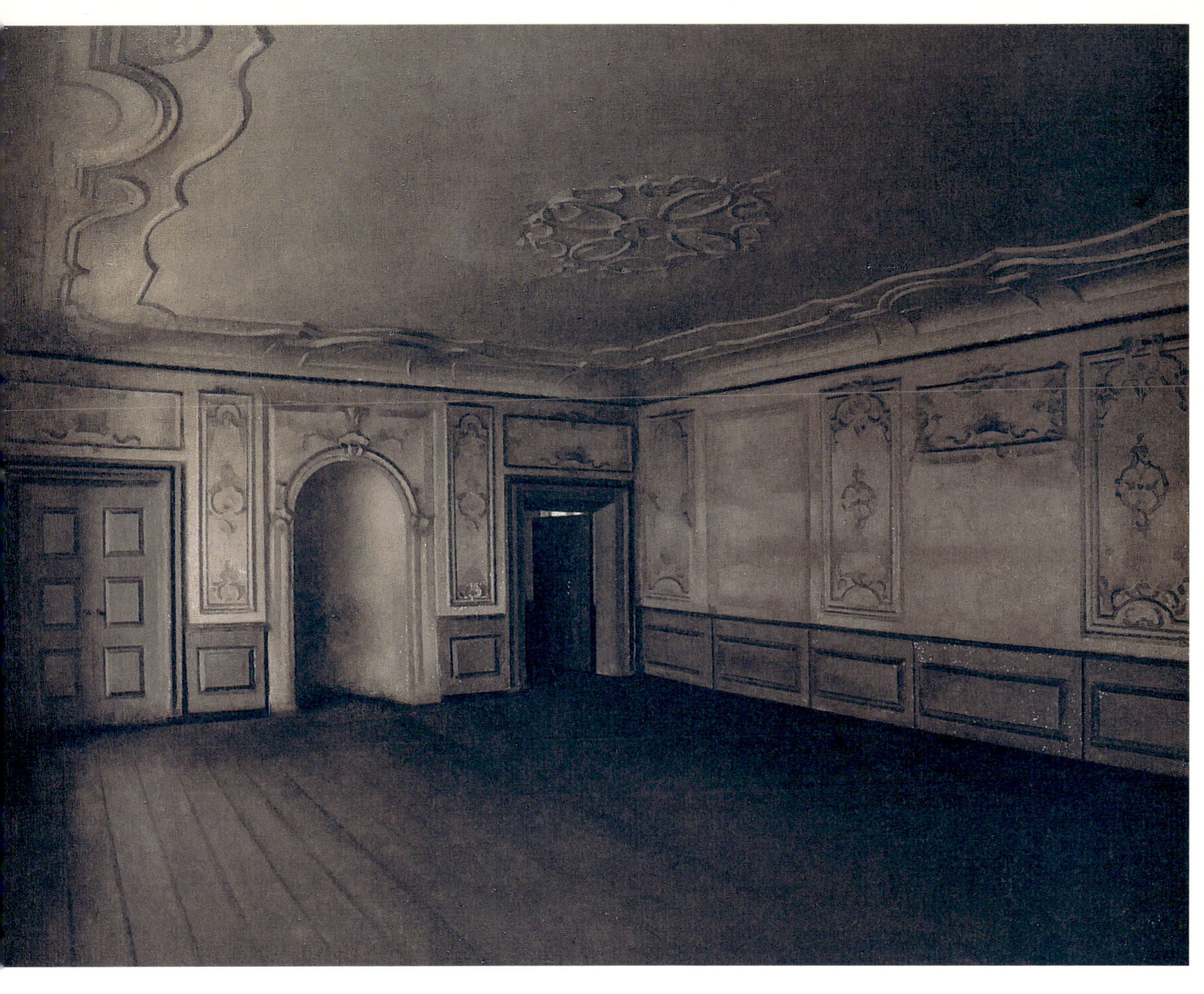

Interior of the Great Hall in Lindegården [Kalundborg], [1909]
Cat. no. 62

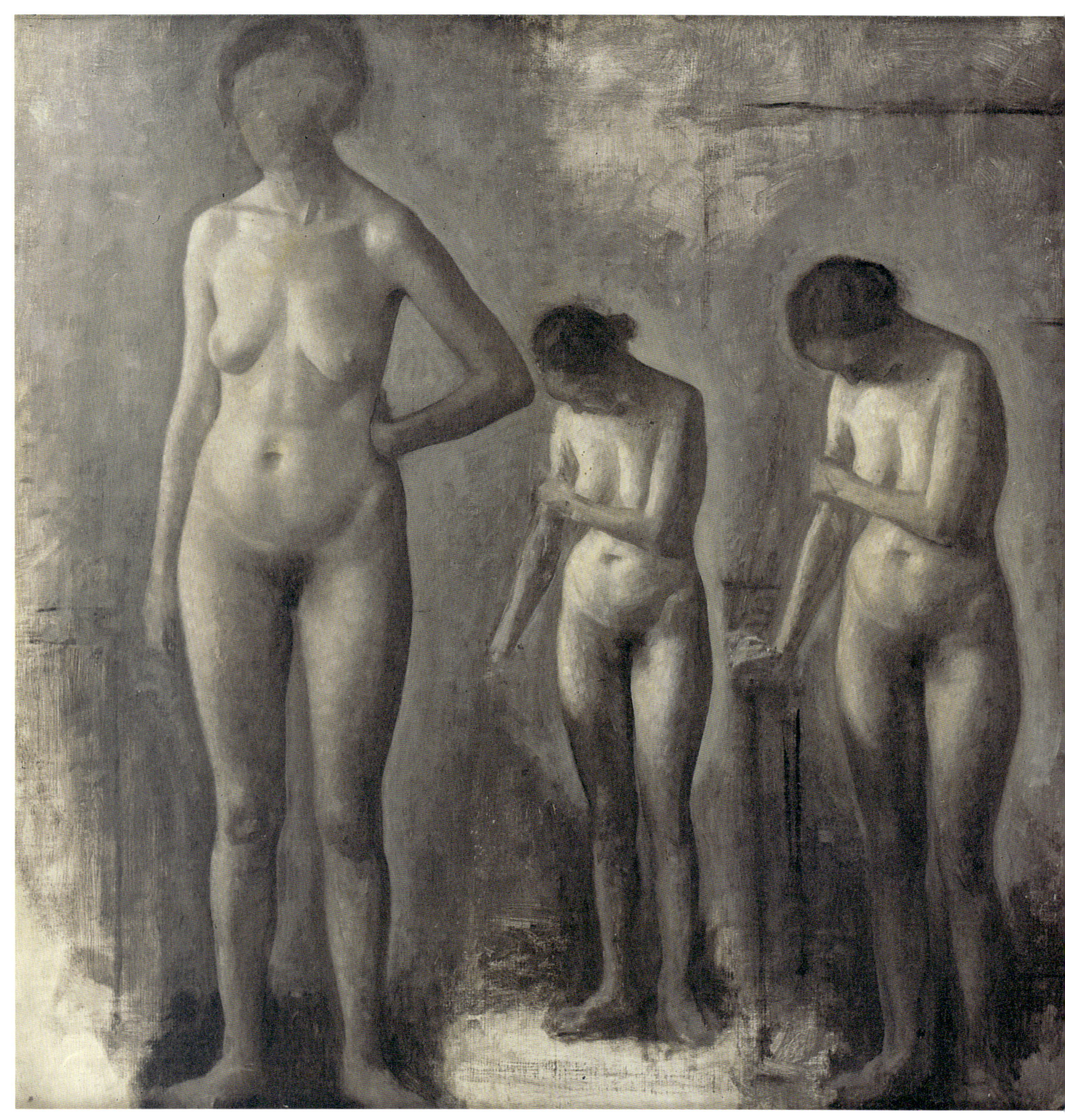

Model, or *Three Studies*, [1909]
Cat. no. 63

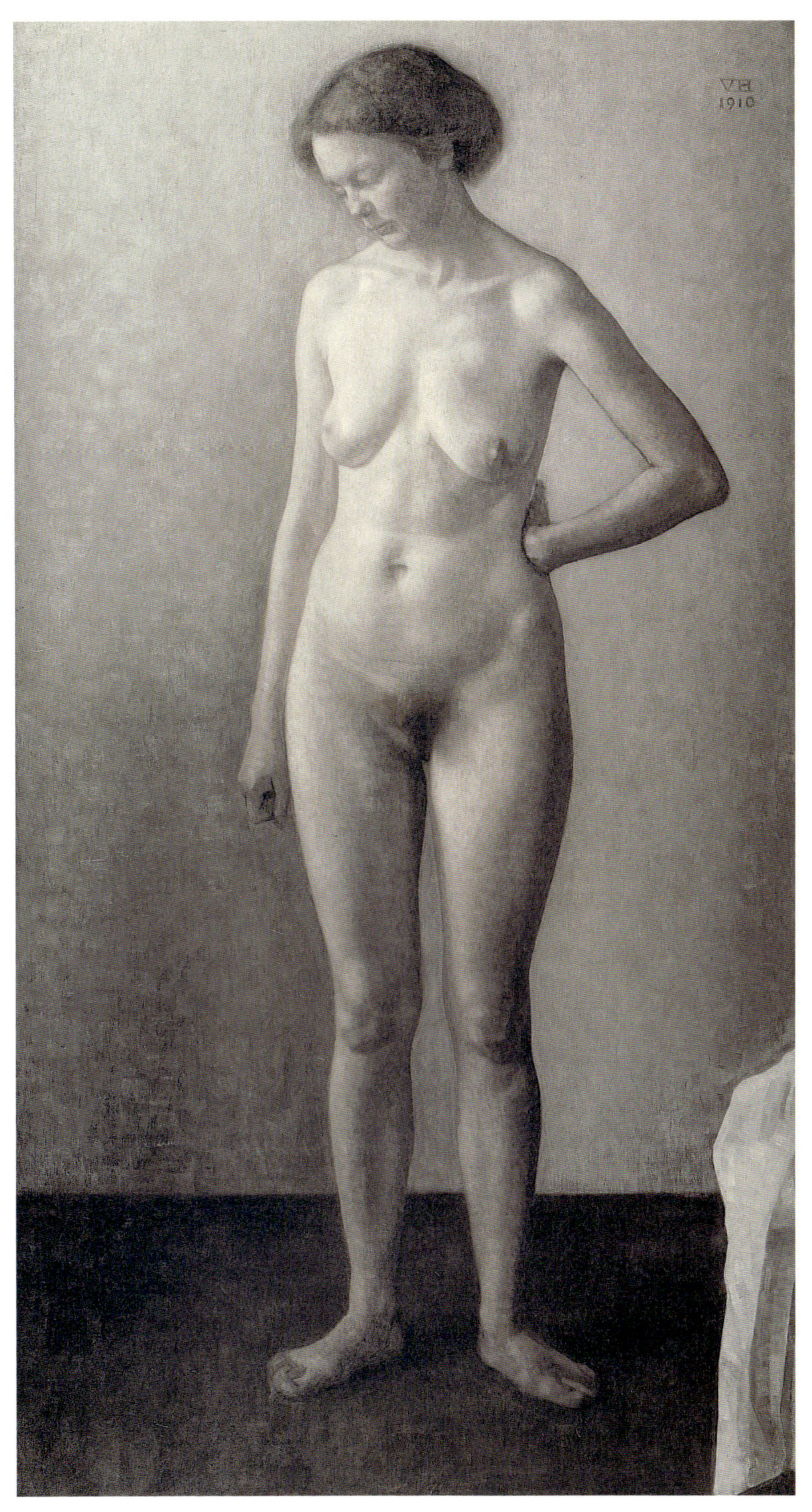

Model, or *Nude Female Model*, [1910]
Cat. no. 65

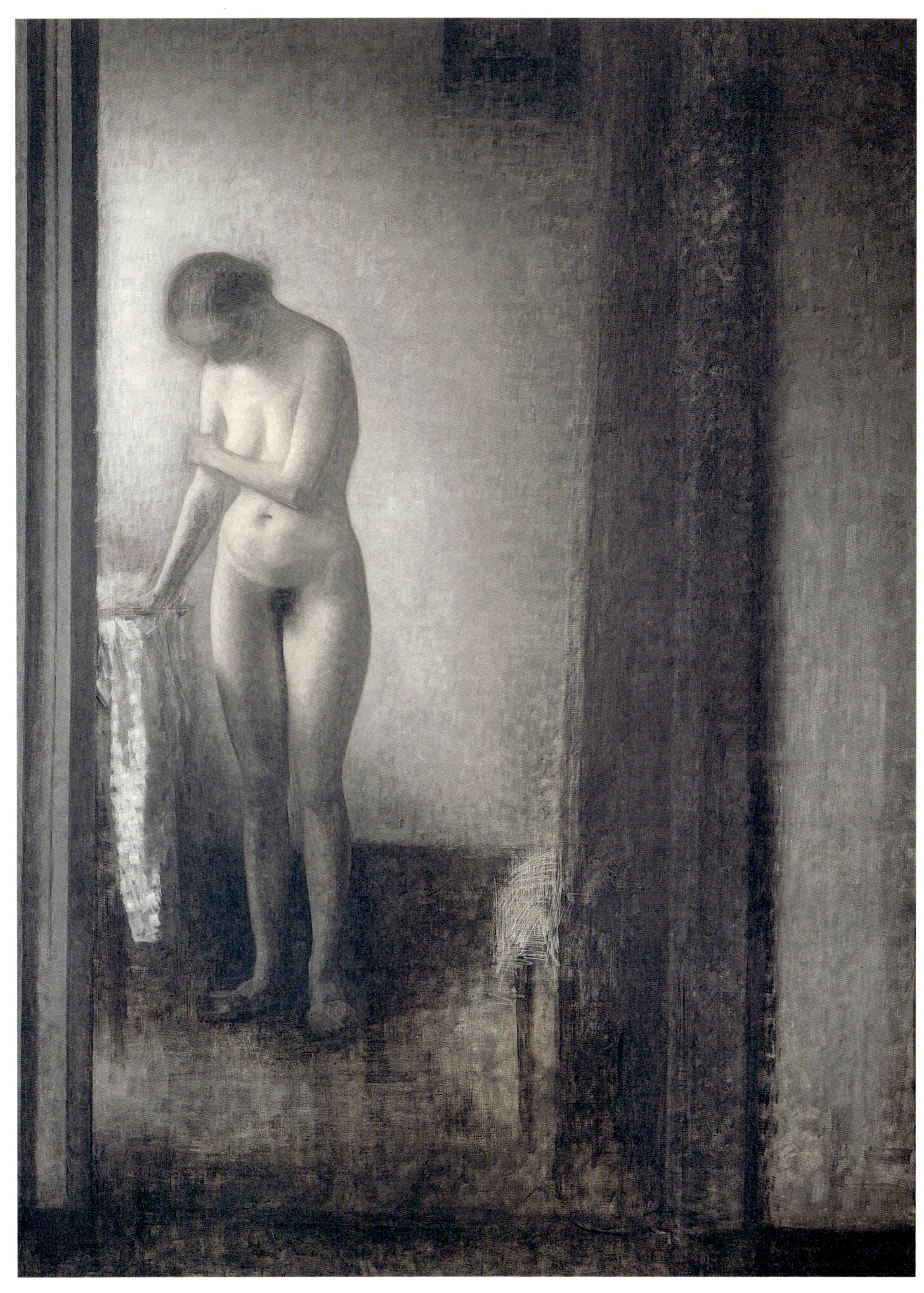

Model, or *Nude Female Model,* [1909]
Cat. no. 64

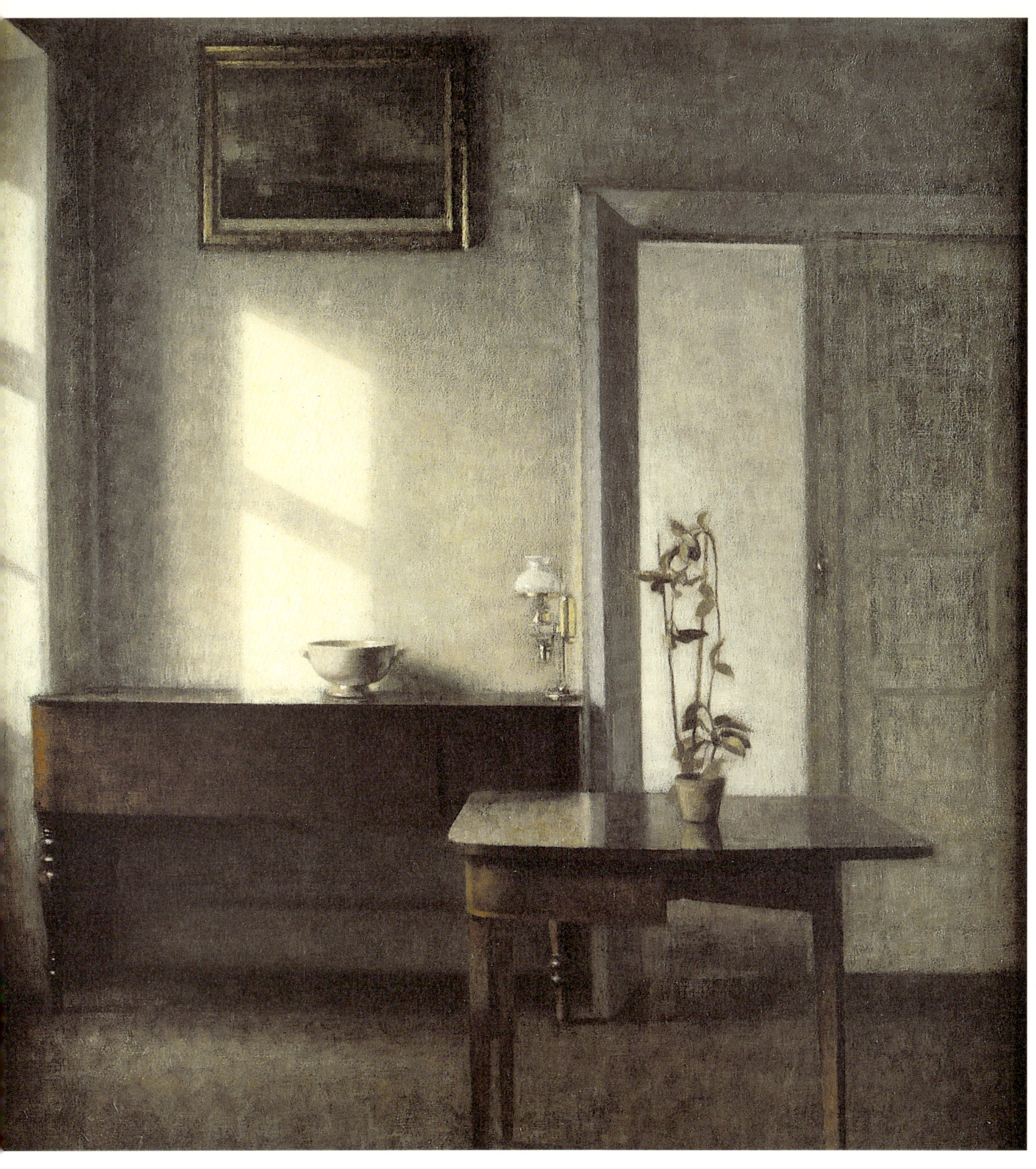

Interior [with potted plant on card table, Bredgade 25], [1910–1911]
Cat. no. 69

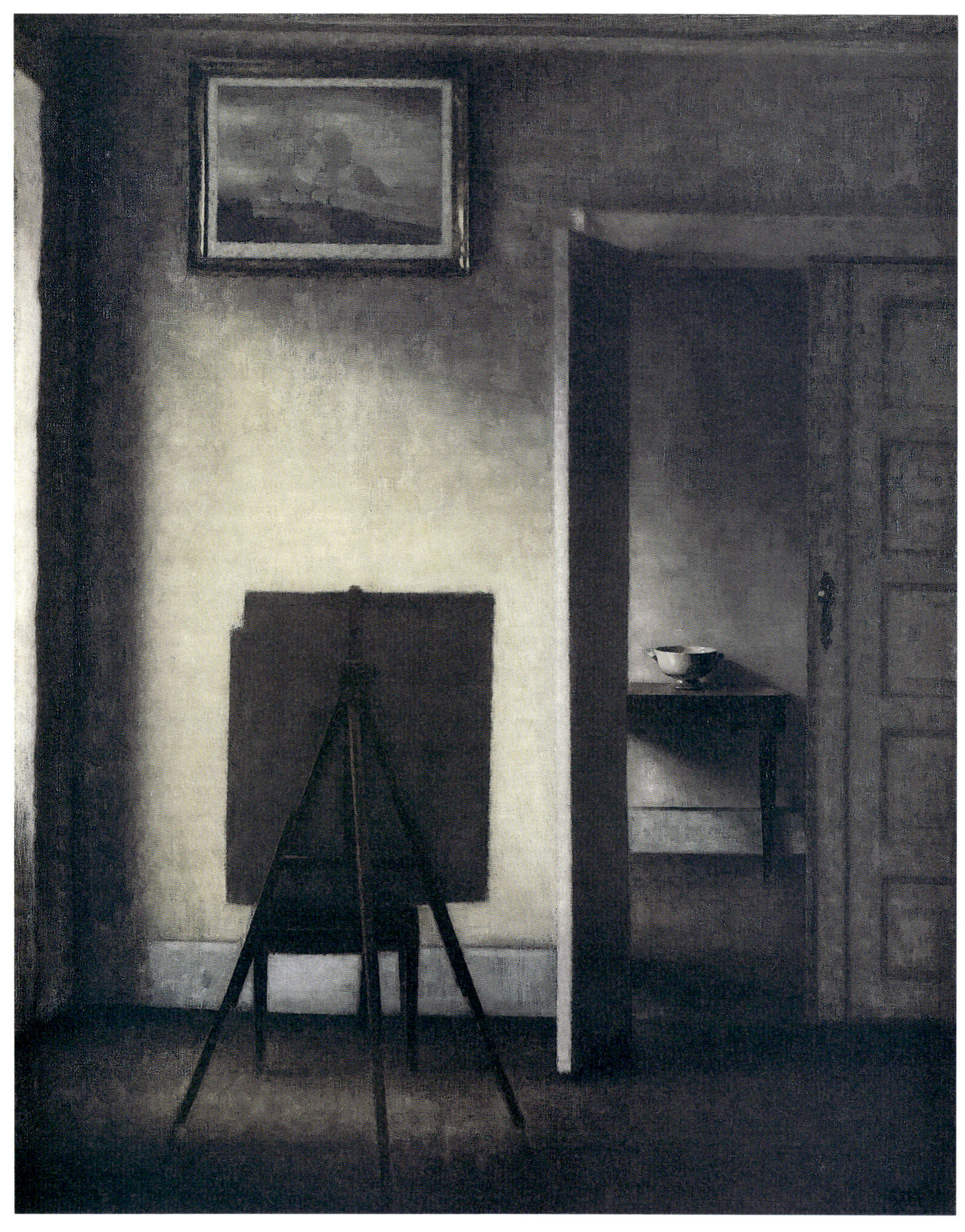

Interior [with easel, Bredgade 25], [1910]
Cat. no. 68

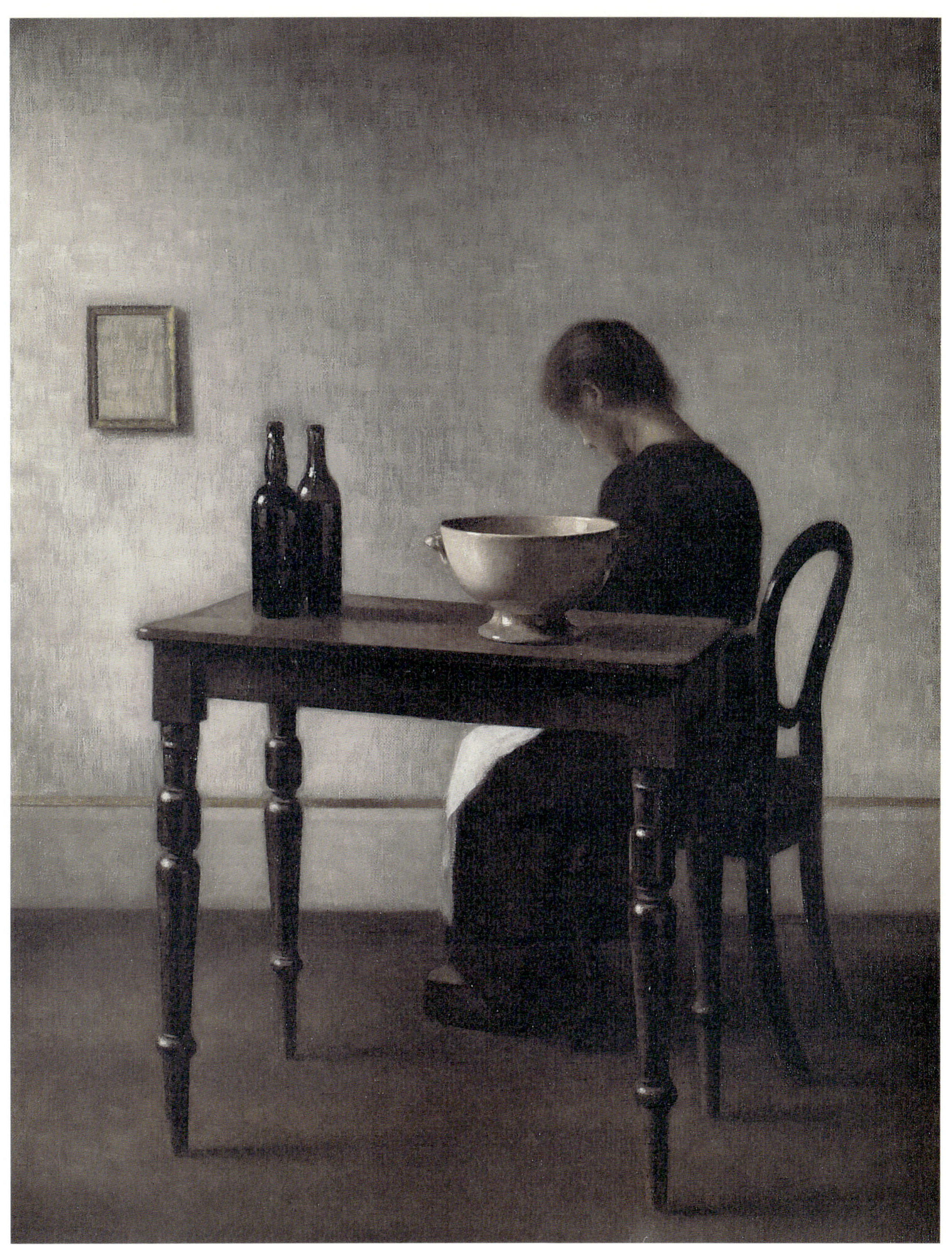

Interior [with woman sitting at a table], [ca. 1910]
Cat. no. 67

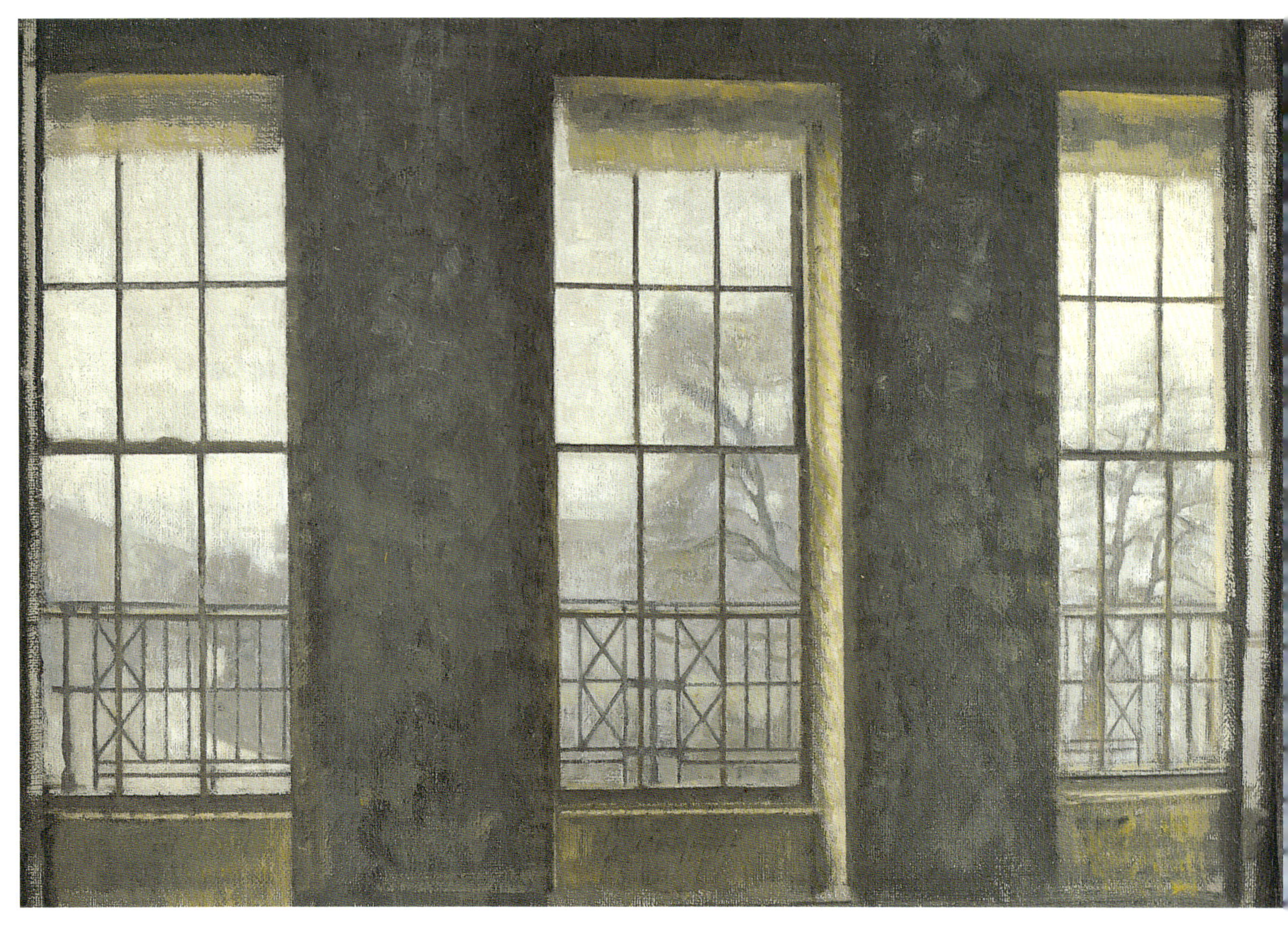

Interior in London: Brunswick Square, [1912]
Cat. no. 70

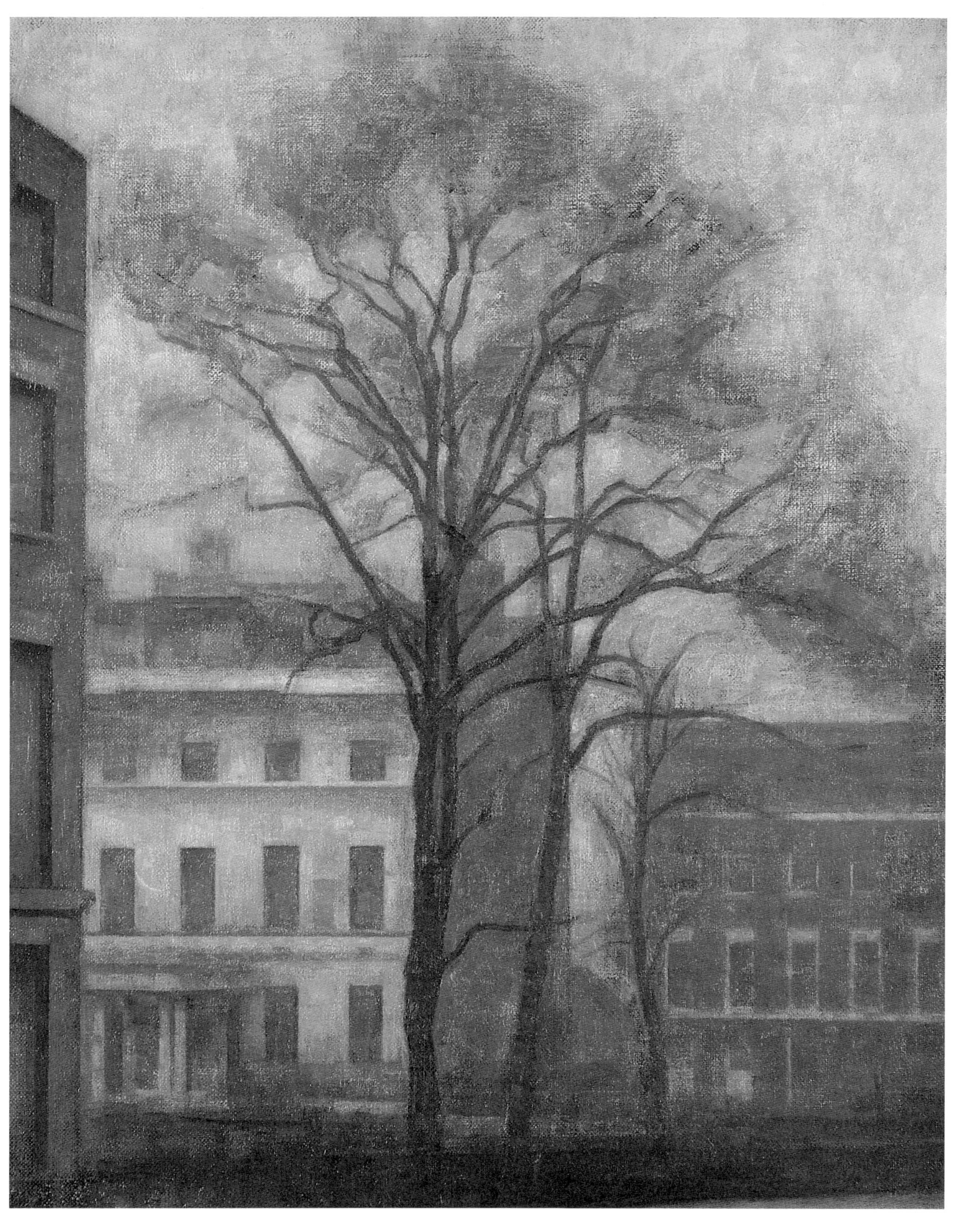

The Jewish School in Guilford Street [London], [1912–13]
Cat. no. 71

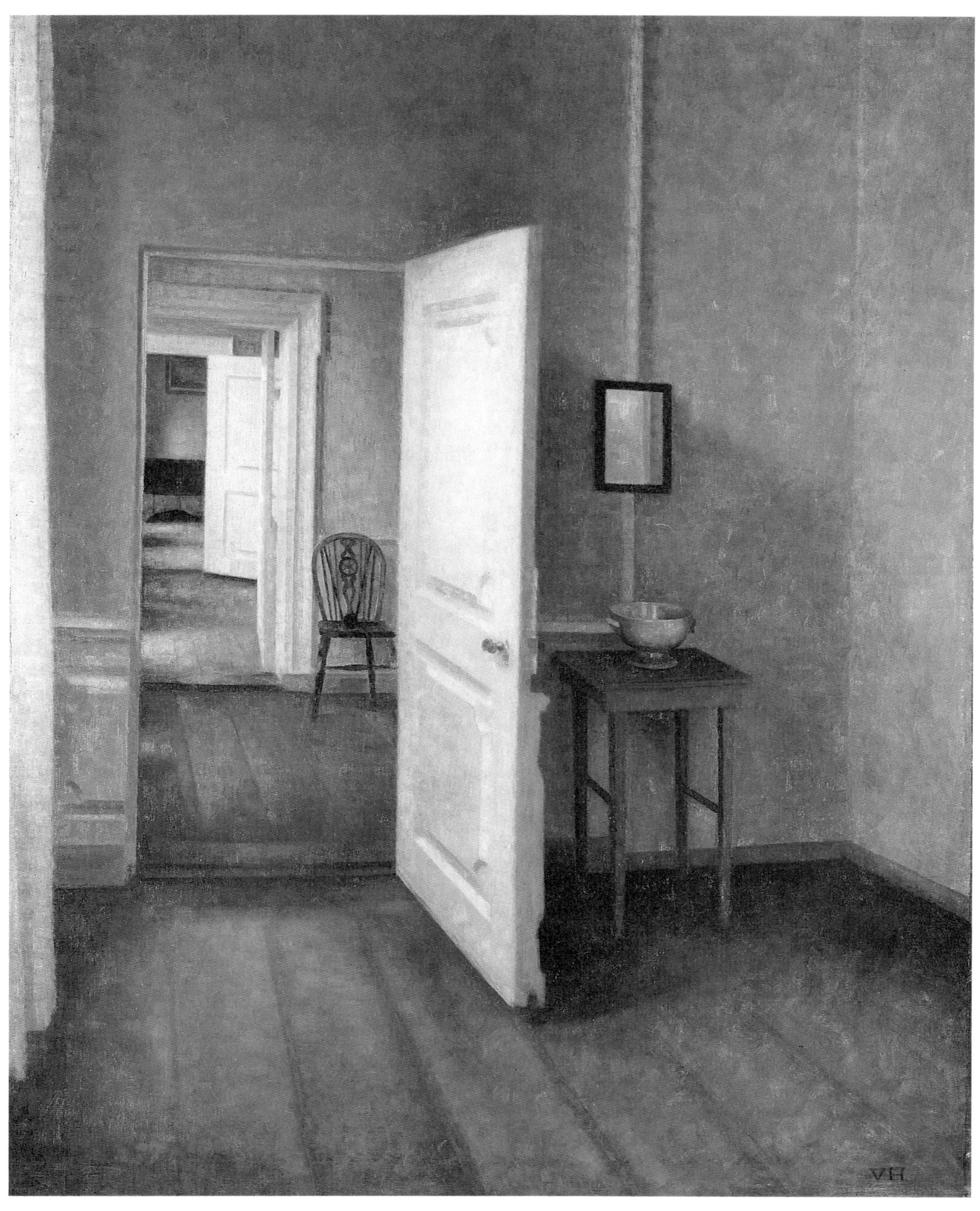

Interior, also called *The Four Rooms* [Strandgade 25], [1914]
Cat. no. 72

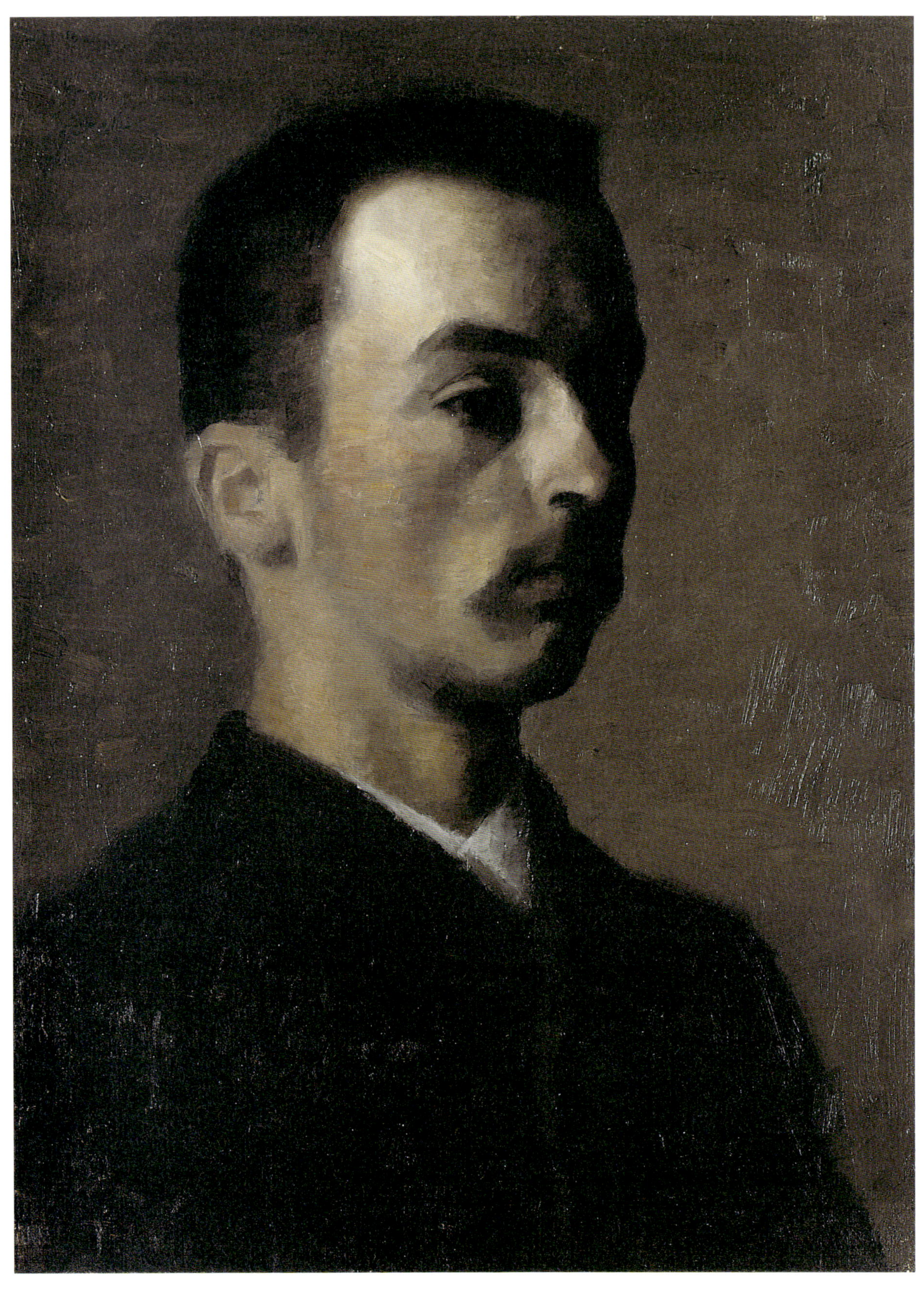

Vilhelm Hammershøi, *Self-Portrait*, [1889]. Oil on canvas. 52.5 x 39.5 cm.
Statens Museum for Kunst, Copenhagen

Catalogue

by Susanne Meyer-Abich,
editing and notes by
Anne-Birgitte Fonsmark
and Mikael Wivel

The titles of the paintings are in italics. The artist's own titles (translated into English) have been used as far as possible in this catalogue; where it has not been possible to trace these, Alfred Bramsen's titles from the list of works in *Vilhelm Hammershøi. Kunstneren og hans Værk* (1918) have been used. In addition to Hammershøi's generally simple, straightforward titles, more poetic titles were given to several pictures, sometimes even during the artist's own lifetime. If a work has more than one title, all of them are usually given, with Hammershøi's or Bramsen's title(s) first, then the more poetic title whenever one exists (preceded by "also called"). For about half the work, further information has been added more recently at the ends of titles, usually identifying a person or place or distinguishing among various interior views; these are given in roman type and enclosed in brackets.

Brackets around the date given for a work indicate that no date appears on the work itself and that the date given has been deduced from other sources. Measurements are given in centimeters (height before width).

References to bibliographic sources and exhibitions have been given in abbreviated form. The full titles can be found in the Selected Bibliography and list of Selected Exhibitions at the back of the catalogue.

The following abbreviations have been used in the catalogue entries:

Bramsen:
Alfred Bramsen

Bruun Rasmussen:
Bruun Rasmussen Art Auctions, Copenhagen

Charlottenborg:
The Charlottenborg Exhibition Building, Copenhagen

Sale of Effects 1916:
The posthumous sale of Hammershøi's effects, Charlottenborg, Copenhagen, October 30, 1916

Kunstforeningen:
The Copenhagen Art Society

Kunsthallen:
The Kunsthallen Art Auctions, Copenhagen

Winkel & Magnussen:
V. Winkel & Magnussens Art Auctions, Copenhagen

1 (repr. p. 51)
***Farm Building*, [1883]**
Oil on canvas, 34 x 38 cm
Private collection

Provenance:
Sale of Effects 1916, no. 14; Grosserer Abrahamson (Bramsen 1918); Johs. C. Bock; Winkel & Magnussen, sale 380, May 19, 1953, no. 33 (with incorrect measurements 50 x 67 cm); Winkel & Magnussen, sale 383, Oct. 26, 1953, no. 76 (still with incorrect measurements)

Literature:
Bramsen 1918, no. 8; Vad 1957, p. 6, ill. 1; Bühlmann 1985, p. 139, ill. 2; Vad 1988, ill. p. 26; Varnedoe 1988, p. 99

Exhibitions:
Kunstforeningen 1916 (vol. 1), no. 9; Ordrupgaard 1981, no. 6; New York 1993, no. 2

This picture of a farm building is among Hammershøi's very earliest oil paintings, but already reveals an unusual degree of artistic independence. His depiction of the building in an unbroken expanse from edge to edge gives the work a quality of abstraction that was rare in the art of that time.

2 (repr. p. 53)
Portrait of a Young Girl
[Anna Hammershøi], [1885]
Oil on canvas, 112.4 x 91.3 cm
Den Hirschsprungske Samling, Copenhagen

Provenance:
Acquired by Heinrich Hirschsprung, 1896; given by him and Pauline Hirschsprung to the nation, 1902

Literature:
Madsen 1899 (unpaginated), p. [5]; Bramsen 1900, no. 11; Bramsen 1905, pp. 178, 180; Emil Hannover, *Fortegnelse over Den Hirschsprungske Samling* (Copenhagen, 1911), no. 144; Wanscher 1915, p. 402f., ill. p. 401; Petersen 1916, p. 524f., ill. p. 520; Jastrau 1916, ill. p. 7; Bramsen 1918, pp. 39, 42f., 61, 63, no. 28; Sass 1946, p. 137; Vad 1957, pp. 5, 7f., 16, ill. 3; Ostenfeld 1981, ill. p. 159; Vad 1988, pp. 33f., 48, 310, ill. p. 37; Wivel 1994, p. 10 (ill.); Billgren and Osipow 1995, p. 90, ill. p. 19; Wivel 1996, p. 13, ill. p. 7

Exhibitions:
Charlottenborg 1885, no. 149; Oslo 1887, no. 282; Copenhagen 1888, no. 161; Charlottenborg 1896, no. 88; Stockholm 1897, no. 1219; Kunstforeningen 1900 (no number); Charlottenborg 1902, no. 112; London, Guildhall 1907, no. 139; Paris 1928, no. 53; Stockholm 1930, no. 1; Oslo 1955, no. 3; Kunstforeningen 1955, no. 3; Ordrupgaard 1981, no. 13; New York 1983, no. 8

This portrait of a young girl is Hammershøi's entry in a competition held by the Kunstakademiet (Royal Academy of Fine Arts) in Copenhagen in 1885. The assigned subject was "female portrait, three-quarter length, lifesize," and the best painting submitted would receive the Neuhausen Prize. Hammershøi's entry did not win the prize, but it was much discussed, in both positive and negative terms. It attracted attention because it was unusual for that time on account of his particularly subdued use of color and the bold, angled composition. The model he used was his sister Anna, then aged nineteen. The pose is modeled after Rembrandt's *Bathsheba* in the Louvre, which Hammershøi might have known from a photograph.

3 (repr. p. 54)
Young Girl Sewing
[Anna Hammershøi], [1887]
Oil on canvas, 37 x 35 cm
Ordrupgaard, Copenhagen

Provenance:
Alfred Bramsen; sale, Winkel & Magnussen, January 1904, no. 20; Wilhelm Hansen (Bramsen 1918), bequest from Wilhelm and Henny Hansen to the nation, 1951

Literature:
Madsen 1899 (unpaginated), p. [10], ill. p. [5]; Bramsen 1900, no. 19; Bramsen 1905, p. 181; Jastrau 1916, ill. p. 9; Bramsen 1918, pp. 39, 43, 61, 63, no. 58; Rostrup 1940, ill. p. 182; Sass 1946, p. 138; Madsen 1946, ill. 2; Leo Swane, *Katalog over Kunstværkerne på Or-*

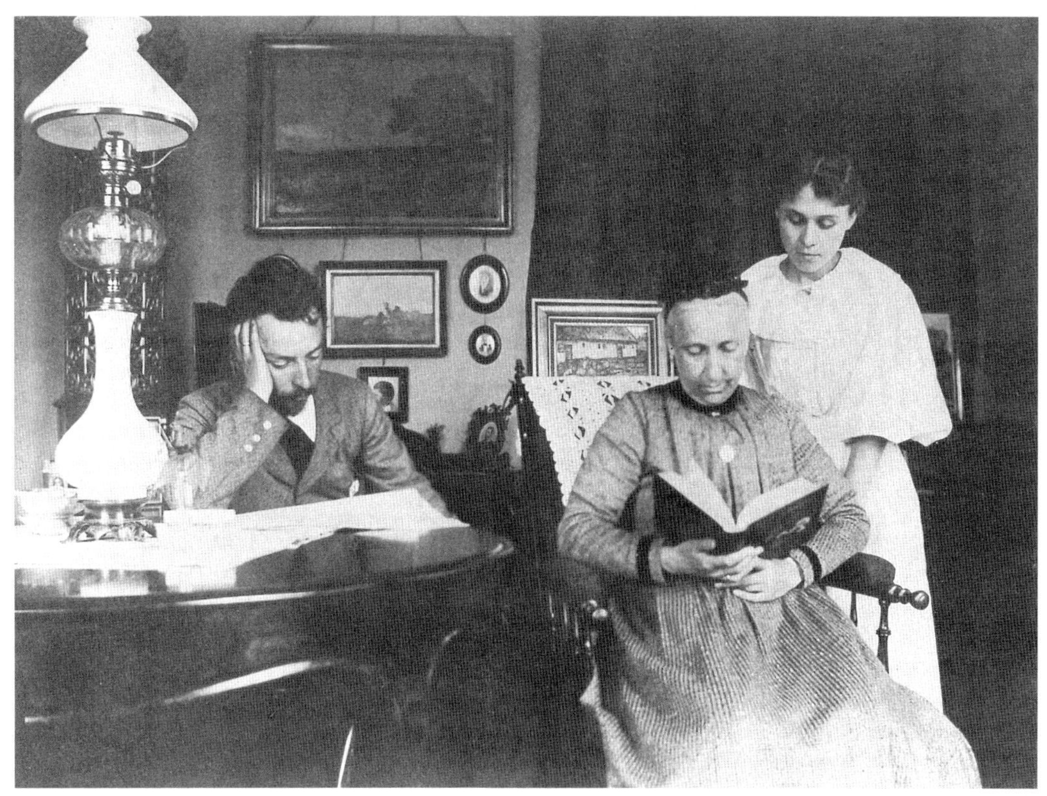

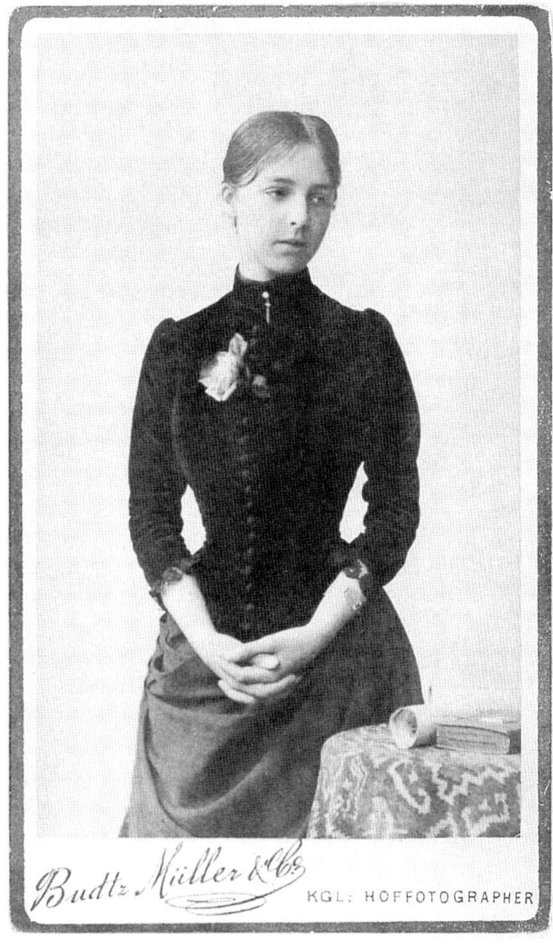

Vilhelm Hammershøi with his mother, Frederikke, and his wife, Ida, ca. 1895. Det Kongelige Bibliotek, Copenhagen

Anna Hammershøi, the artist's sister, 1886. Det Kongelige Bibliotek, Copenhagen

drupgaard (Copenhagen, 1954), no. 125, ill.; Vad 1988, p. 67, ill. p. 79; Werenskjold 1991, p. 228; Wivel 1993, p. 72, ill.

Exhibitions:
Charlottenborg 1888; Paris 1889, no. 46; Kunstforeningen 1890, no. 45; Munich 1891; Charlottenborg 1896, no. 90; Stockholm 1897, no. 1220; St. Petersburg 1897, no. 230; Kunstforeningen 1900 (no number); Berlin 1900, no. 463; Winkel & Magnussen, Copenhagen 1904, no. 20; London, Guildhall 1907, no. 125; Kunstforeningen 1916 (vol. 1), no. 45; Stockholm 1918, no. 97; Paris 1928, no. 55; Ordrupgaard 1981, no. 22; New York 1983, no. 13

The model was Hammershøi's sister, Anna (see also cat. no. 2). In 1888 he submitted the picture to the Charlottenborg Exhibition, the annual juried exhibition organized by the Kunstakademiet (Royal Academy of Fine Arts), but it was not accepted. The rejection angered the younger artists, and together with other rejected pictures it was shown in a protest exhibition, also held in Charlottenborg. Here, it was purchased by Alfred Bramsen (1851–1932), a dentist who subsequently became Hammershøi's mentor and biographer (ill. p. 188). The following year it was shown at the Paris World's Fair, where it was awarded a bronze medal. Hammershøi painted it after visiting Holland and Belgium, and one can see in its treatment of light his admiration of Dutch painters, especially Vermeer.

4 (repr. p. 55)
***Study: Baker's Shop*, [1889]**
Inscription on reverse of label: Studie (bagerbutik) malet i Pile Allé / 1889/ V. Hammershøi
Oil on canvas, 113.5 x 90 cm
Vejen Kunstmuseum, Vejen

Provenance:
Acquired by Alfred Bramsen, 1896 (Bramsen 1918); Gustav Falck; Karen Falck; Bruun Rasmussen, sale 267, Sept. 28, 1971, no. 6; purchased at that sale by the Ny Carlsbergfondet and presented to the Vejen Kunstmuseum

Literature:
Bramsen 1900, no. 27; Bramsen 1918, no. 60; Vad 1957, p. 8, ill. 5; Jørgen Rømer, *Vejen Kunstmuseum, 1991, Katalog over samlingen* (Vejen, 1991), p. 87, ill. p. 88; Varnedoe 1983, ill. p. 110; Bühlmann 1985, p. 139; Vad 1988, pp. 56, 63, ill. p. 57; Werenskjold 1991, p. 217f., ill. p. 218; Billgren and Osipow 1995, ill. p. 24

Exhibitions:
Paris 1889, no. 44; Den frie Udstilling 1891, no. 10; St. Petersburg 1897; Kunstforeningen 1900 (no number); Berlin 1903, no. 4; Kunstforeningen 1916, no. 54; Stockholm 1919, no. 413; New York 1927, no. 41; Paris 1928, no. 58; Kunstforeningen 1955, no. 5; Oslo 1955, no. 5; Stockholm 1976, no. 4; Ordrupgaard 1981, no. 25; New York 1983, no. 14; Kunstforeningen 1983, no. 25; London 1986, no. 30

This painting of a figure seen from behind in an interior is one of Hammershøi's first large-scale works. He painted it while he had a studio in the garden house at Allégade 6 in the Frederiksberg district of Copenhagen; according to an inscription on the reverse, the subject was based on a baker's shop in the nearby Pile Allé. However, Hammershøi was not concerned here with the specific but with the general, as is evident from his flattening of deep space and from his positioning of the figure in the middle ground. Together with *Young Girl Sewing* (cat. no. 3), the picture was shown at the Paris World's Fair and thus contributed to Hammershøi's being awarded a bronze medal there.

5 (repr. p. 56)
***Study of a Model*,**
or *Nude Female Model*, [1889]
Oil on canvas, 126 x 92 cm
Statens Museum for Kunst, Copenhagen

Provenance:
Oscar Wandel; posthumous sale of Wandel's effects, Feb. 16, 1926, no. 72; purchased at that sale by the Statens Museum for Kunst

Literature:
Bramsen 1900, no. 31; Bramsen 1918, no. 74; Petersen 1939, ill. p. 78; Vad 1957, p. 8, ill. 6; Marianne Brøns et al., *Statens Museum for Kunst. Nyere dansk malerkunst. Katalog* (Co-

penhagen, 1970), inv. no. 3766; Vad 1988, p. 44f., 298, ill. p. 49; Usselmann 1990, p. 196; Billgren and Osipow 1995, p. 111f., ill. p. 20; Wivel 1996, p. 24f., ill. p. 22

Exhibitions:
Den frie Udstilling 1894, no. 104; Charlottenborg 1896, no. 82; Kunstforeningen 1900 (no number); Kunstforeningen 1916 (vol. 1), no. 57; Kunstforeningen 1955, no. 7; Oslo 1955, no. 7

This is Hammershøi's first large-scale painting of a female nude. It is closely related to two slightly earlier works: his full-length male nude *Job* (see Vad 1988, p. 39f.; see also Hammershøi's study for *Job*, repr. p. 13 of this catalogue), and his 1885 portrait of his sister (cat. no. 2). Here, the figure is three-quarter-length, as in the portrait; and her pose—sitting slightly turned, with one hand on her lap and the other down at her side—is similar to that of the figure in *Job*. Hammershøi probably painted it just after his first visit to Paris, in the summer of 1889.

6 (repr. p. 57)
***View of Christiansborg Palace*, [1890–92]**
Oil on canvas, 115.5 x 147.5 cm
Statens Museum for Kunst, Copenhagen

Provenance:
Alfred Bramsen (Bramsen 1918); Gustav Falck; Karen Falck; Alice Falck; acquired by the Statens Museum for Kunst, 1972

Literature:
Madsen 1899 (unpaginated), ill. p. [7]; Bramsen 1900, no. 50. *Vilhelm Hammershøi* (Copenhagen: Winkel & Magnussens Kunstforlag, undated [1905]), no. 2; Bramsen 1905, p. 185; Jastrau 1916, ill. p. 13; Bramsen 1918, p. 45, no. 120, ill.; Vad 1988, pp. 56, 146, ill. p. 82; Billgren and Osipow 1995, p. 45f., ill. p. 35

Exhibitions:
Den frie Udstilling 1893, no. 22; Charlottenborg 1896, no. 104; Stockholm 1897, no. 1222; Kunstforeningen 1900 (no number); Berlin 1905, no. 15; Kunstforeningen 1916 (vol. 1), no. 94; Kunstforeningen 1955, no. 15; Oslo 1955, no. 14; Paris 1993, no. 6

Hammershøi painted this, his first architectural picture, looking out from Alfred Bramsen's apartment at the corner of Stormgade and Frederiksholms Kanal in the center of Copenhagen beginning in November 1890.
It is the first of several paintings that he did of Christiansborg Palace (see cat. nos. 29, 56, and 66); a catastrophic fire in 1884 destroyed all but the western sections of the original palace (1733–45), designed by architects Elias David Häusser and Nicolai Eigtved. This picture encompasses a broad view of the complex, including an equestrian pavilion and a stable behind the low buildings in the foreground (among the palace's original buildings) and the Marble Bridge, designed by Eigtved.

7 (repr. p. 61)
***A Greek Relief* [Paris], [1891]**
Oil on canvas, 95.5 x 96 cm
Private collection, on loan to Ny Carlsberg Glyptotek, Copenhagen

Provenance:
Acquired by Alfred Bramsen, 1892; Gustav Falck; Karen Falck

Literature:
Bramsen 1900, no. 47; Bramsen 1905, p. 187f., ill. p. 188; Jastrau 1916, ill. p. 20; Bramsen 1918, p. 51, no. 107; Sass 1946, p. 143, ill. p. 142; Vad 1957, p. 10, ill. 17; Bodelsen 1959, p. 170; Varnedoe 1985, p. 111, ill. p. 112; Vad 1988, p. 105f., 277, ill. p. 109; Usselmann 1990, p. 194, ill. 2; Billgren and Osipow, pp. 76, 110, 115, ill. p. 59; Wivel 1996, p. 26, ill. p. 27; Vad 1996, ill. p. 370

Exhibitions:
Den frie Udstilling 1892, no. 13; Charlottenborg 1896, no. 98; Stockholm 1897, no. 1231; Kunstforeningen 1900 (no number); Berlin 1905, no. 122; Kunstforeningen 1916 (vol. 1), no. 85; Oslo 1955, no. 12; Kunstforeningen 1955, no. 12; Ordrupgaard 1981, no. 38; New York 1983, no. 24; Nivaagaard 1993, no. 37

Hammershøi painted this in the Louvre during his second visit to Paris, in the autumn and winter of 1891–92, working on it without a break from the end of October until Christmas. The relief, executed in archaic style at the beginning of the 5th century B.C., and featuring *Hermes and the Three Graces*, originally adorned the Prytaneum on Thasos. Hammershøi's picture represents the left-hand section of the frieze (ill. p. 151). The picture is the same size as the relief, but according to Poul Vad it should be ragarded as a painterly paraphrase rather than a literal copy. What interested Hammershøi was the light falling across the relief and making the three Graces seem to emerge from the stone. He elaborated on the subject and style of this picture on a much larger scale in his *Artemis* (cat. no. 10), which he painted just over a year later.

8 (repr. p. 59)
Landscape
[Kongevejen near Gentofte], [1892]
Oil on canvas, 115 x 147 cm
Private collection

Provenance:
Acquired by Alfred Bramsen from Kleis Kunsthandel, 1894 (Bramsen 1918); Gustav Falck

Literature:
Madsen 1899 (unpaginated) p. [12], ill. p. [9]; Bramsen 1900, no. 52; Jastrau 1916, ill. p. 22; Bramsen 1918, p. 44, no. 115, ill.; Vad 1957, p. 10f., ill. 18; Vad 1988, p. 154f., ill. p. 140

Exhibitions:
Den frie Udstilling 1893, no. 21; Kunstforeningen 1900 (no number); Berlin 1900, no. 469; Berlin 1905, no. 16; Malmö 1914, no. 2348; Kunstforeningen 1916 (vol. 1), no. 96; Stockholm 1919, no. 426; Kunstforeningen 1955, no. 14; Oslo 1955, no. 13; Ordrupgaard 1981, no. 42

In his landscapes, Hammershøi often depicted the cultivated and farmed countryside around Copenhagen, showing such characteristic elements as a row of trees along a country road. He found the subject for this painting just ten kilometers (about six miles) from the center of the city, along the Kongevejen (the "king's road," today called Lyngbyvej). In 1892 Hammershøi spent his summer holiday here, at Ørnegården, about a kilometer north of Gentofte Lake, staying until August 19.

9 (repr. p. 63)
***Study of a Head*, [1893]**
Oil on canvas, 42 x 42 cm
Private collection

Provenance:
Anna Hammershøi (Bramsen 1918); Bruun Rasmussen, sale 61, Apr. 26, 1955, no. 188

Literature:
Bramsen 1918, no. 134; Vad 1988, p. 117, ill. p. 116

This unfinished painting of a woman's head is related to Hammershøi's *Artemis* (cat. no. 10), according to Bramsen. However, it is not at all similar to any of the four heads in that picture. It could perhaps be regarded as a study suggesting the atmosphere that Hammershøi wanted to achieve in *Artemis*.

10 (repr. p. 64)
***Artemis*, [1893–94]**
Oil on canvas, 193 x 251.5 cm
Statens Museum for Kunst, Copenhagen

Provenance:
Sale of Effects 1916, no. 18; purchased at that sale by the Statens Museum for Kunst

Literature:
Ballin 1894; Madsen 1899 (unpaginated), p. [12]; Jastrau 1916, ill. p. 29; Bramsen 1900, no. 66; Bramsen 1918, p. 59, no. 133; Petersen 1916, pp. 518–20; Rostrup 1940, pp. 178, 181f.; Sass 1946, p. 143f., ill. p. 141; Vad 1957, pp. 12f., 16, 23, 25, ill. 19–21; Bodelsen 1959, pp. 161–74, ill. p. 161; Ditzel 1959, p. 19f., ill.; Marianne Brøns et al., *Statens Museum for Kunst. Nyere dansk malerkunst. Katalog* (Copenhagen, 1970), inv. no. 3358; Nykjær 1981, pp. 71–80, ill. pp. 15, 70; Vad 1988, pp. 117f., 142, 176, 222, ill. p. 120f.; Usselmann 1990, p. 194f., ill. 3; Nykjær 1991, p. 143f., ill. p. 145; Wivel 1994, p. 104, ill.; Wivel 1996, p. 27f., ill. p. 28

Exhibitions:
Den frie Udstilling 1894, no 103; Charlottenborg 1896, no. 84; Kunstforeningen 1900 (no number); Kunstforeningen 1916 (vol. 1),

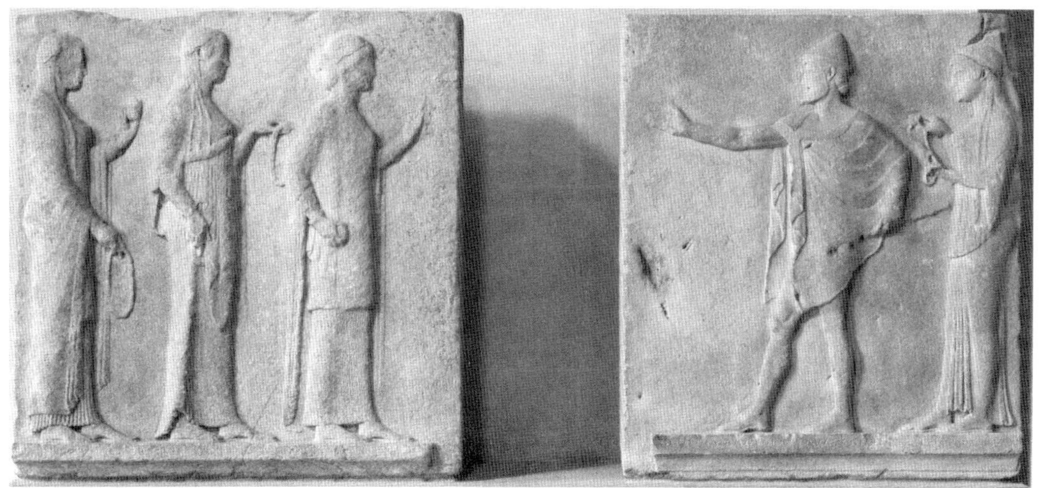

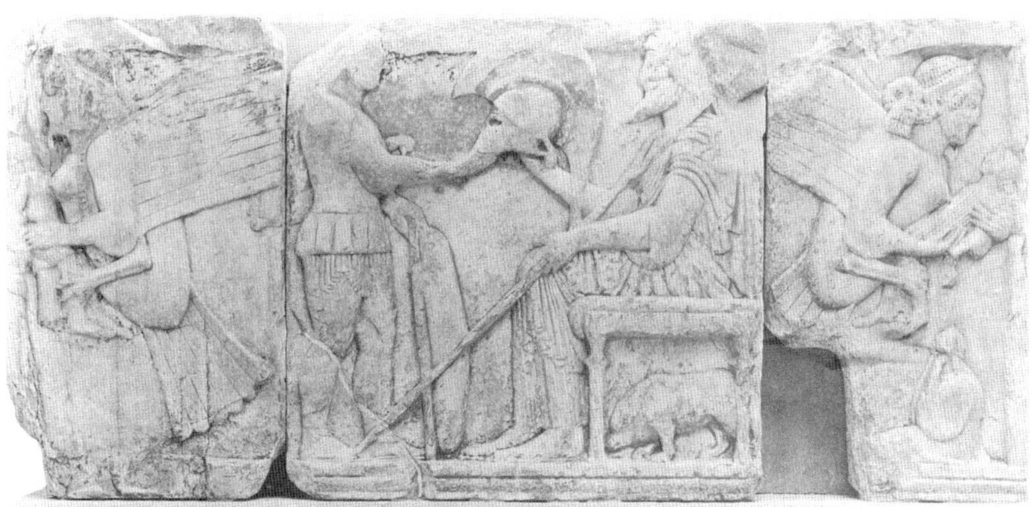

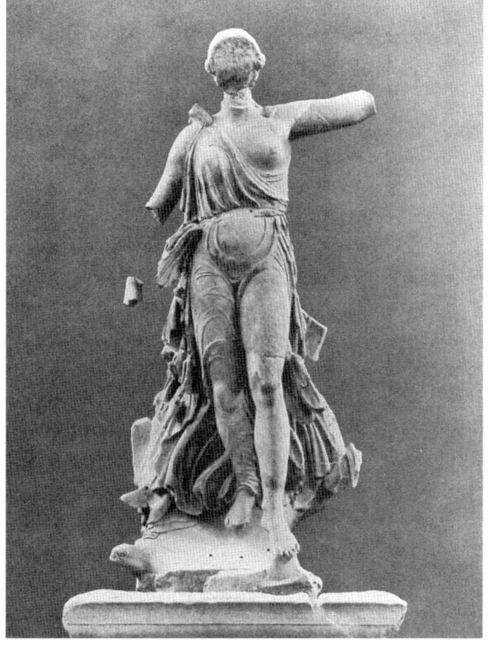

Hermes and the Three Graces,
from Thasos, Greece, ca. 480 B.C.
The Louvre, Paris

Ancient relief from the north side of the Harpy Tomb, Xanthos, Greece, ca. 480 B.C. Marble, ca. 100 x 227 cm. British Museum, London

Paionios, *Nike*, ca. 420–410 B.C.
Marble, 216 cm.
The Museum of Archaeology, Olympia

no. 101; Kunstforeningen 1955, no. 17; Paris 1960, no. 218; Kunstforeningen 1976, no. 70; Ordrupgaard 1981, no. 48

Besides *Job* (1887), which, unfortunately, has darkened so much over time that it is all but lost to us, *Artemis* represents Hammershøi's only other attempt at historical painting. He began it immediately after returning from a lengthy visit to Italy, basing it on his impressions of both Classical and Renaissance art interpreted in a very personal way. According to art historian Karl Madsen, who followed the evolution of the picture at close quarters, the most influential work in this regard was Luca Signorelli's *Pan*, which Hammershøi had seen during a visit to Berlin on his way home; however, the impact of the frescoes of Adam and Eve by Masolino and Masaccio in the Brancacci Chapel in Florence is more clearly discernible. One might also note the similarities to a sculpture by Praxiteles and a painting by Perugino, as well as a Pompeiian mosaic of *The Three Graces*, which Hammershøi might have seen in a photograph (ill. p. 159). In subject, the picture is related to the classical representation of the Judgment of Paris; but Hammershøi's version, with Paris choosing Artemis rather than Aphrodite, is not the usual one. The picture must be regarded as one of Hammershøi's few genuine attempts to adopt the Symbolist approach taken by many artists at that time.

11 (repr. p. 67)
***Landscape in Snow*, [Søndermarken], [1896]**
Oil on canvas, 83.2 x 64.8 cm
Den Hirschsprungske Samling, Copenhagen

Provenance:
Acquired by Heinrich Hirschsprung, 1897 (Bramsen 1918); given by him and Pauline Hirschsprung to the Danish nation, 1902

Literature:
Bramsen 1900, no. 82; Emil Hannover, *Fortegnelse over Den Hirschsprungske Samling* (Copenhagen, 1911), no. 147; Bramsen 1918, no. 152; Vad 1988, pp. 156f., 365, ill. p. 367

Exhibitions:
Paris 1900, no. 23; Charlottenborg 1902, no. 115; Oslo 1955, no. 19; Kunstforeningen 1955, no. 22; Stockholm 1976, no. 15; Ordrupgaard 1981, no. 54; New York 1983, no. 31

Hammershøi married Ida Ilsted in 1891, and the following year the couple moved into Ny Bakkehus in Rahbeks Allé, in the Frederiksberg district on the west side of Copenhagen. Their house was close to Søndermarken, a large park next to Frederiksberg Castle, which had been laid out between 1733 and 1736 and later that century turned into a park in the English style. Here, Hammershøi found his winter motif one day when snow was covering the forest floor and silhouetting the patterns of the twisting tree branches.

12 (repr. p. 69)
***View of Amalienborg Square*, [1896]**
Oil on canvas, 136.5 x 136.5 cm
Statens Museum for Kunst, Copenhagen

Provenance:
Acquired by the Statens Museum for Kunst, 1896

Literature:
Bramsen 1900, no. 83; Bramsen 1905, p. 184; Jastrau 1916, ill. p. 32; Bramsen 1918, pp. 40, 46f., no. 153, ill.; Sass 1946 p. 139, ill. p. 40; Rostrup 1940, ill. p. 191; Vad 1957, p. 12, ill. 25; Marianne Brøns et al., *Statens Museum for Kunst. Nyere dansk malerkunst. Katalog* (Copenhagen, 1970), inv. no. 1542; Bühlmann 1985, p. 141, ill.; Vad 1988, pp. 149f., 355, ill. p. 148; Billgren and Osipow 1995, pp. 15, 27, ill. p. 37

Exhibitions:
Paris 1928, no. 67; Oslo 1955, no. 20; Kunstforeningen 1955, no. 23; Ordrupgaard 1981, no. 59; New York 1983, no. 35

After painting Christiansborg Palace in 1890–92 (cat. no. 6), Hammershøi went on to make paintings of three more Danish castles and palaces: Frederiksborg (1893), Amalienborg (1896), and Kronborg (1897). This view of one of Amalienborg's four rococo palaces is from the second floor in the Christian X Palace, which housed the Ministry of Foreign Affairs at that time. Hammershøi's original intention is said to have been "as far as possible to reproduce the beautiful palace with the lovely appearance it originally had, before the pavilions were raised"—i.e., before C. F. Harsdorff raised Nicolai Eigtved's galleries one entire story when the royal family moved into Amalienborg after the first Christiansborg Palace fire in 1784. Hammershøi failed to carry out this idea, but he omitted the street lamps, which he felt would disturb the harmony of the square. In the middle of the square is French sculptor Jacques-François-Joseph Saly's equestrian statue of King Frederik V, which was erected there in 1771.

13 (repr. p. 68)
***Forest Interior*, also called *The Big Trees* [Halskov Vænge, Falster], [1896]**
Oil on canvas, 84.5 x 84 cm
Private collection

Provenance:
Sale, Winkel & Magnussen (Bramsen 1918)

Literature:
Bramsen 1900, no. 85; Bramsen 1918, no. 156; Vad 1988, p. 156f., ill. p. 157

Exhibitions:
Den frie Udstilling 1897, no. 43; Kunstforeningen 1900 (no number); Den frie Udstilling 1915, no. 74b; Kunstforeningen 1916 (vol. 1), no. 121

After working during the winter on *Landscape in Snow* (cat. no. 11), Hammershøi produced a summer variation, with trees in full foliage. He came across this spot in late summer in Halskov Vænge, in the southeastern part of the island of Falster, near where he and Ida had rented a small house. We get some idea of the special nature of the forest there from a letter written by Hammershøi's brother, Svend, also a painter, who had come on a visit: "After dinner, I went with Vilhelm to inspect the countryside, which is unique in many respects, including a small wood, the likes of which you will have difficulty in finding elsewhere; it is situated just opposite our house. There are the most beautiful oak trees imaginable, burial mounds with large boulders, standing almost side by side, and then there are huge dead tree trunks towering high in the air, and looking extremely ominous after nightfall; amidst all this there are small thickets of elder and small beech trees. . . . Vilhelm is painting in this same wood, not far from where I am sitting; today we were frightened off by a sudden outburst of thunder, and as the woods do not appear particularly inviting in any case, it made us want to run away" (quoted in Vad 1988, pp. 156–57). Poul Vad has emphasized the striking contrast "between Svend's Gothic clichés and the forest that we see in *The Big Trees*, where there are neither burial mounds nor dead trees." With its intangible light and its floating, immaterial quality, the woodland scene evokes a world singularly devoid of specific points of reference.

14 (repr. p. 74)
***Landscape*, or *Ryet* [Farum], [1896]**
Oil on canvas, 44.5 x 56.5 cm
Private collection

Provenance:
Aage Mantzius; E. Aug. Bloch (Bramsen 1918); posthumous sale of Bloch's effects, Charlottenborg, Feb. 17, 1920, no. 35; Martha Schibler; Bruun Rasmussen, sale 149, Nov. 29, 1962, no. 12

Literature:
Madsen 1899 (unpaginated), p. [12]; Bramsen 1918, no. 165

Exhibitions:
Kunstforeningen 1916 (vol. 1), no. 126; Ordrupgaard 1981, no. 61

In summer 1895, Hammershøi stayed at Lille Værløse, north of Copenhagen. It was apparently during that visit that he painted two landscapes from nearby Ryet, near Farum Lake (Bramsen 1918, nos. 141 and 146). At the same time, he probably also made the drawing (Vad 1988, ill. p. 159) that served as a preparatory study for this landscape, which he painted the following year.

15 (repr. p. 62)
Sketch Done in a Room of Ancient Greek Art in the British Museum
[London], [1897]
Oil on canvas, 61 x 46 cm
C. W. Obel A/S

Provenance:
Mrs. Oscar Hansen (Bramsen 1918); Winkel & Magnussen, sale 330, May 1, 1946, no. 95; Winkel & Magnussen, sale 331, June 7, 1946, no. 747; C. W. Obel A/S

Literature:
Bramsen 1900, no. 104; Bramsen 1918, no. 169

Exhibition:
Kunstforeningen 1916 (vol. 1), no. 123

In London, as he had in Paris, Hammershøi attempted to reproduce in oil the image of an antique sculpture, this time in one of the rooms of ancient Greek art in the British Museum. He started this painting on November 11, 1897, but soon gave up. He recalls the events as follows: "I stopped working on the picture I began in the British Museum, partly because I was not really particularly interested in it from the start—mostly, I just wanted to be doing something—and partly because it was so dark in that room that several days would often pass without my being able to paint at all, while the electric lights were lit in [the rest of] the museum all day long" (quoted from Vad 1988, p. 170). Here, unlike the Parisian picture (cat. no. 7), Hammershøi was not simply trying to paint a free copy of a single museum object but rather to create a scene of a museum interior by combining two unrelated works, as if in a photographic collage. The two works are: in the foreground, a section of one of the archaic reliefs on the Harpy Tomb from Xanthus in Lycia, and, in the background, a plaster cast of Paionios's *Nike* from Olympia (both ill. p. 151).

16 (repr. p. 71)
***Two Figures* (*The Artist and His Wife*), or *Double Portrait* [London], [1898]**
Inscription on stretcher: Malet i London 1898 V. Hammershøi (Painted in London 1898 V. Hammershøi)
Oil on canvas, 71.5 x 86 cm
Aarhus Kunstmuseum, Århus

Provenance:
Acquired by Alfred Bramsen, 1899; Gustav Falck; Karen Falck; Bruun Rasmussen, sale 267, Sept. 28, 1971, no. 1; purchased at that sale by the Ny Carlsbergfondet and presented to the Aarhus Kunstmuseum

Literature:
Madsen 1899 (unpaginated), pp. [6], [10], ill. p. [1]; Bramsen 1900, no. 103; Bramsen 1905, p. 180, ill.; Jastrau 1916, ill. p. 36; Bramsen 1918, pp. 51, 60, 65, 68, no. 182, ill.; Petersen 1916, p. 521; Vad 1957, p. 16, ill. 26, 48; Mikael Andersen, *Katalog over malerisamlingen. 1854–1983, Aarhus Kunstmuseum* (Århus, 1984), no. 627, ill.; Nykjær 1980, p. 76, ill. p. 77; Wivel 1982, p. 37, ill. p. 38; Vad 1988, pp. 170f., 290, ill. p. 175; Usselmann 1990, p. 195, ill. 4; Nykjær 1991, p. 145f., ill. p. 146; Wivel 1994, p. 106, ill.; Billgren and Osipow 1995, ill. p. 34; Wivel 1996, p. 40f., ill. p. 41

Exhibitions:
Kunstforeningen 1900 (no number); Berlin 1900, no. 477; Berlin 1905, no. 33; Den frie Udstilling 1908, no. 72; Munich 1909, no. 600; Rome 1911, no. 35; Malmö 1914, no. 2354; Kunstforeningen 1916 (vol. 1), no. 140; Stockholm 1919, no. 436; Paris 1928, no. 69; Oslo 1955, no. 23; Kunstforeningen 1955, no. 26; Ordrupgaard 1981, no. 66; New York 1983, no. 41; Nivaagaard 1995, no. 39

Hammershøi painted this picture during his first visit to London, which lasted from October 8, 1897 to May 28, 1898 (with a single break for the Christmas holidays, which he spent in Denmark from December 22 to January 8). He began it in January, immediately after his return, and did not finish it until the beginning of May. It shows the artist and his wife, Ida, sitting together at a table. However, this is no conventional double portrait, but rather a symbolic representation of their marriage itself. The title *Two Figures* is Hammershøi's own, and he described the picture as follows: "The one picture I am painting away at, and which I have worked on since we came back here after Christmas, is a kind of double portrait of Ida and myself, although my back is almost completely turned to the viewer; and, actually, they are not intended to be portraits in the strictest sense. I am fairly satisfied with it" (quoted in Vad 1988, p. 176).

17 (repr. p. 73)
An Old Courtyard in Christianshavn
or *Interior of Courtyard*
[Strandgade 30], [1899]
Inscribed bottom right:
V. Hammershøi
Oil on canvas, 66 x 47 cm
Private collection

Provenance:
Purchased by Kunstforeningen, 1899; Otto Bull (Bramsen 1918); Winkel & Magnussen, sale 136, May 18, 1933, no. 62

Literature:
Bramsen 1900, no. 110; Bramsen 1918, p. 60, no. 193; Vad 1988, ill. p. 193

Exhibitions:
Den frie Udstilling 1899, no. 50; Paris 1900, no. 29; Kunstforeningen 1916 (vol. 1), no. 146; Kunstforeningen 1930, no. 10; Nivaagaard 1993, no. 40

Hammershøi and his wife moved into the apartment on the second floor of no. 30 Strandgade in the Christianshavn district of Copenhagen in the middle of September 1899, and there they lived until the house changed ownership in 1909. The house, which was built in about 1636 and still stands, is called "Mikkel Vibes Gård" (Mikkel Vibe's town house) after the mayor of Copenhagen who owned the first deed to the site. It is built of brick in Dutch Renaissance style, but had undergone a series of major changes before Hammershøi's time: At the rear of the site two side wings had been built, and at the back of the original apartment an external gallery had been added—all with half-timbered construction—and the original apartment had been renovated twice during the 18th century, so that the building now exhibits both late Baroque and neoclassical features. The building was somewhat dilapidated in 1899, but both it and the apartment fascinated Hammershøi and provided him with numerous subjects for paintings. This one was painted from a courtyard window in the left wing looking toward the corner where the gallery meets the right wing, and where the street entrance and the steps leading up to the apartment are located. Hammershøi painted this motif several times (see cat. nos. 40 and 41).

18 (repr. p. 72)
***Interior*, or *The Corner of a Dining Room* [Strandgade 30], [1899]**
Inscr. bottom right: VH
Oil on canvas, 64 x 57 cm
Tate Gallery, London

Provenance:
Leonard Borwick (Bramsen 1918); presented to the Tate Gallery in 1926 in memory of Leonard Borwick by one of his friends

Literature:
Bramsen 1918, p. 97, no. 196; *National Art Collectors' Fund, 23rd Annual Report* (London, 1927), p. 40; Ronald Alley, *Tate Gallery Catalogues: The foreign paintings, drawings and sculpture* (London, 1959), p. 102; Vad 1988, pp. 267, 367, ill. p. 368

Exhibitions:
London 1904, no. 196; London, van Wisselingh 1907, no. 8; *Opening Exhibition of the Modern Foreign Gallery* (London: Tate Gallery, 1926) (no number)

Like cat. nos. 19, 38, 49, 57, 58, and 60, this picture was painted in the middle room of the main wing overlooking the street. Hammershøi gave it to his English friend, Leonard Borwick, a concert pianist, because it had played a crucial part in their friendship. During a visit to Odense in 1903 to give a recital, Borwick had seen it reproduced on a Christmas card and liked it so much that he visited Alfred Bramsen in his apartment in Copenhagen in order to see more works by the artist; that same afternoon he bought his first picture by Hammershøi, from the art dealer Valdemar Kleis. Borwick did much to promote the work of Hammershøi in Britain, and the artist and his wife visited him in

London several times (see the entries for cat. nos. 44, 46, and 70).

19 (repr. p. 75)
Open Doors
[Interior with woman in black on white chair, Strandgade 30], [1900]
Inscr. bottom right: VH
Oil on canvas, 57 x 49 cm
Private collection

Provenance:
Mrs. Simon, Berlin (Bramsen 1918); Winkel & Magnussen, sale 74, Feb. 4, 1930, no. 39; Knud Neye ; Bruun Rasmussen, sale 345, May 4, 1976, no. 26 ; sale, Christie's London, Mar. 29, 1990, no. 42

Literature:
Vilhelm Hammershøi (Copenhagen: Winkel & Magnussens Kunstforlag, undated [1905]), no. 4; Jastrau 1916, ill. p. 41; Bramsen 1918, no. 206, ill.; Varnedoe 1988, p. 110

Exhibitions:
Ordrupgaard 1981, no. 70; New York 1983, no. 44

The original apartment at Strandgade 30—the front wing overlooking the street—had been renovated between 1730 and 1750, during which the beautifully proportioned rooms were fitted with stuccoed ceilings and panels, and wooden doors and window frames, all distinguished by simple but striking moldings. Hammershøi painted the walls a very pale gray and the woodwork and moldings white, and this strict accentuation of the architecture of the rooms provided him with a wealth of motifs that he could explore at length in many variations. To paint this interior view, Hammershøi stood in the middle room of the front wing with his back to the light, looking through the dark entrance hall toward the sunlit gallery. It was a motif to which he returned again and again (see cat. nos. 18, 38, 49, 57, 58, and 60).

20 (repr. p. 79)
Sunbeams*, or *Sunlight*, also called *Dust Motes Dancing in the Sunbeams
[Strandgade 30], [1900]
Oil on canvas, 70 x 59 cm
Ordrupgaard, Copenhagen

Provenance:
Alfred Bramsen (Bramsen 1918); Jacob Olsen; E. De Foguel; Bruun Rasmussen, sale 210, Oct. 12, 1967, no. 81; Steen Kristensen; acquired by Ordrupgaard, 1989

Literature:
Vilhelm Hammershøi (Copenhagen: Winkel & Magnussens Kunstforlag, undated [1905]), no. 5; Bramsen 1905, p. 183, ill. p. 187; Wanscher 1915, p. 410, ill. p. 408; Jastrau 1916, ill. p. 42; Bramsen 1918, no. 207; Petersen 1916, p. 516f.; Sass 1946, p. 139; Vad 1957, p. 21f., ill. p. 27; Bühlmann 1985, p. 139; Vad 1988, p. 190, ill. p. 197; Varnedoe 1988, p. 100, ill. p. 101; Wivel 1993, p. 73, ill.; Wivel 1994, p. 107, ill. p. 106; Billgren and Osipow 1995, ill. p. 82; Wivel 1996, p. 35, ill. p. 33; Wad 1996, ill. p. 568

Exhibitions:
Berlin 1905, no. 42; London, Guildhall 1907, no. 127; Den frie Udstilling 1908, no. 75; Rome 1911, no. 34; New York 1912–13, no. 63; Malmö 1914, no. 2355; Kunstforeningen 1916 (vol. 1), no. 154; Paris 1928, no. 72; Kunstforeningen 1930, no. 12; Oslo 1955, no. 25; Kunstforeningen 1955, no. 29; Ordrupgaard 1981, no. 71; New York 1983, no. 44; Montreal 1995, no. 141; Kunstforeningen 1996 (no number)

The motif here is from the middle room of the left wing, where Hammershøi stood looking through the courtyard window toward the wing opposite. The closed door leads to the gallery. The motif is a recurrent one in Hammershøi's work and has acquired an almost emblematic character. He repeated it both with and without furniture, and with and without human figures (see cat. nos. 45 and 46), but never as concisely as here, where everything extraneous has been left out in order to focus attention on his depiction of sunlight falling into the room. On the several occasions when Hammershøi exhibited this painting, he called it *Sunbeams* or, alternatively, *Sunlight*; the more lyrical title *Dust Motes Dancing in the Sunbeams*, by which the picture is now known, probably comes from the poet Sophus Michaëlis or from Alfred Bramsen (see Bramsen 1918).

21 (repr. p. 76)
***Farm* [Refsnæs], [1900]**
Inscr. bottom right: VH
Oil on canvas, 53 x 62 cm
Davids Samling, on loan to the Statens Museum for Kunst, Copenhagen

Provenance:
Salomonsen (a factory owner); Klas Fåhræus, Stockholm (Bramsen 1918); acquired by C. L. David before 1930; transferred to the C. L. Davids Fond og Samling, 1945

Literature:
Bramsen 1918, no. 203; Varnedoe 1983, ill. p. 112; Varnedoe 1988, p. 99, ill.; Vad 1988, p. 256f., ill. p. 281; Billgren and Osipow 1995, ill. p. 38

Exhibitions:
Den frie udstilling 1901, no. 52b; Kunstforeningen 1930, no. 11; Ordrupgaard 1981, no. 69; London 1986, no. 31; New York 1982, no. 28; Nivaagaard 1993, no. 41; Davids Samling 1995, no. 33

During a summer holiday in 1900 on the peninsula of Refsnæs in the western part of Zealand, Hammershøi painted this crystalline picture of a farm, probably Kildevang near the village of Kongstrup, where he and Ida had rented lodgings. He also painted a landscape there (cat. no. 22). There is a "floating" quality to the buildings in *Farm*, giving the lifeless scene a dreamlike atmosphere. *Farm* is somewhat of a sequel to his series of works from the early 1880s featuring a whitewashed farm building (including cat. no. 1); and it is also closely related to his architectural pictures from the 1890s (such as cat. nos. 6 and 12).

22 (repr. p. 77)
***View of Refsnæs*, [1900]**
Oil on canvas, 63 x 78 cm
Thielska Galleriet, Stockholm

Provenance:
Alfred Bramsen; Winkel & Magnussen; Ernest Thiel (Bramsen 1918); acquired for the Swedish nation, 1924

Literature:
Bramsen 1918, no. 209; Ulf Linde, *Thielska Galleriet* (Stockholm, 1979), no. 118; Vad 1988, p. 260f., ill. p. 363; Billgren and Osipow 1995, ill. p. 64

Exhibitions:
Winkel & Magnussen, Copenhagen, no. 26; Stockholm 1957 (no catalogue); Stockholm 1976, no. 17

Hammershøi painted these spreading, desolate hills overlooking the sea during his summer holiday at Refsnæs in 1900 (see the entry for cat. no. 21). The landscape, pale and almost "X-rayed" by the light, is characteristic: depicted without details, without any trace of life (apart from the tiny windmill on the distant horizon), and without any road leading into the world of the picture.

23 (repr. p. 82)
***Portrait* [Daniel Jacobson Salter], [1901]**
Inscr. middle right: VH
Oil on canvas, 55.5 x 34 cm
Den Hirschsprungske Samling, Copenhagen

Provenance:
E. Aage Hirschsprung; his bequest to Den Hirschsprungske Samling, 1909

Literature:
Emil Hannover, *Fortegnelse over Den Hirschsprungske Samling* (Copenhagen, 1911), no. 151; Bramsen 1918, no. 211; Vad 1988, ill. p. 215

Exhibitions:
Kunstforeningen 1916 (vol. 2), no. 7; Ordrupgaard 1981, no. 73

E. Aage Hirschsprung, the son of Heinrich and Pauline Hirschsprung (founders of Den Hirschsprungske Samling), commissioned Hammershøi to paint this portrait of his cousin Daniel Jacobson Salter (Pauline's nephew). The subject who sat for the portrait must have interested Hammershøi more than usual, for he went much further than just creating a true portrait likeness, turning it into a psychological interpretation of Salter's physiognomy.

24 (repr. p. 80)
***Landscape*: *View of Fortunen*, [1901]**
Oil on canvas, 55 x 66.5 cm
Statens Museum for Kunst, Copenhagen

Provenance:
Alfred Bramsen; sale, Winkel & Magnussen, January 1904 (the Bramsen Collection), no. 27; Pietro Krohn; posthumous sale of Krohn's effects, Museum of Decorative Arts, Mar. 19, 1906, no. 23; F. Hendriksen (Bramsen 1918); Knud Hendriksen; Valborg Hendriksen; Bruun Rasmussen, sale 364, June 8, 1977, no. 460; purchased at that sale by the Statens Museum for Kunst

Literature:
Bramsen 1918, no. 214; Vad 1988, p. 258, ill. p. 255

Exhibitions:
Kunstforeningen 1916 (vol. 2), no. 8; Kunstforeningen 1930, no. 13; Ordrupgaard 1981, no. 74; New York 1983, no. 48; Nivaagaard 1993, no. 44

In September 1901 Hammershøi went for a late summer holiday north of Copenhagen, where he painted landscapes on the edge of the Deer Park in the area of Ermelunden and Fortunen. Among them is this picture of a stand of oak trees silhouetted against the light filtered through the twisting branches and sparse foliage of the trees.

25 (repr. p. 92)
***Interior* [with piano and woman in black, Strandgade 30], [1901]**
Inscr. bottom right: VH
Oil on canvas, 63 x 52 cm
Ordrupgaard, Copenhagen

Provenance:
Acquired by Wilhelm Hansen 1901; given by bequest of Henny and Wilhelm Hansen to the Danish nation, 1951

Literature:
Jastrau 1916, ill. p. 43; Bramsen 1918, no. 226; Madsen 1946, ill. 4; Leo Swane, *Katalog over kunstværkerne på Ordrupgaard* (Copenhagen, 1954), no. 127; Hofstadter 1982, ill. p. 73; Vad 1988, ill. p. 182; Billgren and Osipow 1995, ill. p. 88

Exhibitions:
Den frie Udstilling 1906, no. 83; London, Guildhall 1907, no. 36; Stockholm 1918, no. 99; Malmö 1975, no. 6; Ordrupgaard 1981, no. 82; New York 1982, no. 29

Hammershøi's apartment at Strandgade 30 was furnished in a manner as personal as it was unusual. He did not care for the cluttered style of the Victorian era; on the contrary, he gave the apartment an extremely spartan look, using relatively few pieces, all in fine taste: a piano, a couple of sofas, some chairs and tables, a bookcase, a few framed drawings, prints, and photographs, and a small number of handmade objects. The scene shown here—one of his most "furnished" —is the large room at the left of the front of the building (ill. p. 182), which Hammershøi referred to as the living room, and which he painted many times. The light coming in from the left is from the room's windows, which look out onto the street.

26 (repr. p. 83)
***Five Portraits*, [1901–02]**
Oil on canvas, 190 x 340 cm
Thielska Galleriet, Stockholm

Provenance:
Acquired by Ernest Thiel at Valand-Utställningen in Gothenburg, Sweden, 1905; acquired for the Swedish nation, 1924

Literature:
Bramsen 1905, p. 181; Wanscher 1915, p. 407f., ill. p. 400; Jastrau 1916, ill. p. 37; Bramsen 1918, pp. 48, 60, 65, no. 216; Petersen 1916, p. 519f.; Rostrup 1940, p. 186, ill. p. 177; Sass

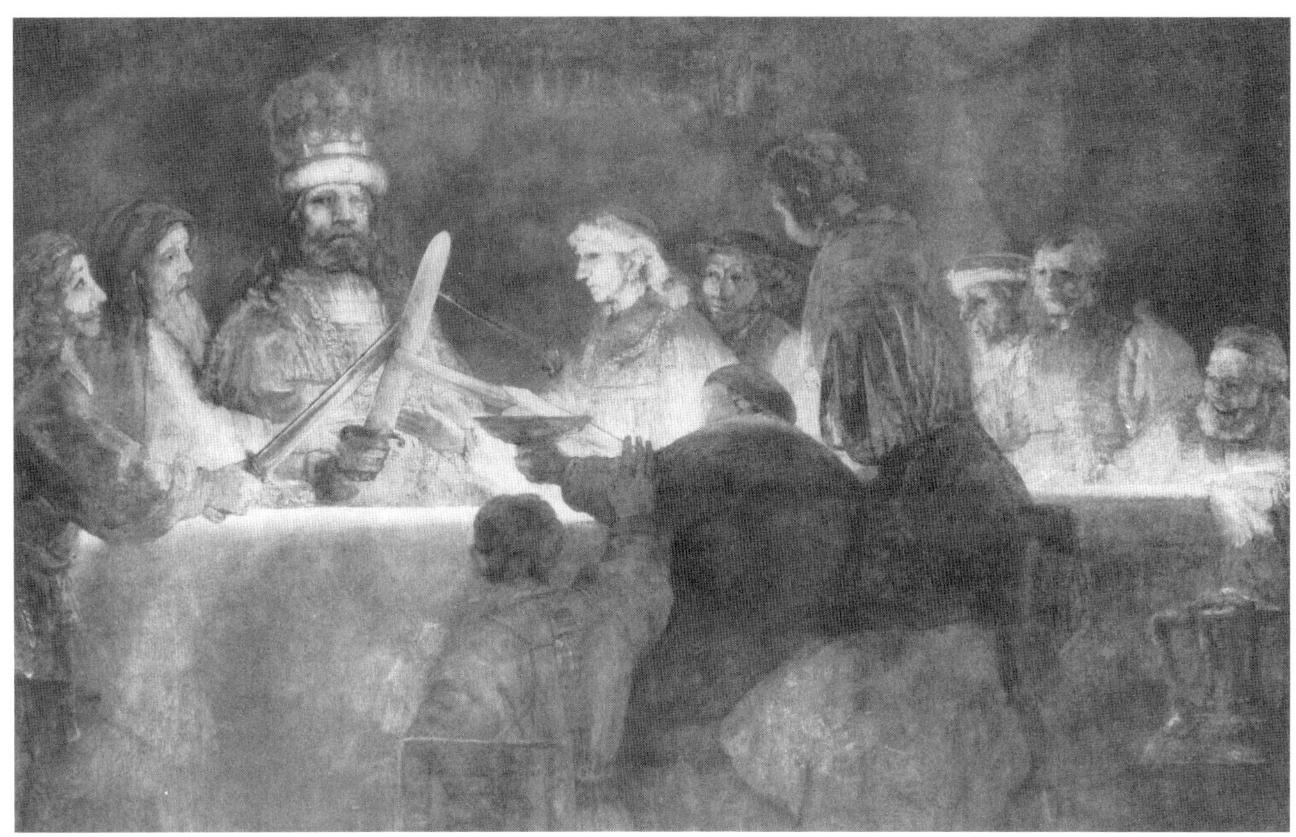

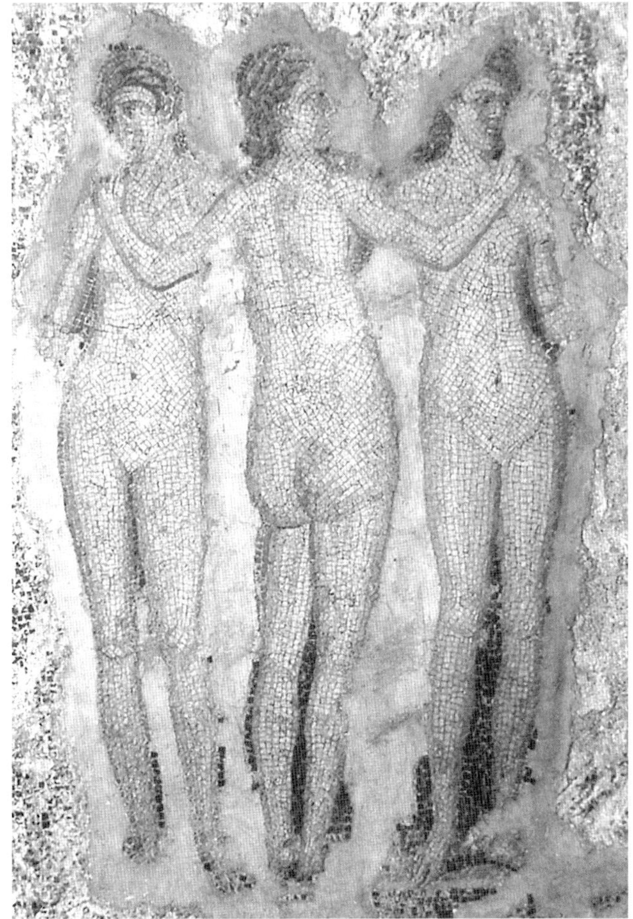

Rembrandt, *The Conspiracy of Julius Civilis,* 1661.
Oil on canvas, 196 x 309 cm.
Nationalmuseum, Stockholm

The Three Graces, Pompeii, fourth style, ca. A.D. 50.
Mosaic, 98 x 87 cm.
Museo Archeologico Nazionale, Naples

1946, p. 141f., ill. p. 137; Vad 1957, pp. 16f., 21, 23, ill. p. 29; Ulf Linde, *Thielska Galleriet*, Stockholm 1979, no. 117, ill.; Varnedoe 1983, p. 116; Varnedoe 1988, p. 102f., ill.; Vad 1988, pp. 213, 218f., ill. p. 216f.; Wivel 1994, p. 102, ill.; Billgren and Osipow 1995, pp. 41, 91, ill. p. 60f; Wivel 1996, p. 46f., ill. p. 48f.

Exhibitions:
Den frie Udstilling 1902, no. 50; Venice 1903 (no real catalogue); Berlin 1904, no. 78; Gothenburg 1905, no. 443; Stockholm 1976, no. 18. Ordrupgaard 1981, no. 81. New York 1982, no. 30; London 1986, no. 32

This picture is the largest of Hammershøi's entire oeuvre. Its setting is the living room at Strandgade 30 (see cat. no. 25), and the five men portrayed are (from left to right): architect and designer Thorvald Bindesbøll (1846–1908), painter and ceramic artist Svend Hammershøi (1873–1948), painter and art historian Karl Madsen (1855–1938), painter Jens Ferdinand Willumsen (1863–1958) and painter Carl Holsøe (1863–1935). Svend Hammershøi was the artist's younger brother, and the other four were friends and colleagues. The picture thus falls into the category of "friendship paintings," but its large scale imbues it with Symbolist overtones. Wanscher noted its kinship to Renaissance paintings of the Last Supper, and Vad identified a specific source of Hammershøi's inspiration in a more modern version of the subject by C. W. Eckersberg (1783–1853) in Frederiksberg Church in Copenhagen, a painting with which Hammershøi was familiar. Moreover, because of its size and Hammershøi's close cropping of the scene, *Five Portraits* bears a striking similarity to the only remaining fragment (the main section) of Rembrandt's huge painting *The Conspiracy of Julius Civilis*, 1661 (Nationalmuseum, Stockholm; ill. p. 159). Karl Madsen was the first art historian to identify the fragment as part of Rembrandt's painting, the rest of which Rembrandt himself had destroyed. There are three compositional sketches for Hammershøi's painting, and six portrait studies of the individual figures (Statens Museum for Kunst, Copenhagen; Koldinghus, Kolding; and private collections). The picture deservedly attracted attention when it was first exhibited in 1902, but to Hammershøi's great disappointment it was not bought for the Kongelige Malerisamling (Royal Collection of Paintings, which is now the Statens Museum for Kunst), and in 1905 he sold it to Ernest Thiel, a great Swedish collector.

27 (repr. p. 86)
***The Asiatic Company Buildings*, [1902]**
Oil on canvas, 146.5 x 140.5 cm
Statens Museum for Kunst, Copenhagen

Provenance:
Sale of Effects 1916, no. 24; Alfred Bramsen (Bramsen 1918); sale, Charlottenborg, June 6, 1944, no. 68; Th. Hagedorn-Olsen; acquired by the Statens Museum for Kunst, 1970

Literature:
Bramsen 1918, pp. 50, 74, no. 237; Vad 1988, p. 241f., ill. p. 243; Billgren and Osipow 1995, pp. 51f., 68, 112, ill. p. 57

Exhibitions:
Kunstforeningen 1930, no. 48; London 1986, no. 33

From his windows in the apartment at Strandgade 30, Hammershøi had a view of the Asiatic Company buildings. The architect, Philip de Lange, had originally built a mansion in late Baroque style for the offices of the company; and in 1780 a warehouse annex was built next to it, duplicating the original mansion for the sake of symmetry. The two buildings were linked by a wall with a great gateway in it providing access to the dock. This beautiful complex came to play a special role in Hammershøi's life, for not only did it become his principal view and frequent subject, but he also ended up living there (at Strandgade 25) during the last years of his life. After having executed a small study of the buildings in 1899 (now in a private collection), Hammershøi took up the subject again in 1902 in two major paintings. In this, the first of them, painted on an almost square canvas, the vanishing point is a little to the left of the gateway, and Hammershøi omitted the gable of the building on the left (which is visible in the photograph that he had taken as a study; a similar photograph is on p. 26 of this catalogue). Thus, paradoxically, a small asymmetry has been built into the picture's symmetry, and this almost imperceptible disharmony has been interpreted by Poul Vad as the source of the vague sense of unease and dissonance caused by the work. The painting was never finished, and the explanation is presumably in a comparison with the following painting (cat. no. 28).

28 (repr. p. 87)
View of the Old Asiatic Company,
or *The Asiatic Company Buildings,*
[1902]
Oil on canvas, 158 x 166 cm
Private collection

Provenance:
Alfred Bramsen (Bramsen 1918)

Literature:
Bramsen 1905, p. 184, ill.; Jastrau 1916, ill. p. 47; Bramsen 1918, pp. 50, 60, 63, 74f., no. 236, ill.; Sass 1946, p. 139; Varnedoe 1983, ill. p. 116; Vad 1988, p. 241f., ill. p. 240; Varnedoe 1988, p. 106, ill.; Billgren and Osipow 1995, pp. 13, 27f., ill. p. 40

Exhibitions:
Den frie Udstilling 1903, no. 219; London, Guildhall 1907, no. 130; Kunstforeningen 1916 (vol. 2), no. 24; Kunstforeningen 1930, no. 48; Ordrupgaard 1981, no. 84

In the preceding painting of the Asiatic Company buildings (cat. no. 27), the masts of two ships docked there can just barely be made out, lightly sketched in under the paint. But Hammershøi changed his mind about the composition he wanted, and decided instead to put a single mast at the right of the central space. Meanwhile, the need to balance the assymetry created by the single, off-center mast meant that the work had to be redone. As has been demonstrated by Poul Vad, the vanishing point had to be shifted slightly to the right, and so Hammershøi started on a new, slightly larger canvas. At the same time, he decided to include in the revised composition the corners of the two buildings at the intersection of Strandgade and Sankt Annægade. As in several other of his pictures, the absence of street surfacing and sidewalk contributes to its somewhat "unreal" quality.

29 (repr. p. 89)
View of Old Christiansborg Palace,
[1902]
Oil on canvas, 117 x 139 cm
Private collection

Provenance:
Victor A. Goldschmidt, Horsens (Bramsen 1918); sale, Charlottenborg, Feb. 7, 1934, no. 21; P. Carl Petersen; Winkel & Magnussen, sale 321, May 25, 1945, no. 178; Christie's London, Mar. 24, 1988, no. 60

Literature:
Bramsen 1918, no. 239; Vad 1957, p. 20, ill. 32; Bühlmann 1985, p. 142, ill.; Vad 1988, pp. 246, 436, ill. p. 245

Exhibitions:
Kunstforeningen 1916 (vol. 2), no. 25; Oslo 1955, no. 29; Kunstforeningen 1955, no. 33; Ordrupgaard 1981, no. 85

This is the second in a series of three paintings that Hammershøi did of this particular view of Christiansborg Palace (the other two are cat. no. 6, and Bramsen 1918, no. 323). The view is from Frederiksholms Kanal 4, where the Art Society was housed at that time. In 1902, one of the most productive years in Hammershøi's career, he painted such works as *Five Portraits* (cat. no. 26) and, for the offices of the administrator of social services in the new Copenhagen City Hall, two large architectural paintings, of Ladegården (the Copenhagen workhouse) and Almindeligt Hospital (the General Hospital). In these, he had successfully attempted a larger format than in any of his earlier architectural pictures, thus encouraging him to try even larger-scale works when that same year he tackled other architectural motifs, including this painting of Christiansborg Palace. For this project, he once again had to work against the light, as he had done when painting landscapes in 1900 and 1901 (cat. nos. 22 and 24). Poul Vad concluded that it took

Hammershøi the entire summer to complete, for he painted no landscapes in 1902.

30 (repr. p. 91)
Interior of the Church of San Stefano Rotundo in Rome*, or *Church Interior
[1902–03]
Oil on canvas, 67.5 x 72.8 cm
Fyns Kunstmuseum, Odense

Provenance:
Alfred Bramsen (Bramsen 1918); Gustav Falck; Hans Tobiesen; Winkel & Magnussen, sale 388, Sept. 23, 1954, no. 16; purchased at that sale by the Ny Carlsbergfondet and presented to the Fyns Kunstmuseum

Literature:
Bramsen 1903, p. 184; Jastrau 1916, ill. p. 46; Bramsen 1918, pp. 51, 55, 60f., 65, 68, no. 232, ill.; Rostrup 1940, p. 188; Madsen 1946, ill. 15; *Fortegnelse over malerier og skulpturer; Fyns Stifts Kunstmuseum* (Odense, 1977), no. 509; Vad 1988, p. 250f., ill. p. 253; Billgren and Osipow 1995, ill. p. 58; Wivel 1996, p. 35, ill. p. 34

Exhibitions:
Den frie Udstilling 1903, no. 48; Berlin 1905, no. 44; London, Guildhall 1907, no. 133;. Rome 1911, no. 43; Malmö 1914, no. 2356; Kunstforeningen 1916 (vol. 2), no. 22; Stockholm 1919, no. 444; Stockholm 1930, no. 18; Kunstforeningen 1930, no. 18; Kunstforeningen 1955, no. 32; Malmö 1975, no. 8; Stockholm 1976, no. 20; Ordrupgaard 1981, no. 86; New York 1983, no. 56

On October 7, 1902, Vilhelm and Ida went to Rome. The artist spent a long time looking for a suitable subject to paint, and finally chose the interior of an ancient church that was not a popular tourist attraction: Santo Stefano Rotundo, on Monte Celio not far from SS. Giovanni e Paolo. In Hammershøi's day it was believed that the church—actually from the fifth century—was a building dating from antiquity. The circular building's interior, adorned with twenty-two granite columns, was decorated in the sixteenth century with frescoes, which Stendhal described as "awful paintings" (quoted in Vad 1988, p. 250)—but in Hammershøi's picture they are just barely visible. Johannes Jørgensen, a Danish writer then living in Rome, had obtained permission for Hammershøi to work in the church. Hammershøi roughed out the composition in a pencil sketch, and painted it from December 2, 1902 to January 29, 1903, broken only by a "weeklong holiday." He intended to paint a bigger version after returning to Denmark, but nothing ever came of it.

31 (repr. p. 106)
***View of Gentofte Lake*, also called *Sunshower*, [1903]**
Oil on canvas, 83 x 78 cm
Private collection

Provenance:
Alfred Bramsen (Bramsen 1918); Theodor Jensen; Bruun Rasmussen, sale 154, May 28, 1963, no. 6

Literature:
Bramsen 1903, ill. p. 189; *Vilhelm Hammershøi* (Copenhagen: Winkel & Magnussens Kunstforlag, undated [1905]), no. 6; Jastrau 1916, ill. p. 10; Bramsen 1918, pp. 44, 60, 66, no. 241, ill.; Madsen 1946, ill. 18; Sass 1946, p. 139f., ill. p. 144; Vad 1988, p. 259f., ill. p. 257; Wivel 1996, ill. p. 37

Exhibitions:
Berlin 1905, no. 45; Den frie Udstilling 1908, no. 76; Kunstforeningen 1916 (vol. 2), no. 29; Stockholm 1919, no. 445; Kunstforeningen 1930, no. 15; Kunstforeningen 1955, no. 34; Ordrupgaard 1981, no. 90

In 1903 Hammershøi appears to have spent his summer holiday in Gentofte, just north of Copenhagen. While there, he painted this large, cool landscape of Gentofte Lake in front of a row of trees along the Kongevejen (the "king's road"), which he had already painted in 1892 (cat. no. 8). He worked out the composition in a drawing and four painted preparatory studies, but in the finished picture he changed the oblong format of the studies into an upright and added a cloudscape of impressive dimensions.

32 (repr. p. 93)
Interior
[with young woman seen from behind, Strandgade 30], [ca. 1903–04]
Inscr. bottom left: VH
Oil on canvas, 61 x 50.5 cm
Randers Kunstmuseum, Randers

Provenance:
The Heyman family; Sven Risom; acquired by the Ny Carlsbergfondet and presented to the Randers Kunstmuseum, 1948

Literature:
Villads Villadsen, *Randers Kunstmuseum* (Randers, 1952), p. 31, ill. p. 32; Wivel 1982, ill. p. 34; Signe Jacobsen in *Randers Kunstmuseum, 100 år. 1887–1987* (Randers, 1987), p. 32, ill. p. 33; Vad 1988, pp. 203, 205f., ill. frontispiece; Wivel 1994, p. 103, ill.; Wivel 1996, p. 43, ill. p. 44

Exhibitions:
Ordrupgaard 1981, no. 93

The subject here is a portion of the living room (see the entry for cat. no. 25). A woman (the artist's wife) is standing with her face turned away and is holding a pewter dish in her hands. There is a framed print on the wall, and right below it on the piano (shown closed here) there is a large punch bowl of Copenhagen porcelain, which Hammershøi often used as a striking feature in his pictures of the apartment at Strandgade 30 (including cat. nos. 33 and 49).

33 (repr. p. 95)
Interior with Punch Bowl
[Strandgade 30], [1904]
Oil on canvas, 78.5 x 57.5 cm
H.M. Queen Ingrid of Denmark

Provenance:
Alfred Bramsen; Conrad M. Pineus (Bramsen 1918); King Gustav IV Adolf of Sweden; H.M. Queen Ingrid of Denmark

Literature:
Bramsen 1905, ill. p. 185; Bramsen 1918, no. 267; C. Nordenfalk, *Katalog over Conrad M. Pineus Konstsamling* (Gothenburg, 1940), no. 223

Exhibitions:
Berlin 1905, no. 46; London, Guildhall 1907, no. 13; Den frie Udstilling 1908, no. 329; Malmö 1914, no. 2352; Stockholm 1957 (no catalogue); Ordrupgaard 1981, no. 102

Here is another, larger view of the section of the living room that Hammershøi painted in cat. no. 32, with the punch bowl on top of the closed piano, and showing more of the furniture. The same punch bowl also appears in an interior scene from 1907 (cat. no. 49), where it is set on top of a table in an adjoining room.

34 (repr. p. 113)
The Cabinet Sofa
[Strandgade 30], [1904]
Inscr. bottom right: VH
Oil on canvas, 69 x 53 cm
Private collection

Provenance:
A. W. Simmelhag (Bramsen 1918); Bruun Rasmussen, sale 76, Oct. 3, 1956, no. 76

Literature:
Vilhelm Hammershøi (Copenhagen: Winkel & Magnussens Kunstforlag, undated [1908]), no. 10; Ritter 1910, ill. p. 166; Jastrau 1916, ill. p. 50; Bramsen 1918, no. 266, ill.; Madsen 1946, ill. 16; Vad 1988, ill. p. 189

Exhibition:
Ordrupgaard 1981, no. 101

This view of the living room of Strandgade 30 (see the entry for cat. no. 25) is the first in a series of paintings that Hammershøi did with the cabinet sofa as the dominant motif (see also cat. nos. 37 and 48). On the wall above the sofa is an unframed canvas (a landscape sketch?), and on the table in front of it is a ceramic vase that could be the work of Thorvald Bindesbøll (see the entry for cat. no. 26).

35 (repr. p. 97)
Young Beech Forest
[Arresødal, Frederiksværk], [1904]
Oil on canvas, 47 x 73 cm
Davids Samling, on loan to Den Hirschsprungske Samling, Copenhagen

Provenance:
Alfred Bramsen (Bramsen 1918); Winkel & Magnussen, sale 173, May 14, 1938, no. 101; acquired by C. L. David; transferred to the C. L. Davids Fond og Samling, 1945

Literature:
Bramsen 1918, no. 262; Erik Zahle, in *C. L. Davids Samling, Nogle Studier I* (Copenhagen, 1948), p. 207; Borneville 1960, ill. p. 199; Vad 1988, p. 256, ill. p. 354

Exhibitions:
Berlin 1905, no. 48; London, van Wisselingh, 1907, no. 13; Den frie Udstilling 1908, no. 330; Kunstforeningen 1916 (vol. 2), no. 44; Kunstforeningen 1930, no. 21; Stockholm 1976, no. 22; Ordrupgaard 1981, no. 99; Davids Samling 1995, p. 98, ill. p. 99

During a visit to Arresødal near Frederiksværk in the summer of 1904, one of the pictures Hammershøi painted was this scene of a young beech forest. Although the subject is in the tradition of Denmark's Golden Age of painting (i.e., the first half of the nineteenth century), the strange, dreamlike atmosphere of Hammershøi's treatment removes any hint of national romanticism.

36 (repr. p. 98)
***Soirée in the Living Room*, [1904]**
Oil on canvas, 101 x 123.5 cm
Statens Museum for Kunst, Copenhagen

Provenance:
Alfred Bramsen (Bramsen 1918); Gustav Falck; Th. Hagedorn-Olsen; acquired by the Statens Museum for Kunst, 1970

Literature:
Jastrau 1916, ill. p. 52; Bramsen 1918, pp. 48, 60, 72, no. 250, ill.; Sass 1946, p. 142; Vad 1957, pp. 18f., 21, ill. 35; Vad 1988, p. 234, ill. p. 233

Exhibitions:
Malmö 1914, no. 2366; Kunstforeningen 1916 (vol. 2), no. 37; Stockholm 1919, no. 448; Stockholm 1930, no. 21; Ordrupgaard 1981, no. 96; New York 1983, no. 62

This picture must be considered in connection with Hammershøi's *Five Portraits* (cat. no. 26), to which it is related thematically. It, too, was painted in the living room of Strandgade 30 (see the entry for cat. no. 25) and portrays a group of people around a table in candlelight. The four figures include two from the earlier picture: Thorvald Bindesbøll and Svend Hammershøi, both shown sitting sideways. The other two, behind the table and with their backs to the windows, are writer Henry Madsen (Karl Madsen's son), and Hammershøi's wife, Ida. Hammershøi left the picture unfinished, due—according to Bramsen—to his great disappointment that *Five Portraits*, into which he had put his entire soul, was not bought for the Kongelige Malerisamling (Royal Collection of Paintings, which is now the Statens Museum for Kunst). Hammershøi made a compositional sketch for *Soirée in the Living Room* in a slightly different format (Ordrupgaard) and a series of preparatory studies for the individual figures (Statens Museum for Kunst; Koldinghus, Kolding; and private collections).

37 (repr. p. 114)
***Interior*, also called *The Old Cabinet Sofa* [Strandgade 30], [1905]**
Oil on canvas, 49.5 x 40 cm
Staatliche Museen zu Berlin, Preußischer Kulturbesitz, Nationalgalerie

Provenance:
Acquired by Alfred Beit and presented to the Nationalgalerie, 1906

Literature:
Karl Scheffler, *Die Nationalgalerie zu Berlin* (Berlin, 1912), p. 223; Bramsen 1918, no. 273; Vad 1988, ill. p. 189; Vad 1996, ill. p. 369

Exhibition:
Berlin 1905, no. 52

Here, Hammershøi has painted the same part of the living room as in cat. no. 34, but from a different angle and with some of the décor changed, so that the cabinet sofa emerges more clearly as a motif. He repeated this composition with slight modifications two years later (cat. no. 48).

38 (repr. p. 101)
White Doors* or *Open Doors
[Strandgade 30], [1905]
Oil on canvas, 52 x 60 cm
Davids Samling, on loan to Den Hirschsprungske Samling, Copenhagen

Provenance:
Alfred Bramsen (Bramsen 1918); Gustav Falck; Hans Tobiesen; Winkel & Magnussen, sale 382, Oct. 5, 1953, no. 610; purchased at that sale for Davids Samling

Literature:
Vilhelm Hammershøi (Copenhagen: Winkel & Magnussens Kunstforlag, undated [1905]), no. 4; Jastrau 1916, ill. p. 38; Bramsen 1918, pp. 57, 60f., 66, no. 275, ill.; Erik Zahle, in *C. L. Davids Samling, Nogle Studier III* (Copenhagen, 1948), p. 127, ill.; Vad 1957, pp. 21, 23, ill. p. 34; Wivel 1982, p. 35, ill.; Varnedoe 1983, ill. p. 107; Vad 1988, pp. 199, 364, ill. p. 277; Wivel 1994, p. 100, ill.; Billgren and Osipow 1995, ill. p. 85; Wivel 1996, p. 45, ill. p. 38

Exhibitions:
Berlin 1905, no. 57; London, Guildhall 1907, no. 128; Den frie Udstilling 1908, no. 80; Rome 1911, no. 33; New York 1912–13, no. 65; Malmö 1914, no. 2365; Kunstforeningen 1916, no. 55; Oslo 1955, no. 32; Kunstforeningen 1955, no. 37; Malmö 1975, no. 11; Stockholm 1976, no. 26; Kunstforeningen 1976, no. 72; Ordrupgaard 1981, no. 106; New York 1982, no. 31; Davids Samling 1995, p. 109, ill. p. 101; Kunstforeningen 1996 (no number)

Hammershøi painted this picture in the same middle room at the front of Strandgade 30 as cat. nos. 18 and 19, but here he omitted anything that would distract attention from the white doors, with their distinct moldings and shiny brass handles. The view through a succession of open doors is one of Hammershøi's most original motifs, and he painted it again several times later in his career, as in cat. no. 72, one of his last pictures. When he first exhibited this picture, in Berlin in 1905, he called it *White Doors*, a title he retained when showing it in Den frie Udstilling (The Independent Exhibition) three years later.

39 (repr. p. 103)
Young Lady*, also called *Resting
[Strandgade 30], [1905]
Oil on canvas, 49.5 x 46.5 cm
Musée d'Orsay, Paris

Provenance:
Alfred Bramsen (Bramsen 1918); The Heyman family; Eva Kiær; acquired by the Musée d'Orsay, 1996

Literature:
Vilhelm Hammershøi (Copenhagen: Winkel & Magnussens Kunstforlag, undated [1905]), no. 9; Jastrau 1916, ill. p. 44; Bramsen 1918, pp. 60f., 63, 66, 68, no. 274, ill.; Vad 1988, p. 209f., ill. p. 208

Exhibitions:
Berlin 1905, no. 53; London, Guildhall 1907, no. 131; Den frie Udstilling 1908, no. 79; Rome 1911, no. 32; Malmö 1914, no. 2361; Kunstforeningen 1916 (vol. 2), no. 53; Kunstforeningen 1930, no. 24; Stockholm 1930, no. 26; Ordrupgaard 1981, no. 105

This picture should be regarded as a kind of "portrait" of the artist's wife, Ida, and also as one of Hammershøi's most important depictions of one of his favorite motifs, a figure seen from behind. The room that serves as the setting here has not been identified.

40 (repr. p. 105)
Interior of Courtyard
[Strandgade 30], [1905]
Oil on canvas, 74 x 60 cm
Private collection

Provenance:
Arnbaks Kunsthandel, Copenhagen; Thorsten Laurin, Stockholm (Bramsen 1918); Bruun Rasmusssen, sale 273, Feb. 8, 1972, no. 46

Literature:
Bramsen 1918, no. 268, ill. (N.B.: the illustration erroneously shows the following version, cat. no. 41)

Exhibitions:
Berlin 1905, no. 50 (this or the following version); London, Guildhall 1907, no. 124; Kunstforeningen 1916 (vol. 2), no. 51; Stockholm 1919, no. 450; Stockholm 1957 (no catalogue); Ordrupgaard 1981, no. 104

This and the following picture were painted from the window of the middle room in the left wing of Strandgade 30. The motif is closely related to cat. no. 17, except that here there is a figure in the open window in the corner, the angle of the view is different, and there is more sunlight on the gallery.

41 (repr. p. 104)
Interior of Courtyard
[Strandgade 30], [1905]
Oil on canvas, 75 x 63 cm
Ambassador John L. Loeb, Jr., New York, on loan to the Busch-Reisinger Museum, Harvard University Art Museums, Cambridge, Mass.

Provenance:
William Bendix (Bramsen 1918); Winkel & Magnussen, sale 224, Nov. 11, 1937, no. 25; G. Espersen; John L. Loeb, Jr.

Literature:
Vilhelm Hammershøi (Copenhagen: Winkel & Magnussens Kunstforlag, undated [1905]), no. 8; Jastrau 1916, ill. p. 49; Bramsen 1918, no. 269, ill. (erroneously listed as no. 268); Rostrup 1940, ill. p. 192 (as belonging to Thorsten Laurin; see cat. no. 40); Vad 1988, ill. p. 373

Exhibitions:
Den frie Udstilling 1906, no. 82; Cambridge 1994, no. 9

The picture was painted from the same angle as cat. no. 40, but the model appears to be different and the lighting conditions have also been slightly changed.

42 (repr. p. 107)
***Landscape: View of Lejre*, [1905]**
Oil on canvas, 41 x 68 cm
Nationalmuseum, Stockholm

Provenance:
Carl Robert Lamm, Stockholm (Bramsen 1918); sale, Bukowski, Stockholm, Sept. 28, 1920, no. 79; purchased at that sale by the Nationalmuseum

Literature:
Bramsen 1918, p. 44, no. 278; Wivel 1982, ill. p. 39; Görel Cavalli Björkmaan, *Nationalmuseum, Stockholm. Illustrerad katalog över äldre måleri från Danmark, Finland och Norge* (Stockholm, 1996), p. 11; Vad 1988, p. 261, ill.; Wivel 1996, p. 33., ill. p. 30

Exhibitions:
Kunstforeningen 1916 (vol. 2), no. 50; Stockholm 1957 (no catalogue); Stockholm 1976, no. 27; Ordrupgaard 1981, no. 108; New York 1982, no. 32; London 1986, no. 35

During a visit to Lejre in central Zealand in the summer of 1905, Hammershøi painted a series of pictures of a splendid, gently rolling landscape under blue skies and white clouds. In this picture, the clouds hang like strings of beads in parallel rows that curve almost imperceptibly toward the hills below.

43 (repr. p. 109)
***Montague Street in London*, or**
***Side View of the British Museum: Corner of Montague Street*, [1905–06]**
Inscr. bottom right: VH
Oil on canvas, 56 x 64 cm
Ny Carlsberg Glyptotek, Copenhagen

Provenance:
Alfred Bramsen (Bramsen 1918); Gustav Falck; acquired by the Ny Carlsbergfondet for the Ny Carlsberg Glyptotek, 1939

Literature:
Jastrau 1916, ill. p. 56; Bramsen 1918, pp. 52, 60, 63, 68, no. 289, ill.; Rostrup, *Danske malerier og tegninger* (Copenhagen: Ny Carlsberg Glyptotek, 1977), no. 787; Vad 1988, p. 320f., ill. p. 269; Billgren and Osipow 1995, ill. p. 98

Exhibitions:
London, van Wisselingh 1907, no. 12; Den frie Udstilling 1908, no. 333; Rome 1911, no. 38; New York 1912–13, no. 66; Malmö 1914, no. 2369; Kunstforeningen 1916 (vol. 2), no. 60; Stockholm 1919, no. 451; Kunstforeningen 1930, no. 29; Ordrupgaard 1981, no. 110

In 1905–06, Vilhelm and Ida visited London for the third time (see the entry for cat. no. 15). They arrived about November 10 and found accommodations at 67 Great Russell Street. From here, Hammershøi painted two street scenes looking toward the British Museum: this painting and cat. no. 44. The visit lasted until the beginning or middle of January 1906.

44 (repr. p. 108)
View of the British Museum
[London], [1905–06]
Inscr. on reverse: LB from VH in memory of happy times in London 1906
Oil on canvas, 50.5 x 45 cm
Storstrøms Kunstmuseum, Maribo

Provenance:
Leonard Borwick, London (Bramsen 1918); Bruun Rasmussen, sale 46, Nov. 5, 1953, no. 51; Bruun Rasmussen, sale 272, Dec. 7, 1971, no. 89; purchased at that sale by the Ny Carlsbergfondet and presented to the Storstrøms Kunstmuseum

Literature:
Bramsen 1918, pp. 52, 60, 63, 66, no. 290; *Lolland-Falsters Stiftsmuseums Årsskrift* (Maribo, 1972), p. 17, ill.; Henrik Hertig, *Fortegnelse over malerier og skulpturer* (Maribo: LollandFalsters Kunstmuseum, 1975), no. 83; Vad 1988, pp. 266, 320f., ill. p. 267; Wivel 1996, p. 52, ill.

Exhibitions:
London, van Wisselingh 1907, no. 7; New York 1912–13, no. 66

This picture was painted from the same place as cat. no. 43, but looking to the right rather than the left. Hammershøi gave it to his friend Leonard Borwick (see the entries for cat. nos. 18 and 46).

45 (repr. p. 111)
Study in Sunlight
[Strandgade 30], [1906]
Oil on canvas, 55 x 47 cm
Davids Samling, on loan to Den Hirschsprungske Samling, Copenhagen

Provenance:
Alfred Bramsen (Bramsen 1918); Winkel & Magnussen, sale 176, May 24, 1935, no. 46; purchased at that sale by C. L. David; transferred to the C. L. Davids Fond og Samling, 1945

Literature:
Bramsen 1918, pp. 60, 63, no. 283; Erik Zahle, in *C. L. Davids Samling, Nogle Studier I* (Copenhagen, 1948), p. 207; Billgren and Osipow 1995, ill. p. 100

Exhibitions:
London, van Wisselingh 1907, no. 4; Den frie Udstilling 1908, no. 332; Kunstforeningen 1916 (vol. 2), no. 62; Stockholm 1919, no. 453; Kunstforeningen 1930, no. 27; Malmö 1975, no. 12; Stockholm 1976, no. 30; Ordrupgaard 1981, no. 112; New York 1982, no. 33; Davids Samling 1995, p. 106, ill. p. 107

This picture and cat. no. 46 are later variations on the motif in cat. no. 20.

46 (repr. p. 110)
Interior*, also called *The Quiet Room
[Strandgade 30], [1906]
Inscr. bottom right: VH
Oil on canvas, 51.5 x 55 cm
Tate Gallery, London

Provenance:
Leonard Borwick, London (Bramsen 1918); Mrs. Ethel Hales, Whittle, 1924 ; acquired from her for the Tate Gallery, 1930

Literature:
Bramsen 1918, p. 105, no. 284; *The Studio* 16, no. 198, London (Sept. 15, 1909), ill. p. 256; Vad 1988, p. 265

Exhibition:
Opening Exhibition of the Modern Foreign Gallery (London: Tate Gallery, 1926) (no number)

Hammershøi gave this picture to Leonard Borwick, as he had cat. nos. 18 and 44. It is one of several versions he painted of the middle room in the left wing of Strandgade 30, including cat. nos. 20 and 45. This one was originally somewhat larger in width, and included a woman dressed in black on the left, standing behind the table covered by the white tablecloth. Borwick felt that this figurative aspect of the picture was not of the same artistic quality as the rest, and he therefore folded the canvas and thus gave the picture its present shape and dimensions. This must have happened fairly soon after he acquired it, as a reproduction of the picture in its present form appeared in the periodical *The Studio* in 1909.

47 (repr. p. 112)
***Avenue of Rowan Trees near Snekkersten*, [1906]**
Oil on canvas, 42 x 54 cm
Davids Samling, on loan to Marienlyst Palace, Elsinore

Provenance:
Alfred Bramsen; Wilhelm Tegner (Bramsen 1918); acquired by C. L. David, 1923; transferred to the C. L. Davids Fond og Samling, 1945

Literature:
Bramsen, no. 287; Vad 1988, p. 327, ill. p. 331; Vad 1995, p. 104, ill. p. 105

Exhibitions:
Den frie Udstilling 1908, no. 83; Winkel & Magnussen 1913, no. 3; Kunstforeningen 1916 (vol. 2), no. 63; Stockholm 1976, no. 29; Ordrupgaard 1981, no. 113; Davids Samling 1995, no. 137

Hammershøi found this avenue of rowan trees next to rolling cornfields during a summer visit to Snekkersten near Elsinore in northern Zealand in 1906. The tree trunks stand silhouetted against the bright sky and white cumulus clouds in the background—a composition that Poul Vad compares with Japanese art.

48 (repr. p. 115)
Interior with Cabinet Sofa
[Strandgade 30], [1907]
Inscr. bottom right: VH
Oil on canvas, 55 x 55 cm
Private collection

Provenance:
Art dealer Martin Grosell (Bramsen 1918); posthumous sale of Grosell's effects, Winkel & Magnussen, sale 109, Mar. 4, 1932, no. 37; Winkel & Magnussen, sale 141, Oct. 12, 1933, no. 119; Gulmann; posthumous sale of Gullman's effects, Bachs Kunsthandel, Copenhagen, Oct. 26, 1934, no. 17

Literature:
Bramsen 1918, no. 304; Vad 1988, ill. p. 189; Billgren and Osipow 1995, ill. p. 87

Exhibitions:
Den frie Udstilling 1908, no. 336; London, van Wisselingh 1907, no. 3 (dated 1906); Kunstforeningen 1916 (vol. 2), no. 1

This picture is a variation of the motif in cat. no. 37.

49 (repr. p. 116)
***Interior* [with easel and punch bowl, Strandgade 30], [1907]**
Inscr. bottom right: VH
Oil on canvas, 64 x 59 cm
Private collection

Provenance:
K. Brandt (Bramsen 1918); Winkel & Magnussen, sale 77, Apr. 30, 1930, no. 16; Winkel &

Magnussen, sale 340, Oct. 2, 1947, no. 71; Winkel & Magnussen, sale 358, Mar. 30, 1950, no. 49

Literature:
Bramsen 1918, no. 305; Vad 1988, ill. p. 285; Varnedoe 1988, p. 109, ill.; Billgren and Osipow 1995, ill. p. 97; Wivel 1996, ill. p. 47

Exhibitions:
Kunstforeningen 1916 (vol. 2), no. 72; Kunstforeningen 1930, no. 34; Ordrupgaard 1981, no. 118

The view here is from the middle room at the front of Strandgade 30 looking into the living room (see cat. nos. 25, 32, 33, and 50). The porcelain bowl and furniture are the same as in those other pictures, but there are two additional objects depicted in this painting: the artist's easel and a potted plant in the window overlooking the street, both of which are unusual elements in Hammershøi's interiors.

50 (repr. p. 102)
***Music Room* [Strandgade 30], [1907]**
Inscr. bottom right: VH
Oil on canvas, 69 x 59 cm
Private collection

Provenance:
Sale, Winkel & Magnussen, October 1910, no. 17; Ole Olsen (Bramsen 1918); Lady Abrahamsen (1941); posthumous sale of Olsen's effects, Winkel & Magnussen, sale 307, Feb. 28, 1944, no. 717

Literature:
Bramsen 1918, no. 308; Vad 1957, p. 21f., ill. 37; Vad 1988, pp. 189, 195, 377, ill. p. 382

Exhibitions:
Kunstforeningen 1916 (vol. 2), no. 75; Kunstforeningen 1955, no. 42; Oslo 1955, no. 37; Ordrupgaard 1981, no. 119

The subject of this picture is the same section of the living room that Hammershøi painted in cat. nos. 25, 32, and 33. Here, he has added a violin and a cello to the piano to suggest the chamber music that was played in the room. His interest in music is well known, and the two instruments could very well have belonged to Alfred Bramsen's children, Karen and Henry Bramsen, who played the violin and cello, respectively. The framed print above the piano has been identified as F. L. Bradt's *View of the New Road Constructed Outside the Walls of Nørre Port* (ca. 1781).

51 (repr. p. 117)
***View of the Asiatic Company*, or *Entryway to the Asiatic Company Dock*, [1907]**
Inscr. bottom right: VH
Oil on canvas, 50.5 x 45 cm
Private collection

Provenance:
Alfred Bramsen (Bramsen 1918); Gustav Falck; F. C. Kielgast, Kalundborg; Bruun Rasmussen, sale 5, Mar. 10, 1949, no. 54; Bruun Rasmussen, sale 8, Sept. 19, 1949, no. 31

Literature:
Bramsen 1918, pp. 50, 60, 63, 66, 68, no. 303, ill.; Rostrup 1940, ill. p. 188; Madsen 1946, ill. 8; Vad 1957, p. 21, ill. 40; Wivel 1982, p. 33, ill.; Vad 1988, p. 244, ill. p. 320; Wivel 1994, p. 98, ill.; Wivel 1996, p. 55, ill.

Exhibitions:
London, van Wisselingh 1907, no. 9; Den frie Udstilling 1908, no. 335; Rome 1911, no. 36; Malmö 1914, no. 2367; Kunstforeningen 1916 (vol. 2), no. 70; Stockholm 1919, no. 455; Kunstforeningen 1930, no. 33;Oslo 1955, no. 36; Kunstforeningen 1955, no. 41; Ordrupgaard 1981, no. 117

In an interview in 1907, Hammershøi said he was tired of painting interiors and that he would like to "look in a different direction" and "paint architecture" (*Hver 8. Dag*, 1907, pp. 437–38). That same year he returned to the Asiatic Company buildings as a motif (see cat. nos. 27 and 28), this time using a relatively small upright canvas. The picture is of a winter scene, and the white light from the snow dominates the tonality of the painting, which is also marked by touches of green as in other pictures from the same year.

52 (repr. p. 118)
***Portrait* [Ida Hammershøi], [1907]**
Oil on canvas, 91 x 73 cm
Statens Museum for Kunst, Copenhagen

Provenance:
Ida Hammeershøi; given by her to the Statens Museum for Kunst, 1916

Literature:
Bramsen 1918, no. 297; Vad 1957, p. 19, ill. 44, 49; Marianne Brøns et al., *Statens Museum for Kunst. Nyere dansk malerkunst. Katalog* (Copenhagen, 1970), inv. no. 3352; Vad 1988, pp. 287f., 298, ill. p. 293; Wivel 1996, p. 54, ill. p. 57

Exhibitions:
Kunstforeningen 1916 (vol. 2), no. 65; Oslo 1955, no. 35; Kunstforeningen 1955, no. 40; Ordrupgaard 1981, no. 116

Hammershøi's wife, Ida (1869–1949), was his favorite model throughout his life. He painted numerous portraits of her, and she was also frequently the model for the solitary female figures in his many interiors. This portrait was painted when Ida was thirty-eight years old, and it and the following one were the last portraits Hammershøi painted of her. Here, the apparent influence of Constantin Hansen (1804–1880)—specifically, his portrait of Elise Købke (Statens Museum for Kunst, Copenhagen)—is an excellent example of the personal way in which Hammershøi took inspiration from the Golden Age of Danish painting (i.e., from the first half of the nineteenth century). The portrait was left unfinished and must be considered a study for the following, more representative, portrait (cat. no. 53). Hammershøi painted the black frame around this portrait to test the slightly smaller format he wanted for the final version.

53 (repr. p. 119)
***Portrait* [Ida Hammershøi], [1907]**
Oil on canvas, 79.3 x 63.5 cm
Aarhus Kunstmuseum, Århus

Provenance:
Ida Hammershøi (Bramsen 1918); Alice Lønberg; Winkel & Magnussen, sale 302, Oct. 5, 1943, no. 102; Johan Lønberg; Bruun Rasmussen, sale 163, Mar. 16, 1964, no. 13; purchased at that sale by the Ny Carlsbergfondet and presented to the Aarhus Kunstmuseum, 1964

Literature:
Bramsen 1918, p. 106, no. 298; Vad 1957, ill. 49; Mikael Andersen, *Katalog over malerisamlingen. 1854–1983. Aarhus Kunstmuseum* (Århus, 1984), no. 530; Vad 1988, pp. 287f., 298, ill. p. 288; Usselmann 1990, ill. 7; Billgren and Osipow 1995, ill. p. 102

Exhibitions:
London, van Wisselingh 1907, no. 5; Den frie Udstilling 1908, no. 337; Kunstforeningen 1916 (vol. 2), no. 66

Hammershøi painted this portrait immediately after the preceding one (cat. no. 52), not as a copy but as a more complete work. The painting's execution is notably more finished, and the likeness is stronger. In terms of its artistic expression, it must be seen in relation to the portrait of Ida in *Two Figures*, which Hammershøi had painted in London ten years earlier (cat. no. 16).

54 (repr. p. 122)
***Two Oak Trees*, or *Young Oak Trees*, 1907**
Inscr. bottom left: VH 07
Oil on canvas, 55 x 76.5 cm
Private collection

Provenance:
Alfred Bramsen (Bramsen 1918); Gustav Falck; Winkel & Magnussen, sale 185, Nov. 26, 1935, no. 92; Valerius Ragoczy; E. Svendsen

Strandgade 30 and 32, May 1903. Hammershøi's apartment is on the second floor of the building at the right. Københavns Bymuseum, Copenhagen

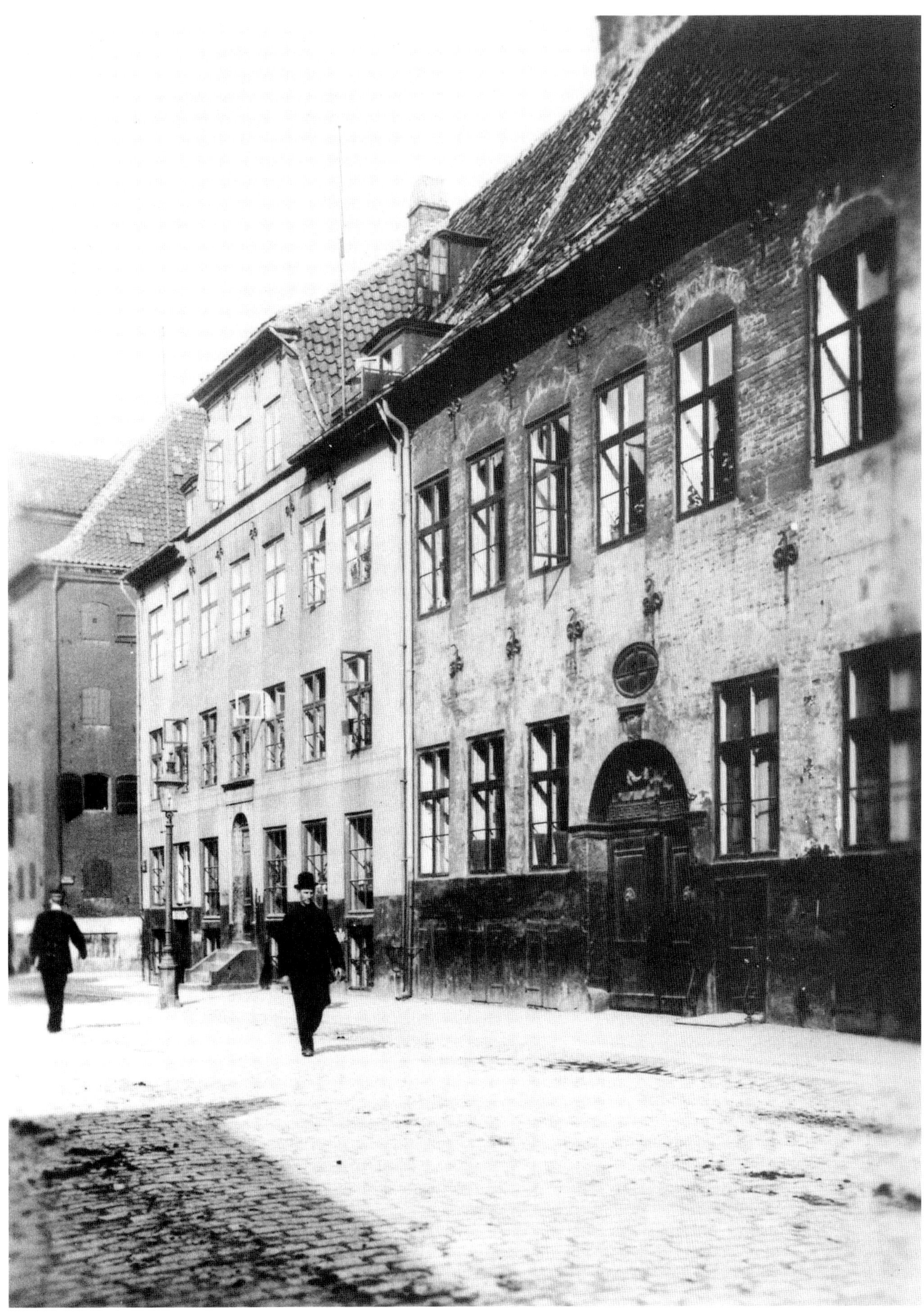

Literature:
Jastrau 1916, ill. p. 59; Bramsen 1918, no. 296, ill.; Vad 1957, p. 20, ill. 39; Vad 1988, p. 327f., ill. p. 330

Exhibitions:
Den frie Udstilling 1908, no. 85; Kunstforeningen 1916 (vol. 2), no. 74; Kunstforeningen 1930, no. 32; Stockholm 1976, no. 32; Ordrupgaard 1981, no. 115

Poul Vad has compared this landscape with young oak trees to Chinese landscape painting, in which two or three carefully chosen elements represent the manifold qualities of nature. The central position given to the two slender trees against the great expanse of the sky and the unintegrated transition between near and far help to raise the picture above narrowly literal naturalism and endow it with an abstract dimension.

55 (repr. p. 120)
***Trørød Forest*, also called *Young Forest*, [1907]**
Oil on canvas, 43 x 66 cm
Private collection

Provenance:
Alfred Bramsen (Bramsen 1918); Bruun Rasmussen, sale 38, May 13, 1953, no. 51; Bruun Rasmussen, sale 53, Oct. 7, 1954, no. 31; Bruun Rasmussen, sale 57, Feb. 4, 1955, no. 104; Bruun Rasmussen, sale 61, Apr. 26, 1955, no. 104

Literature:
Bramsen 1918, no. 295

Exhibitions:
Den frie Udstilling 1908, no. 338; Kunstforeningen 1916 (vol. 2), no. 69; Kunstforeningen 1930, no. 31; Ordrupgaard 1981, no. 114

In the summer of 1907, during a visit to Trørød, north of Copenhagen, Hammershøi painted this forest scene. It differs from his others in its focus on the foreground, a thicketlike mass of young trees, and in the presence of the woodland path at the right, which leads into the pictorial space of the composition.

56 (repr. p. 121)
***View of Old Christiansborg Palace*, [1907]**
Inscr. bottom right: VH
Oil on canvas, 58 x 45 cm
Statens Museum for Kunst, Copenhagen

Provenance:
Acquired at Den frie Udstilling by the Statens Museum for Kunst, 1908

Literature:
Vilhelm Hammershøi (Copenhagen: Winkel & Magnussens Kunstforlag, undated [1908]), no. 9; Ritter 1910, ill. p. 264; Jastrau 1916, ill. p. 58; Bramsen 1918, no. 307, ill.

Exhibitions:
Den frie Udstilling 1908, no. 86; Stockholm 1976, no. 34

In the first pictures that Hammershøi painted of the western end of Christiansborg Palace (cat. nos. 6 and 29), he had chosen a viewpoint that encompassed the entire section of the complex visible from that side, including the Marble Bridge and an equestrian pavilion. When he returned to the motif in 1907, he selected a more northerly angle, where one of the two stables (prominently visible at the left of cat. no. 29) can be seen in pure "profile," without any of the other buildings or the bridge. It was winter when he painted it, and there is a thin covering of snow on the roof. Behind it, at the right, are the tops of the masts on ships in Frederiksholms Kanal.

57 (repr. p. 127)
***Interior* [with woman dressed in black sitting on yellow-brown chair, Strandgade 30], [1908]**
Inscr. bottom left: VH
Oil on canvas, 69 x 56 cm
Aarhus Kunstmuseum, Århus

Provenance:
Acquired from Winkel & Magnussen by the Aarhus Kunstmuseum, 1908

Literature:
Bramsen 1918, p. 107, no. 310; Varnedoe

1983, ill.; Mikael Andersen, *Katalog over malerisamlingen, 1854-1983. Aarhus Kunstmuseum* (Århus, 1984), no. 121; Vad 1988, ill. p. 317; Varnedoe 1988, ill. p. 110; Usselmann 1990, ill. 5; Billgren and Osipow 1995, ill. p. 63

Exhibitions:
Malmö 1975, no. 13; Stockholm 1976, no. 35; New York 1982, no. 35; London 1986, no. 36

This picture of the middle room at the front of Strandgade 30 is a variation on the motif in cat. no. 19.

58 (repr. p. 125)
Woman Reading
[Strandgade 30], [1908]
Inscr. bottom right: VH
Oil on canvas, 68 x 56 cm
Kunstmuseet Brundlund Slot, Åbenrå

Provenance:
Alfred Bramsen (Bramsen 1918); acquired by the Ny Carlsbergfondet and presented to the Kunstmuseet Brundlund Slot, 1950

Literature:
Vilhelm Hammershøi (Copenhagen: Winkel & Magnussens Kunstforlag, undated [1908]), no. 10; Jastrau 1916, ill. p. 55; Bramsen 1918, pp. 60, 66, 68, no. 316, ill.; Vad 1988, ill. p. 319

Exhibitions:
Den frie Udstilling 1908, no. 87; Rome 1911, no. 44; Malmö 1914, no. 2368; Kunstforeningen 1916 (vol. 2), no. 76; Kunstforeningen 1930, no. 35; Kunstforeningen 1996 (no number)

Like cat. nos. 18, 19, 38, 49, 57, and 60, this picture shows the middle room at the front of Strandgade 30. It is a variation on cat. no. 19 and on one of the first pictures Hammershøi painted after moving into the apartment (Bramsen 1918, no. 187, private collection).

59 (repr. p. 129)
***View of the Greenland Trading Company Dock*, [1908]**
Inscr. bottom right: VH
Oil on canvas, 37.5 x 46 cm
Private collection

Provenance:
Ole Olsen (Bramsen 1918); posthumous sale of Olsen's effects, Winkel & Magnussen, sale 305, Jan. 17, 1944, no. 730

Literature:
Bramsen 1918, no. 311; Vad 1988, p. 319, ill. p. 339

Exhibitions:
Kunstforeningen 1916 (vol. 2), no. 79; Ordrupgaard 1981, no. 121

After he began to act on his declaration to break out of his role as a painter of interiors (see the entry for cat. no. 51), Hammershøi wanted to paint not only buildings but also ships, as an integral part of the city scene. He has achieved that in this picture of the Greenland Trading Company Dock in Christianshavn, not far from his apartment at Strandgade 30.

60 (repr. p. 126)
***Interior* [with stove and standing woman dressed in black, Strandgade 30], [1909]**
Inscr. bottom right: VH
Oil on canvas, 67.3 x 55.8 cm
Warren Adelson, New York

Provenance:
Paul Warburg, New York (Bramsen 1918); Mrs. Bettina Warburg Grimson; Warren Adelson, New York, 1991

Literature:
Bramsen 1918, no. 326; Billgren and Osipow 1995, p. 105

This picture, showing the middle room at the front of Strandgade 30, is a close variation of cat. nos. 19 and 57, with some elements of cat. no. 18. It is one of the last pictures that Hammershøi painted in that apartment.

61 (repr. p. 130)
Interior of the Great Hall in Lindegården **[Kalundborg], 1909**
Inscr. on reverse: Lindgaarden. Kallundborg April-Maj 1909
Oil on canvas, 77 x 118 cm
Jane Abdy, London

Provenance:
Jacob S. Meyer (Bramsen 1918); Ove Bendix; Torben Bendix; Bruun Rasmussen, sale 507, Apr. 20, 1988, no. 154; Jane Abdy

Literature:
Bramsen 1918, p. 60, no. 328

Exhibitions:
Kunstforeningen 1916 (vol. 2), no. 88; Kunstforeningen 1930, no. 38; London 1989, no. 5; New York 1991, no. 4

It is not known for certain why Hammershøi visited Kalundborg in western Zealand in April–May 1909, but while there he painted two unusual, nearly identical pictures of the great hall in Lindegården, one of the oldest buildings in the town (see also cat. no. 62). The rococo ornamentation and the panels were probably done on the orders of Rasmus Salten, who bought Lindegården in 1753 and made numerous changes and improvements. Salten had previously been the administrator of the Lerchenborg estate, and thus the similarities between some of the stucco work at Lindegården and in the great hall of Lerchenborg Palace indicate that they were probably done by the same stucco artist. Two years after Hammershøi painted this picture, Lindegården became a museum (today called Kalundborg og Omegns Museum). When Hammershøi was there, the west wing where the great hall is located served as a corn warehouse. This may explain why it is empty in Hammershøi's two pictures, without furniture or any other trace of life; even the stove is missing from its niche in the rear wall. The two pictures are in any case more architectural pictures than interiors, a fact underscored by Hammershøi's deliberate emphasis on the stucco work of the walls and, especially, of the ceiling.

62 (repr. p. 131)
Interior of the Great Hall in Lindegården **[Kalundborg], [1909]**
Inscr. bottom right: VH
Oil on canvas, 71 x 91 cm
Ordrupgaard, Copenhagen

Provenance:
Carl Otto Meyer, Hamburg (Bramsen 1918); Ole Olsen; Kunsthallen, sale 215, Sept. 27, 1956, no. 76; Bruun Rasmussen, sale 618, Feb. 27, 1996, no. 116; purchased at that sale by Ordrupgaard with funds from the State Museum Committee and the Ny Carlsbergfondet.

Literature:
Bramsen 1918, no. 329; Madsen 1946, ill. 7

This is a slightly smaller version of cat. no. 61.

63 (repr. p. 132)
Model, **or** ***Three Studies*****, [1909]**
Oil on canvas, 63 x 63 cm
Malmö Konstmuseum, Malmö

Provenance:
Klas Fåhræus, Stockholm (Bramsen 1918); Herman Gotthardt; given by him to the Malmö Konstmuseum, 1934

Literature:
Bramsen 1918, no. 332; *Herman Gotthardts Konstsamling* (Malmö, 1933), ill. p. 42; Vad 1988, p. 294, ill. p. 295

The three female nudes in this oil sketch are figure studies for two life-size paintings of nudes that Hammershøi did in his new apartment at Kvæsthusgade 6 in 1909 and 1910. The two smaller figures at the right are studies for the first painting (cat. no. 64); the larger, single figure at the left, for the second (cat. no. 65). Hammershøi used the same model for both pictures; her identity is unknown.

64 (repr. p. 133)
Model, **or** ***Nude Female Model*****, [1909]**
Oil on canvas, 205 x 153 cm
Statens Museum for Kunst, Copenhagen

Provenance:
Auction of Effects 1916, no. 25; purchased at that sale by the Statens Museum for Kunst

Literature:
Bramsen 1918, pp. 60, 72, no. 331; Vad 1957, p. 19f., ill. 41; Marianne Brøns et al., *Statens Museum for Kunst. Nyere dansk malerkunst. Katalog* (Copenhagen, 1970), no. 3359; Vad 1988, p. 292f., ill. p. 297; Usselmann 1990, ill. 6; Billgren and Osipow 1995, p. 111, ill. p. 103

Exhibitions:
Kunstforeningen 1916 (vol. 2), no. 82; Oslo 1955, no. 38; Kunstforeningen 1955, no. 43; Charlottenborg 1959, no. 3359; Ordrupgaard 1981, no. 123; New York 1982, no. 36

This is the first of the two large pictures of a nude female figure that Hammershøi painted in 1909 and 1910 (see the entry for cat. no. 63). His source of inspiration for these was C. W. Eckersberg's nudes in the Kunstakademiet (Royal Academy of Fine Arts). With its photographlike cropping and its suggestion of the woman's intimate surroundings, the present picture can be seen as a grand paraphrase of Eckersberg's *Nude Female Model Seen from Behind* (private collection). Hammershøi evidently left certain parts of the painting unfinished—perhaps because the task of completing the other nude occupied his attention more, or because he felt that he could go no further here without diminishing the effect.

65 (repr. p. 133)
***Model,* or *Nude Female Model,* [1910]**
Inscr. bottom right: VH 1910
Oil on canvas, 171 x 95 cm
Davids Samling, on loan to Den Hirschsprungske Samling, Copenhagen

Provenance:
Sale of Effects 1916, no. 7; acquired at that sale by C. L. David; transferred to the C. L. Davids Fond og Samling, 1945

Literature:
Jastrau 1916, ill. p. 64; Bramsen 1918, pp. 60, 72, no. 330; Vad 1988, pp. 292, 296f., ill. p. 301; Usselmann 1990, p. 196; Vad 1995, p. 108, ill. p. 109; Wivel 1996, p. 59

Exhibitions:
Kunstforeningen 1916 (vol. 2), no. 94; Davids Samling 1995, no. 39

This picture is different from the preceding one (cat. no. 64) both in its having been finished and in Hammershøi's depiction of his model in an anonymous and almost clinical interior—which Poul Vad even compares to a doctor's observations during an examination. According to Bramsen, the work on the two enormous pictures was extremely wearing on Hammershøi: "The two large nude pictures represented an unusual expense of energy and a corresponding effort of will. It was the kind of work to which he was simply not accustomed, and which always saps one's energy. He never completely recovered from this, his last great achievement as an artist" (quoted in Vad 1988, p. 302).

66 (repr. p. 123)
***Christiansborg Palace Chapel, Copenhagen,* [1910]**
Inscr. bottom right: VH
Oil on canvas, 65 x 70 cm
Nationalmuseum, Stockholm

Provenance:
Winkel & Magnussen (Bramsen 1918); Winkel & Magnussen, sale 91, Mar. 25, 1931, no. 64; Kunsthallen, sale 280, Feb. 14, 1968, no. 88; purchased at that sale by the Nationalmuseum

Literature:
Jastrau 1916, ill. p. 63; Bramsen 1918, no. 340, ill.; Görel Cavalli-Björkman, *Nationalmuseum, Stockholm. Illustrerad katalog över äldre måleri från Danmark, Finland och Norge* (Stockholm, 1996), p. 11

Exhibitions:
Kunstforeningen 1916 (vol. 2), no. 81; Stockholm 1976, no. 38

The picture of the Palace Chapel belongs to the series that Hammershøi painted of Christiansborg Palace (see cat. nos. 6, 29, and 56).

After the 1884 fire, the chapel was the only part of the building remaining from C. F. Hansen's neoclassical rebuilding of the palace (1803–33). According to Bramsen, the view here is from Nybrogade, across the canal from the chapel.

67 (repr. p. 139)
***Interior* [with woman sitting at a table], [ca. 1910]**
Oil on canvas, 82.5 x 64 cm
Ordrupgaard, Copenhagen

Provenance:
The Heyman family; The Dessau family; Galerie Römer, Zürich; Entwistle, London; purchased from Entwistle by Ordrupgaard with funds from the Ny Carlsbergfondet, 1989

Literature:
Vad 1988, pp. 316, 390, ill. p. 386; Wivel 1993, p. 74, ill.

This picture appears to have been painted after Hammershøi had moved from Strandgade 30—either to the apartment at Kvæsthusgade 6, where he painted the two large nudes (cat. nos. 64 and 65), or to the apartment at Bredgade 25, where he lived from 1910 to 1913. The subject appears to be the interior of a kitchen. The earthenware bowl on the table is a mass-produced design of English manufacture.

68 (repr. p. 138)
Interior
[with easel, Bredgade 25], [1910]
Inscr. bottom right: VH
Oil on canvas, 84 x 69.3 cm
Statens Museum for Kunst, Copenhagen

Provenance:
Winkel & Magnussen (Bramsen 1918); Winkel & Magnussen, sale 31, Apr. 29, 1925, no. 27; Einer Madvig; Winkel & Magnussen, sale 308, Mar. 20, 1944, no. 9; Ole Gangsted Rasmussen; art market, Sweden; sale, Christie's London, Mar. 24, 1988, no. 126; acquired at that sale by the Statens Museum for Kunst

Literature:
Bramsen 1918, p. 60, no. 341; Georg Kleis, *Valdemar Kleis, 1843 7. Januar–1943, Den gamle Kunsthandel paa Vesterbro* (Copenhagen, 1943), ill. p. 33

Exhibitions:
Kleis Kunsthandel, Copenhagen 1913, no. 54; Munich 1913, no. 1196

Hammershøi's new apartment at Bredgade 25 (see the entry for cat. no. 67) did not inspire him to the same extent as the one at Strandgade 30. Apparently, only one motif here interested him: the view from the living room into a smaller room through open double doors. The rooms of this apartment were furnished in the same sparse style as before: a few pieces of fine furniture, the piano, the punch bowl, the pewter dish, and the framed prints. Unlike the other pictures he did of this subject, this one has the artist's easel—or his work—as the principal motif. High on the wall above the easel hangs J. F. Clemens's print after C. A. Lorentzen's painting *The Battle of Copenhagen, April 2, 1801*.

69 (repr. p. 137)
***Interior* [with potted plant on card table, Bredgade 25], [1910–1911]**
Oil on canvas, 78.5 x 71 cm
Malmö Konstmuseum, Malmö

Provenance:
English private collection; Danish private collection; sale, Sotheby's London, Feb. 26, 1974, no. 86; Bruun Rasmussen, sale 343, Mar. 16, 1976, no. 34; purchased at that sale by the Malmö Konstmuseum

Literature:
Vad 1988, p. 316, ill. p. 357; Vad 1996, ill., p. 93

Exhibitions:
Stockholm 1976, no. 39; Ordrupgaard 1981, no. 126

Hammershøi painted this picture in the same room and from the same vantage point as in cat. no. 68. It is different from most of his other works in that he has given a potted plant such a central place in the composition.

The English earthenware bowl (see the entry for cat. no. 67) is on top of the piano, and Clemens's print *The Battle of Copenhagen, April 2, 1801* is still hanging in the same spot high on the wall (see cat. no. 68).

70 (repr. p. 140)
***Interior in London: Brunswick Square*, [1912]**
Oil on canvas, 53 x 76 cm
Jane Abdy, London

Provenance:
Ida Hammershøi; Anna Hammershøi (Bramsen 1918); Knud Abildgård; Bruun Rasmussen, sale 494, Apr. 23, 1987, no. 218; Jane Abdy

Literature:
Bramsen 1918, p. 52, no. 357; Vad 1988, p. 331, ill. p. 342; Wivel 1996, ill. p. 58

Exhibitions:
Kunstforeningen 1916 (vol. 2), no. 104; Kunstforeningen 1955, no. 44; Oslo 1955, no. 39; London 1989, no. 4; New York 1991, no. 6

Hammershøi spent the autumn and winter of 1912–13 in London. He rented an apartment in Brunswick Square, where Leonard Borwick (see the entries for cat. nos. 18, 43, and 46) lived. From one of the windows of the apartment, he painted two pictures: a view of the square outside (cat. no. 71) and this one, of a wall with windows, which is more an architectural picture than an interior.

71 (repr. p. 141)
***The Jewish School in Guilford Street* [London], [1912–13]**
Oil on canvas, 51 x 41.5 cm
Schleswig-Holsteinisches Landesmuseum, Schloss Gottorf, Schleswig

Provenance:
Sale of Effects 1916, no. 16; Thomsen, Hellerup (Bramsen 1918); P. F. A. Thomsen; posthumous sale of Thomsen's effects, Charlottenborg, Jan. 28, 1924, no. 33; Bruun Rasmussen, sale 376, Mar. 8, 1978, no. 35; Kunsthallen, sale 462, Feb. 14, 1996; acquired at that sale by the Schleswig-Holsteinisches Landesmuseum

Literature:
Bramsen 1918, p. 52, no. 353; Vad 1988, p. 331, ill. p. 322

Hammershøi painted this picture during his visit to London in 1912–13 (see the entry for cat. no. 70). The view is from one of the windows of his apartment overlooking Brunswick Square, featuring the square's large plane trees and the gray façade of the Jewish School in Guilford Street just beyond.

72 (repr. p. 143)
***Interior*, also called *The Four Rooms* [Strandgade 25], [1914]**
Inscr. bottom right: VH
Oil on canvas, 85 x 70.5 cm
Ordrupgaard, Copenhagen

Provenance:
Acquired by Wilhelm Hansen, 1915; given by bequest of Henny and Wilhelm Hansen to the Danish nation, 1951

Literature:
Bramsen 1918, no. 368; Leo Swane, *Katalog over kunstværkerne på Ordrupgaard* (Copenhagen, 1954), no. 130; Hofstadter 1985, ill., p. 75; Vad 1988, p. 318, ill. p. 388; Usselmann 1990, ill. 1; Wivel 1993, p. 75f., ill.

Exhibition:
Ordrupgaard 1981, no. 130

In 1913, Hammershøi moved back to Copenhagen's Christianshavn district, into an apartment on the second floor of Strandgade 25, the Asiatic Company's main building just opposite his former apartment on that street. The new apartment was on the "sunny side" of the street and thus had more light than the other one, which to some extent is reflected in the pictures he painted there. The rooms were well-proportioned and had high ceilings, and Hammershøi furnished them as was his custom—sparsely, but exquisitely. This picture, one of the last he completed, is a late variation on the motif with open doors from the apartment at Strandgade 30 (see cat. no. 38).

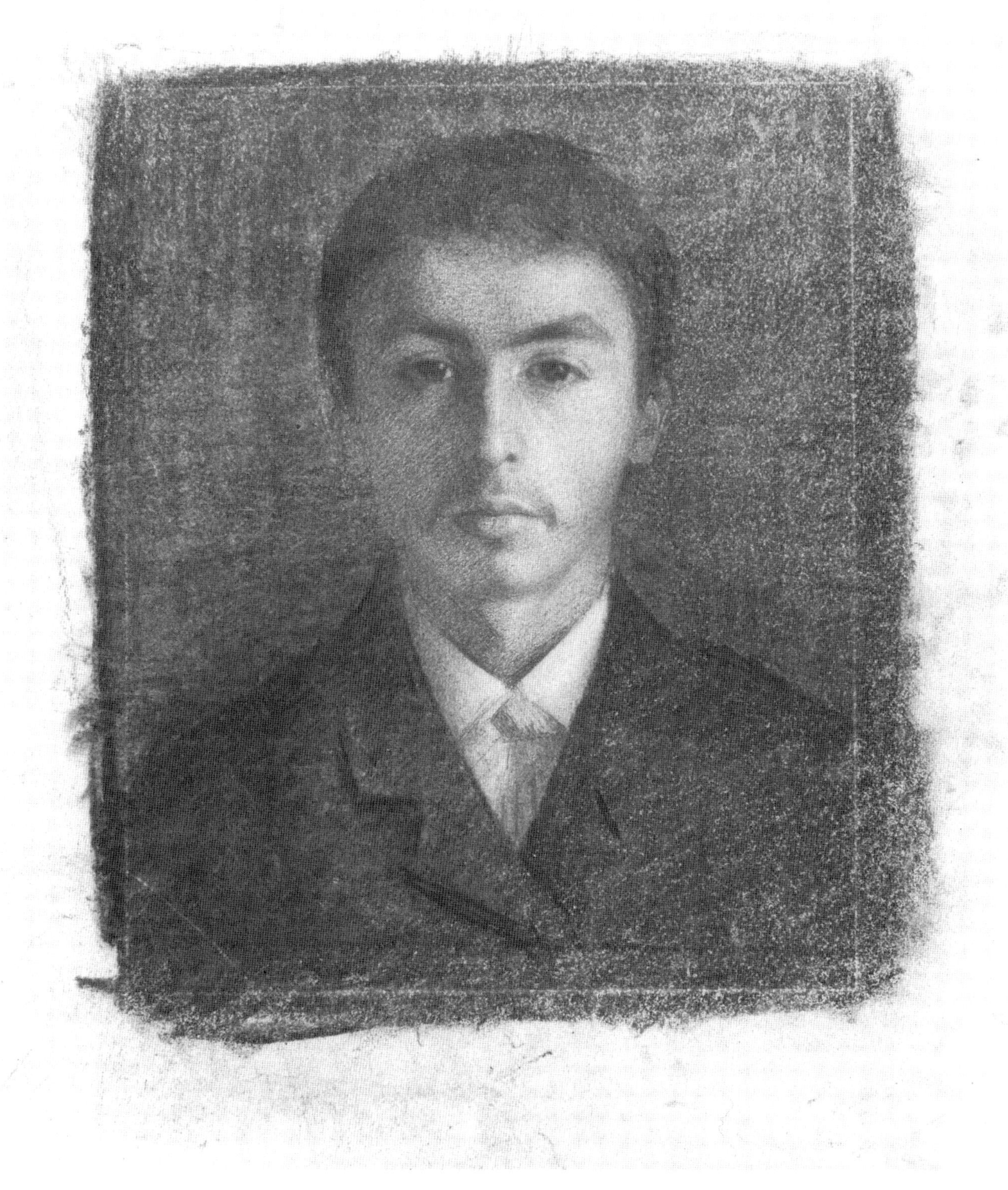

Vilhelm Hammershøi, *Self-Portrait*, ca. 1882. Charcoal on paper, 28.9 x 24.7 cm.
Den Hirschsprungske Samling, Copenhagen

Biography in Brief

by Poul Vad

1864 Vilhelm Hammershøi is born May 15 in Copenhagen, the son of a merchant, Christian Hammershøi (1828–1893), and his wife, Frederikke (née Rentzmann; 1838–1914).

1872–76 Hammershøi receives instruction in drawing from Niels Christian Kierkegaard, a respected teacher who had studied under C. W. Eckersberg at the Kunstakademiet [The Royal Academy of Fine Arts], Copenhagen.

1877–79 Studies privately with various specialists, including drawing teacher Holger Grønvold, who had been a pupil of Henri Lehmann at the Ecole des Beaux-Arts in Paris in 1875–76, and painter Vilhelm Kyhn.

1879–84 Studies at the Kunstakademiet with Frederik Vermehren and other teachers.

1883–85 Studies under Peder Severin Krøyer at De frie Studieskoler [The Independent Study Schools].

1885 Debuts in the Charlottenborg Exhibition that spring with *Portrait of a Young Girl* (cat. no. 2). Visits Berlin and Dresden.

1887 In May visits Hamburg, Holland (Amsterdam, Haarlem, The Hague, Rotterdam), and Belgium (Antwerp, Bruges, Brussels).

1888 *Young Girl Sewing* (cat. no. 3) is rejected by the Charlottenborg Exhibition and is then shown in a protest exhibition together with works by other artists. There, the picture is purchased by Alfred Bramsen (1851–1932), a dentist who subsequently amasses an extensive collection of Hammershøi's works and becomes Hammershøi's mentor and biographer.

1889 Visits Paris during June and July on the occasion of the World's Fair, in which Hammershøi is represented in the Danish section with four pictures.

1890 Becomes engaged to Ida Ilsted (1869–1949). After another painting by Hammershøi (ill. p. 41) is rejected by the Charlottenborg Exhibition, fellow painter Johan Rohde organizes Den frie Udstilling [The Independent Exhibition] with a group of artists including Hammershøi. French art critic Théodore Duret, during a visit to Copenhagen in July, becomes interested in Hammershøi's work.

1891–92 Marries Ida Ilsted on September 5, 1891. On their honeymoon, they travel through Holland and Belgium to Paris, where they stay from the end of September to March 1892. While in Paris, Hammershøi visits Duret and art dealer Paul Durand-Ruel. After returning to Denmark, the couple move into Ny Bakkehus in Rahbeks Allé, in Copenhagen's Frederiksberg district.

1893 The artist's father, Christian Hammershøi, dies on April 27. Hammershøi visits Italy (Florence, Fiesole, Siena, Padua, Venice, Verona) from September to December.

1893–94 That winter, paints *Artemis* (cat. no. 10), which is exhibited in Den frie Udstilling in April–May 1894.

1897 Hammershøi and his wife move to the newly built Åhuset in Åboulevarden. During preparations for a Scandinavian art exhibition in Saint Petersburg, Sergei Diaghilev visits Copenhagen and buys two paintings by Hammershøi. (It has since been impossible to trace these pictures either in Russia or elsewhere.)

1897–98 From October to May, visits London, where he paints *Two Figures* (cat. no. 16). In May he tries to meet James McNeill Whistler in order to show him the picture, but Whistler is in France at the time.

1898 On September 15 Hammershøi and his wife move into an apartment on the second floor of Strandgade 30.

1900 Retrospective exhibition of his work at the Kunstforeningen [Copenhagen Art Society].

1901–02 That winter, paints *Five Portraits* (cat. no. 26), which is exhibited in Den frie Udstilling [The Independent Exhibition] in 1902.

1902 Executes two large architectural paintings for the offices of the administrator of social services in the new Copenhagen City Hall.

1902–03 Visits Rome from October to February. Johannes Jørgensen, a Danish writer living there, obtains permission for Hammershøi to paint in the church of Santo Stefano Rotundo.

1903 During a concert tour in Denmark, English pianist Leonard Borwick (1868–1925) discovers Hammershøi's art and, through Alfred Bramsen, meets him.

1904 Travels to England in September, visiting London and Leonard Borwick's home in Sussex. Austrian poet Rainer Maria Rilke visits Alfred Bramsen to study Hammershøi's art, and meets the artist at the beginning of December.

1905 Solo exhibition at Galerie Eduard Schulte, Berlin.

1905–06 Visits London from November to January, and paints two pictures of the British Museum (cat. nos. 43 and 44).

1907 In London, has a solo exhibition in the Van Wisselingh Gallery and participates in a major exhibition of Danish art. From September to October visits Italy with Ida; the trip ends suddenly when they are wrongly arrested as suspected forgers—an experience that upsets them deeply, especially Ida.

1909–10 They move from Strandgade to Kvæsthusgade in 1909, and then to Bredgade 25 in 1910. Hammershøi becomes a member of the Council of the Kunstakademiet.

1911 Is awarded first prize (10,000 lire) in an international art exhibition in Rome.

1912 Is invited by the Uffizi Gallery in Florence to do a self-portrait for the museum's collection of self-portraits. Visits London in June.

1912–13 Visits London from November to January.

1913 He and Ida move to an apartment in the Asiatic Company building at Strandgade 25 (which today is the Ministry of Foreign Affairs). Visits London in April.

1914 The artist's mother, Frederikke Hammershøi, dies on June 11.

1915 Grows very weak as a result of throat cancer, and paints only one picture the entire year.

1916 Hammershøi dies on February 13. A memorial exhibition is held at the Kunstforeningen (Copenhagen Art Society), April–May.

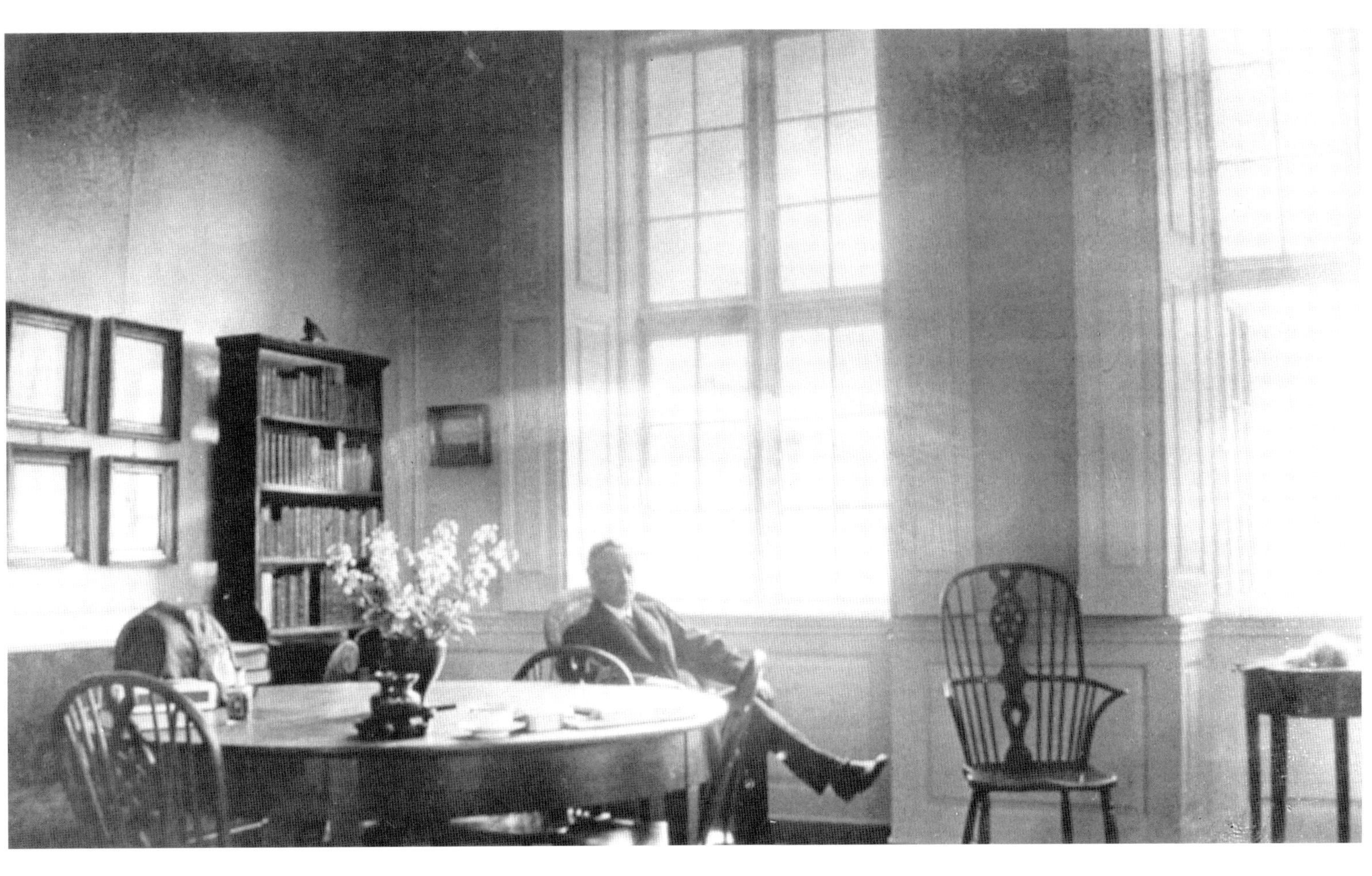

Vilhelm Hammershøi in front of the tall windows in the living room of Strandgade 25, July 1915. Private collection

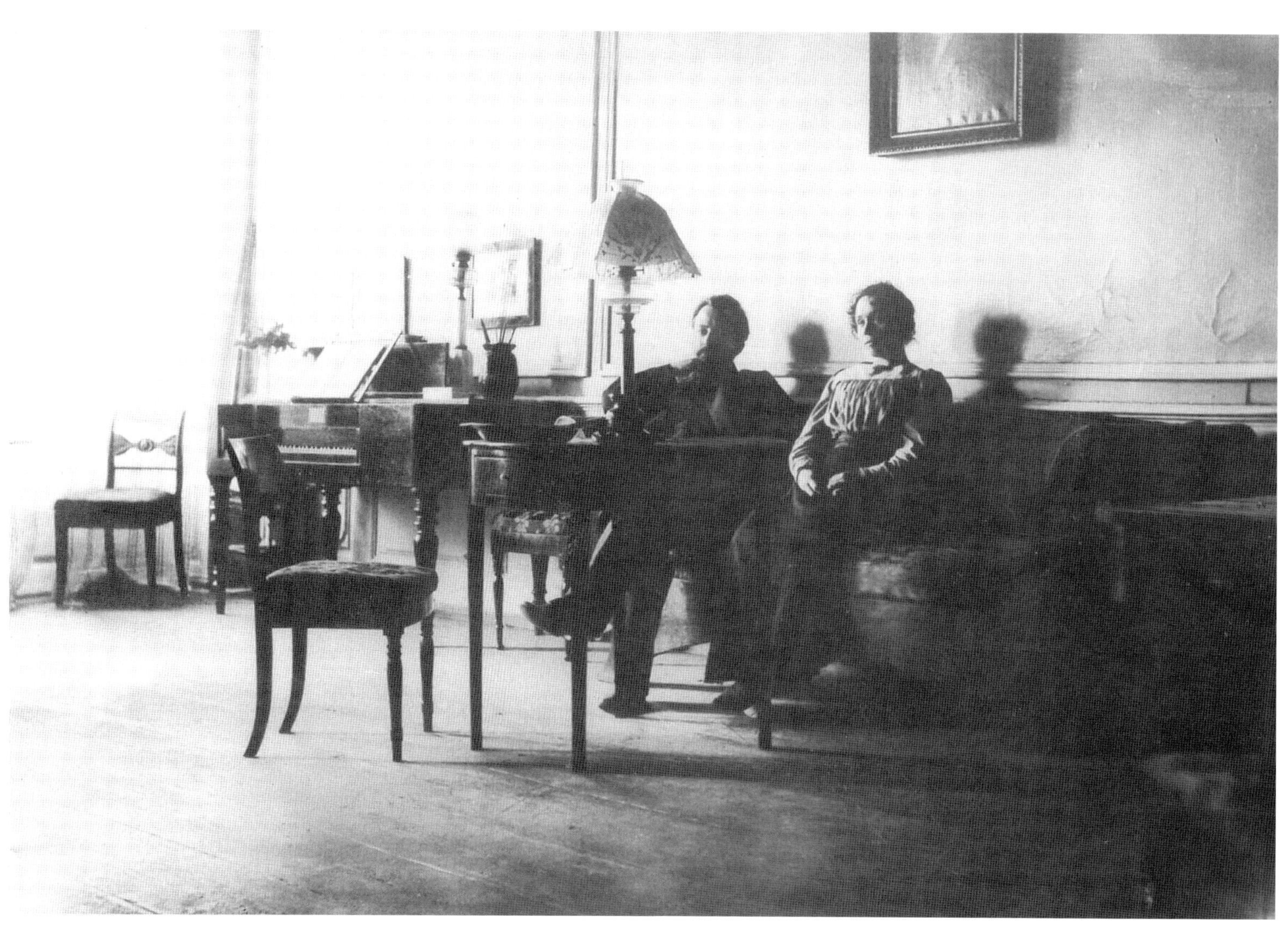

Vilhelm and Ida Hammershøi in the living room of Strandgade 30, ca. 1905.
Det Kongelige Bibliotek, Copenhagen

Selected Exhibitions

- *Charlottenborg*, Copenhagen, 1885.
- *Charlottenborg*, Copenhagen, 1886.
- *Kunstudstillingen*, [The Art Exhibition], Oslo, 1887.
- *Den nordiske Industri-, Landbrugs- og Kunstudstilling*, [The Nordic Industry, Agriculture, and Art Exhibition], Copenhagen, 1888.
- *Udstilling af kasserede arbejder*, [Exhibition of Rejected Works], Charlottenborg, Copenhagen, 1888.
- *Exposition universelle de 1889* [World's Fair], Paris, 1889.
- *En Samling af moderne dansk Kunst*, [A Private Collection of Modern Danish Art], (Alfred Bramsen's collection), Kunstforeningen [Copenhagen Art Society], Copenhagen, 1891.
- *Münchner Jahresausstellung*, Glaspalast, Munich, 1891.
- *VI. Internationale Kunstausstellung*, Glaspalast, Munich, 1892.
- *Den frie Udstilling*, [The Independent Exhibition], Copenhagen, 1891–1904.
- *Münchner Freie Vereinigung*, Salon Gurlitt, Berlin, 1895.
- *Kunstnernes Studieskole*, [The Independent Study School], Charlottenborg, Copenhagen, 1896.
- *Konstafdelningen vid Allmänna Konst- och Industriutställningen*,[The Art Section of The Art and Industry Exhibition], Stockholm, 1897.
- *Saint Petersburg*, 1897. (Exhibition organized by Sergei Diaghilev)
- Vilhelm Hammershøis Arbejder [Alfred Bramsen's collection], Kunstforeningen [Copenhagen Art Society], Copenhagen, 1900.
- *Große Berliner Kunstausstellung*, Berlin, 1900.
- *Exposition universelle de 1900* [World's Fair], Paris, 1900.
- *Raadhusudstillingen af Dansk Kunst til 1890* [The City Hall Exhibition of Danish Art Before 1890], Copenhagen, 1901.
- *Nordische Kunstausstellung*, Kaiser-Wilhelm-Museum, Krefeld, 1902.
- *Den Hirschsprungske Samling af Danske Kunstneres Arbejder* [The Hirschsprung Collection of the Works of Danish Artists], Charlottenborg, Copenhagen, 1902.
- *Esposizione biennale internazionale d'arte*, Venice, 1903.
- *Internationale Kunstausstellung im Städtischen Kunstpalast*, Düsseldorf, 1904.
- *Kunstausstellung der IX. Secession*, Berlin, 1904.
- *En samling malerier og studier forhen tilhørende Dr. Alfred Bramsen* [A Collection of Paintings and Studies Previously Belonging to Dr. Alfred Bramsen], Winkel & Magnussen, Copenhagen, 1904.
- *4th Exhibition of the International Society of Sculptors, Painters and Gravers*, London 1904

- *Valand-Utställningen*, Gothenburg, 1905.
- *Vilhelm Hammershøi, Galerie Eduard Schulte*, Berlin, 1905. (The exhibition also traveled to Cologne, Düsseldorf, and Hamburg.)
- *Den frie Udstilling*, [The Independent Exhibition], Copenhagen, 1906.
- *Exhibition of a Selection of Works by Danish Painters, Guildhall Art Gallery*, London, 1907.
- *Vilhelm Hammershøi, E. Van Wisselingh & Co. Gallery*, London, 1907.
- *Den frie Udstilling*, [The Independent Exhibition], Copenhagen, 1908.
- *X. Internationale Kunstausstellung*, Glaspalast, Munich, 1909.
- *Esposizione Internazionale di Roma*, Rome, 1911.
- *Den frie Udstilling*, [The Independent Exhibition], Copenhagen, 1911–16.
- *Exhibition of Works by Modern Danish Artists*, Brighton, 1912.
- *Contemporary Scandinavian Art*, New York, Buffalo, Toledo, Chicago, Boston, 1912–13.
- *En samling af malerier og studier af danske kunstnere* [A Collection of Paintings and Studies by Danish Artists], Winkel & Magnussen, Copenhagen, 1913.
- *XI. Internationale Kunstausstellung*, Glaspalast, Munich, 1913.
- *Baltiska Utställningen* [The Baltic Exhibition], Malmö, 1914.
- *Vilhelm Hammershøi*, Kunstforeningen [Copenhagen Art Society], Copenhagen, 1916.
- *Etatsrådet Wilhelm Hansens Samling av Dansk Målarkonst* [The Wilhelm Hansen Collection of Danish Painting], Nationalmuseum, Stockholm, 1918.
- *L'art danois depuis la fin du XVIIIe siècle jusqu'à 1900*, Musée du Jeu de Paume, Paris, 1928.
- *Udvalg af Vilhelm Hammershøis arbejder* [Selection of Vilhelm Hammershøi's Works], Kunstforeningen [Copenhagen Art Society], Copenhagen, 1930.
- *Vilhelm Hammershøi, Theodor Philipsen og L.A. ring*, Sveriges Allmänna Konstförening, Stockholm, 1930.
- *Esposizione biennale internazionale d'arte*, Venice, 1932.
- *Danish Art Treasures*, Victoria & Albert Museum, London, 1949.
- *Vilhelm Hammershøi*, Kunstforeningen [Oslo Art Society], Oslo, 1955.
- *Vilhelm Hammershøi*, Kunstforeningen [Copenhagen Art Society], Copenhagen, 1955.
- *Vilhelm Hammershøi*, Prins Eugens Waldemarsudde, Stockholm, 1957.
- *Les Sources du XXe siècle*, Musée national d'art moderne, Paris, 1960–61.
- *Det besjälade rummet* [The Room Endowed with Spirit], Malmö Museum, Malmö, 1975.
- *Vilhelm Hammershøi*, Prins Eugens Waldemarsudde, Stockholm, 1976.
- *Vilhelm Hammershøi. En retrospektiv udstilling*, [A retrospective exhibition] Ordrupgaard, Copenhagen, 1981.
- *Northern Light: Realism and Symbolism in Scandinavian Painting 1880–1910*, Cocoran Gallery of Art, Washington, D. C.; The Brooklyn Museum, New York; and The Minneapolis Institute of Arts, Minneapolis; 1982-83.
- *Vilhelm Hammershøi. Painter of Stillness and Light*, Wildenstein, New York and Phillips Collection, Washington, 1983.
- *Dreams of a Summer Night*, Hayward Gallery, London and Kunstmuseum, Düsseldorf, 1986–87.
- *Lumières du nord*. Musée du Petit Palais, Paris, 1987.
- *Den frie Udstilling / The Free Exhibition*, Bury St. Gallery, London, 1989.
- *Danish Painting at the Turn of the Century*, Adelson Galleries, New York, 1991.
- *Im Licht des Nordens*, Altonaer Museum, Hamburg, 1993.
- *1893, L'Europe des peintres*. Musée d'Orsay, Paris, 1993.
- *Symbolismen i dansk kunst* [Symbolism in Danish Art], Nivaagaard, Nivå, 1993.
- *Danish Paintings of the Nineteenth Century from the Collection of Ambassador John L. Loeb Jr.*, Busch-Reisinger Museum, Harvard University, Cambridge, Mass., 1994.
- *Dansk Kunst i Davids Samling—fra Philipsen til Saxbo*, Davids Samling [The David Collection], Copenhagen, 1995.
- *Paradis Perdus. L'Europe Symboliste*, Musée des Beaux-Arts, Montreal, 1995,
- *Mørkets lys. Nordisk kunst gennem 100 år*. [The Light of Darkness: Scandinavian Art over 100 Years], Kunstforeningen [Copenhagen Art Society], Copenhagen, 1996.

Select Bibliography

- Ballin, Mogens. "Den frie Udstilling I" [The Independent Exhibition I]. *Tårnet* (April–May 1894), pp. 36–41.
- Billgren, Ola and Paul Osipow. *Hammershøi*. Hellerup, 1995.
- Bodelsen, Merete. "Vilhelm Hammershøis Artemis." *Kunst og Kultur* (Oslo), vol. 42 (1959), pp. 161–74.
- Borneville, Edward. "Den grå revolution. Vilhelm Hammershøi og hans værk" [The Gray Revolution: Vilhelm Hammershøi and His Work]. *Kunst* (Copenhagen) 7, no. 8 (1960), pp. 199–204.
- Bramsen, Alfred. *Fortegnelse over Vilhelm Hammershøis Arbejder* [Inventory of Vilhelm Hammershøi's Works]. Copenhagen, 1900.
- ______. "Weltkunst. Der dänische Maler Vilhelm Hammershøi" [World Art: The Danish Painter Vilhelm Hammershøi]. *Zeitschrift für bildende Kunst* (Leipzig), vol. 16 (1905), pp. 176–89.
- ______. "Vilhelm Hammershøi, Meister der Farbe" [Vilhelm Hammershøi, Master of Color]. *Europäische Kunst der Gegenwart* (Leipzig), vol. 3 (1905), p. 85.
- Bramsen, Alfred and Sophus Michaëlis. *Vilhelm Hammershøi. Kunstneren og hans Værk* [Vilhelm Hammershøi: The Artist and His Work]. Copenhagen/Christiania, 1918.
- Bühlmann, René. "Tabte horisonter. Vilhelm Hammershøi og storbyen" [Lost Horizons: Vilhelm Hammershøi and the City] *Konsthistorisk Tidskrift* (Stockholm) 54, no. 3 (1985), pp. 136–44.
- Clutton-Brock, Arthur. "Danish Painting in Guildhall: A New Master." *Tribune*, Apr. 9, 1907; reprinted in Poul Vad, *Vilhelm Hammershøi. Værk og Liv*, Copenhagen, 1988, p. 407f.
- Ditzel, Harald. "Artemis." *Kunst* (Copenhagen), vol. 7 (1959–60), p. 19f.
- Ferreira, Ingrid Fersing. "Hammershøi est-il un peintre symboliste? Quelques observations sur Hammershøi, Khnopff et Mellery" [Is Hammershøi a Symbolist Painter? Some observations on Hammershøi, Khnopff, and Mellery]. *Bulletin du Comité des Historiens d'Art Nordique*, no. 1 (1997), pp. 22–24.
- Finsen, Hanne and Inge Vibeke Raaschou-Nielsen. *Vilhelm Hammershøi. En retrospektiv udstilling*. Exh. cat., Ordrupgaard, Copenhagen, 1981.
- ______. *Vilhelm Hammershøi: Painter of Stillness and Light*. Exh. cat., Wildenstein, New York/ The Phillips Collection, Washington, D.C., 1983
- Giersing, Harald. "Vilhelm Hammershøi" in *Om Kunst*, [On Art], Copenhagen, 1934, pp. 36–38.

- Hansen, Thorkild. "Den sort-hvide kolorist" [The Black and White Colorist], in *Vilhelm Hammershøi*, exh. cat., Ordrupgaard, Copenhagen, 1981, pp. 10–13.
- Hofstadter, Dan. "Hammershøi's rooms." *Art and Antiques* (New York), Dec. 1985, pp. 71–75.
- Jastrau, V., ed. *Vilhelm Hammershøi*. Smaa Kunstbøger, no. 13. Copenhagen, 1916.
- Klange, Else. "Omkring en Job-figur" [On a Figure of Job]. *Ikonografisk Post* (Uppsala), no. 4 (1983), pp. 2–23.
- Madsen, Karl. "Vilhelm Hammershøi." *Kunst* (Copenhagen), vol. 1 (1899) [unpaginated].
- Nasgaard, Roald. *The Mystic North: Symbolist Landscape Painting in Northern Europe and North America 1890–1940*. Exh. cat., Art Gallery of Ontario, Toronto, 1984.
- Nykjær, Mogens. "Hammershøis Artemis," in *Enten Eller*, exh. cat., Sophienholm, Lyngby, 1980–81, pp. 71–80.
- _______. *Kundskabens billeder: Motiver i dansk kunst fra Eckersberg til Hammershøi* [Images of Knowledge: Motifs in Danish Art from Eckersberg to Hammershøi]. Århus, 1991.
- Olsen, Harald. "Vilhelm Hammershøi," in *Vilhelm Hammershøi*, exh. cat., Ordrupgaard, Copenhagen, 1981, pp. 18–24.
- Ostenfeld, Ib. "Var Hammershøi farveblind?" [Was Hammershøi Color Blind?]. *Medicinsk Forum* (Copenhagen) 34, no. 5 (1981), pp. 154–62.
- Petersen, Carl V. "Omkring Hammershøi-Udstillingen i Kunstforeningen" [On the Hammershøi Exhibition at the Copenhagen Art Society]. *Tilskueren* (Copenhagen), vol. 1 (1916), pp. 515–25; reprinted in *Afhandlinger og Artikler om Kunst*, Copenhagen, 1939, pp. 137– 47.
- Ritter, William. "Vilhelm Hammershøi." *L'Art et les artistes* (Paris), no. 10 (1909–10), pp. 264–68.
- Rostrup, Haavard. "Om Vilhelm Hammershøis Kunst" [On the Art of Vilhelm Hammershøi]. *Kunst og Kultur* (Oslo), vol. 26 (1940), pp. 177–92.
- Sass, Else Kai. "Vilhelm Hammershøi." *Danmark* (Copenhagen) 6, nos. 5–6 (1946), pp. 137–44.
- Usselmann, Henri. "L'Art de Hammershøi, rêve poétique et angoissé" [The Art of Hammershøi, Poetic and Anguished Dream]. *Konsthistorisk Tidskrift* (Stockholm) 59, no. 3 (1990), pp. 190–99.
- Vad, Poul. *Vilhelm Hammershøi*. Copenhagen, 1957.
- _______. "Rilke, Hammershøi og tingene" [Rilke, Hammershøi, and Things]. *Signum* (Copenhagen) 4, no. 2 (1964), p. 24f.
- _______. "Om Hammershøis interiører" [On Hammershøi's Interiors], in *Det besjälade rummet*, [The Room Endowed with Spirit], exh. cat., Malmö Museum, Malmö, 1975, pp. 8–11; reprinted in *Det springende punkt* [On the Horns of a Dilemma], Copenhagen, 1997, pp. 89–95.
- _______. *Hammershøi. Værk og liv*. [Work and Life], Copenhagen, 1988. English-language edition: *Vilhelm Hammershøi and Danish Art at the Turn of the Century*. New Haven/London, 1992.
- _______. "Vilhelm Hammershøi," in *Dansk kunst i Davids Samling*, [Danisk Art in the David Collection], exh. cat., Davids Samling [The David Collection], Copenhagen, 1995, pp. 90–109.
- _______. "Vilhelm Hammershøi und Rainer Maria Rilke." *Akzente* 43, no. 6 (1996), pp. 562–71.
- Varnedoe, Kirk. *Northern Light: Realism and Symbolism in Scandinavian Painting 1880–1910*. Exh. cat., Brooklyn Museum, New York, 1982.
- _______. "Private Light." *Art in America* (New York) 71, no. 3 (1983), pp. 110–16.
- _______. *Northern Light.*. New Haven/London, 1988.
- Doctor W. "Vilhelm Hammershøi. Stuernes Maler" [Vilhelm Hammershøi: Painter of Rooms].*Verden og Vi* (Copenhagen), 1913, pp. 3–5.
- Wanscher, Johan Hendrik. "Vilhelm Hammershøis farvesyn" [Vilhelm Hammershøi's Color Vision]. *Medicinsk Forum* (Copenhagen) 35, no. 1 (1982), pp. 16–18.
- Wanscher, Vilhelm. "Vilhelm Hammershøi." *Ord och Bild* (Stockholm) 24, no. 8 (1915), pp. 399–411.
- Werenschold, Marit. "Sergej Djagilevs artikkel 'Moderne skandinavisk maleri,' 1897" [Sergei Diaghilev's article 'Modern Scandinavian painting,' 1897]. *Kunst og Kultur* (Oslo) 74, no. 4 (1991), pp. 194–229.

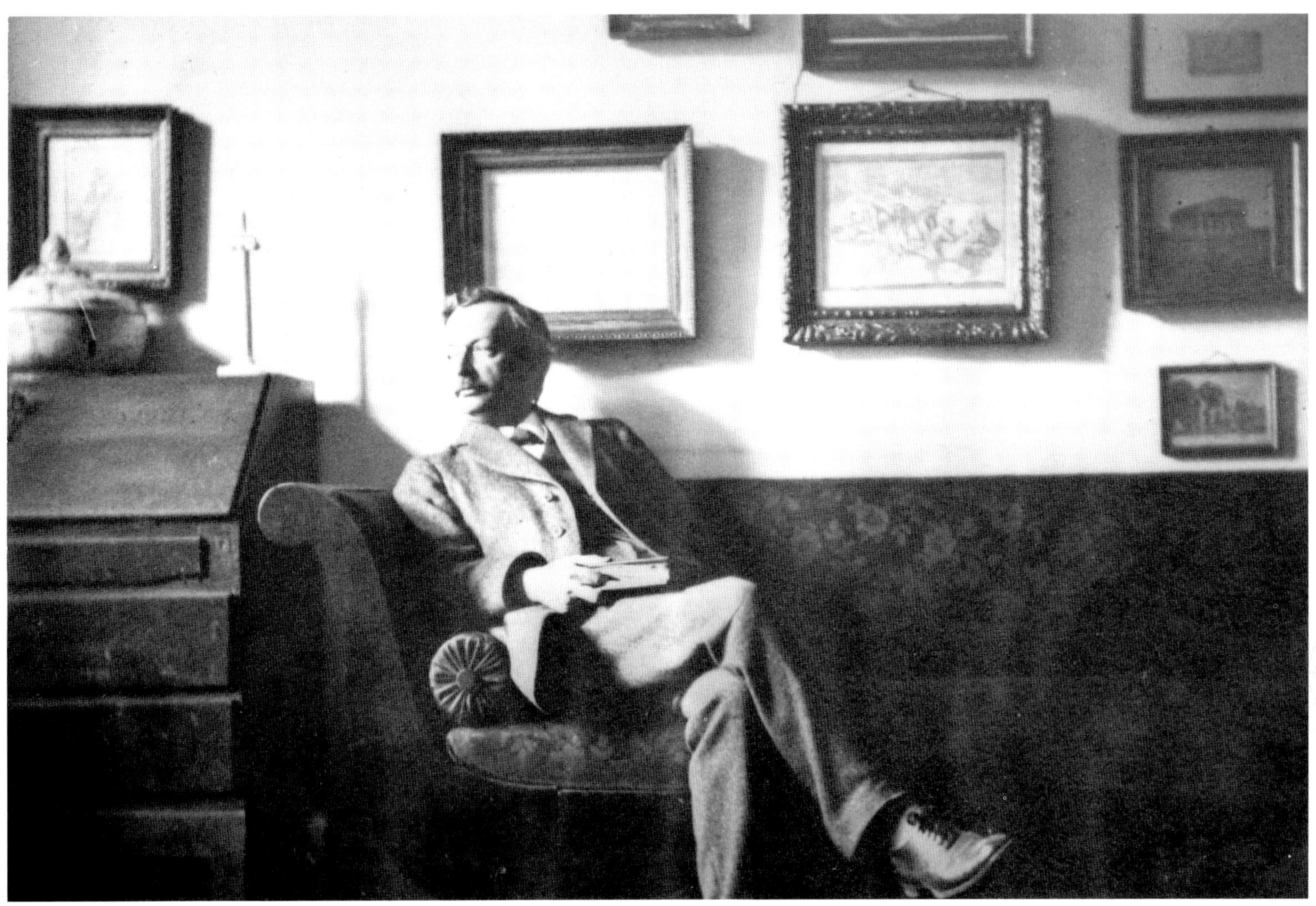

Vilhelm Hammershøi in the living room of Strandgade 25, ca. 1911. The punch bowl of Copenhagen porcelain is on the bureau; in the middle above the sofa is a reproduction of Raphael's *The Miraculous Draft of Fishes* and, to the right of that, a photograph of one of the temples in Paestum. Thorvaldsens Museum, on loan to Den Hirschsprungske Samling, Copenhagen

- Wivel, Henrik. "Den realistiske uhygge. Vilhelm Hammershøis og L. A. Rings motivverden" [Realistic Unease: The motifs of Vilhelm Hammershøi and L. A. Ring]. *Kritik* (Copenhagen), no. 59 (1982), pp. 30–52.
- ______. "Den kølige mystiker" [The Cool Mystic]. *Nordisk tidskrift för vetenskap, konst och industri*, vol. 66, no. 2 (1990), pp. 120–27.
- ______. "Symbolisme og impressionisme." *Ny dansk kunsthistorie*, vol. 5. Copenhagen, 1994.
- ______. *Vilhelm Hammershøi*. Copenhagen, 1996.
- Wivel, Mikael. *Ordrupgaard. Selected Works* (Copenhagen), nos. 72–75 (1993).

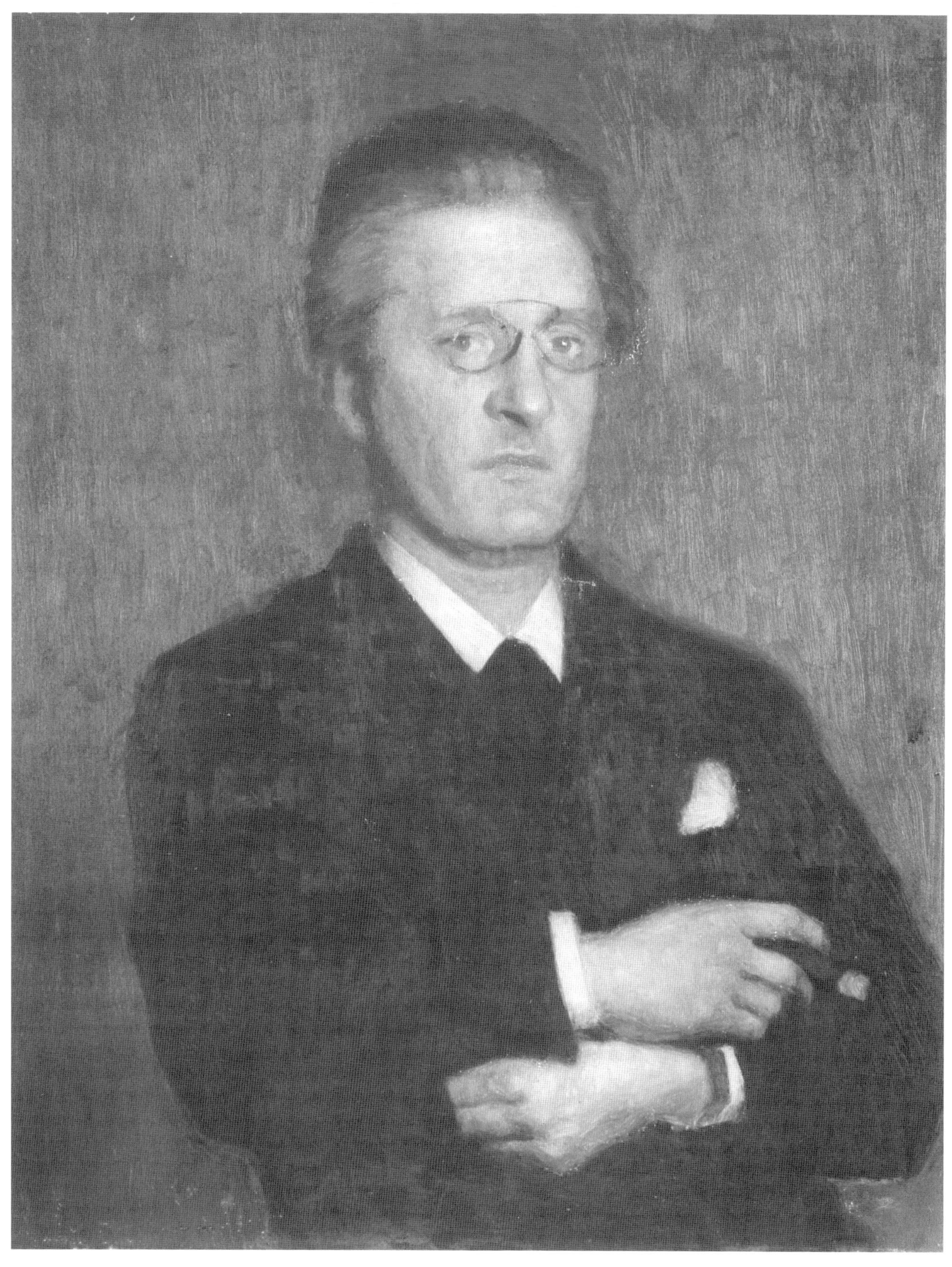

Vilhelm Hammershøi, *Portrait of the Dentist Alfred Bramsen*, [1893]. Oil on canvas, 77 x 61 cm. Schleswig-Holsteinisches Landesmuseum, Schloss Gottorf, Schleswig

Three Letters to Alfred Bramsen

Rainer Maria Rilke

At an international art exhibition in Düsseldorf during the summer of 1904, Austrian poet Rainer Maria Rilke (1875–1926) had the opportunity of seeing some paintings by Vilhelm Hammershøi. While staying in the province of Skåne in southern Sweden that same autumn, he paid several visits to Copenhagen, partly with the aim of extending his knowledge of Hammershøi's art. He was introduced by Danish poet Sophus Michaëlis to Alfred Bramsen (1851–1923), a dentist who since 1888 had built up an extensive Hammershøi collection containing many of the artist's most important works. Rilke's letters to Alfred Bramsen were published in Danish in Poul Vad, *Hammershøi. Værk og Liv* (Copenhagen, 1988); in English in the English-language edition of the same book, *Vilhelm Hammershøi and Danish Art at the Turn of the Century* (New Haven and London, 1992); and then finally in the original German in *Akzente*, vol. 43, no. 6 (December 1996).

Jonsered nr. Gothenburg
Furuborg, the 22nd of November 1904

Esteemed Doctor,

Some two months ago you had the great kindness, on the recommendation of Mr. Sophus Michaëlis, to receive us, my wife and myself, in your beautiful home so that we could enjoy Hammershøi's paintings, which we so desired to see.

This great artist's work has not ceased profoundly to occupy my thoughts; therefore, on returning from here to Germany, I intend to spend a further eight or ten days in Copenhagen, with the sole object of again seeing the pictures which are in your possession and of studying them attentively.

I take the liberty of asking you, esteemed doctor, whether at that time — it will be during the early days of December — you will again receive me and thereby grant me the invaluable opportunity for a thorough examination of the Hammershøi paintings?

Indeed, remembering that you yourself remarked that with a word to the artist you would introduce me to him (as soon as I myself desired it), it will perhaps not seem to you to be too immodest if I put a further question to you and earnestly ask you to inform me whether Mr. Hammershøi is yet returned from London, and whether I dare hope to be able to find him in Copenhagen at the beginning of December, and if possible to visit him.

The result of all this is to be a study of the artist and later perhaps an original essay; I feel also what enormous enrichment could be brought about for me in my deepest and truest poetical strivings as a result of my encounter with this master, whose great and eminent work I believe I understand to a significant degree in my admiration for it.

It is thus a question, esteemed Doctor, of whether you will make arrangements for a stranger to have this joy and this labour?

I request you to send me a line to inform me of the situation.

With the deepest respect and esteem, I remain,

Rainer Maria Rilke

last day of November 1904:

Honored Doctor,

Please accept my deepest gratitude for your kind and accommodating card; I will take the liberty of presenting myself to you in Admiralgade on Sunday the 3rd of December in the afternoon between half past two and half past three. (If the time is not convenient to you, I would ask you to be so kind as to suggest a different one; I will adapt to that as far as possible.) My sojourn in Copenhagen must necessarily be shorter than I had hoped to be able to make it; I can only reckon on five days; it would therefore be very welcome to me to be able to meet and visit Mr. Hammershøi fairly soon after my arrival.

My address for any communication from you will from the morning of the 3rd of December be:
Charlottenlund
Villa Charlottenlund
(c/o Miss Bagger)
With gratitude and appreciation, I remain, esteemed Doctor,
Yours truly:

Rainer Maria Rilke

Villa des Brillants,
Meudon-Val-Fleury
near Paris
The 10th of November 1905

Honored Sir,

Someone has had the kind idea of sending me the little Hammershøi catalogue containing your warm and sensitively descriptive words.

Whether this item has come from you or not, it is at any event high time that I should address a few words to you: first to say that I have not ceased to remember you and your kind wife with the utmost gratitude—and secondly to explain how it could happen that I have still, in any way be it major or minor, been unable to carry out my intention of speaking on Hammershøi's work. To be frank: despite my studies in Copenhagen (for the furtherance and thoroughness of which I owe you many thanks), I nevertheless did not feel sufficiently prepared, initiated, immersed to be able to produce a piece of work entirely and convincingly filled with the essence of this great master, as was my concern.

It certainly appears extremely unfortunate, and so, too, it is. With the bases which you obtained for me, another would probably have been able to achieve something valuable and distinctive; but, as I am increasingly aware, my manner of gathering and transforming such thing presupposes very thorough labor; my little book on Rodin could only come into being on the basis of months spent on his work, and although I will not say that Hammershøi would have been obliged to tolerate me in his proximity for months in order to give me the possibility of writing an article, I would nevertheless have needed a few more occasions on which to see and understand and perhaps not have been able to discover by asking, but as it were to understand and discover from the works some dates and circumstances of life in order to form a whole, as I so powerfully desired and still desire with all my heart.

There is, it seems to me, no urgency. Hammershøi is not one of those of whom it is necessary to speak to *quickly*. His work is long and slow, and at whatever moment one grasps it, it will always give ample opportunity to speak about what is important and essential in art.

I am sure that by this circuitous path I shall again return to Hammershøi's work and one day to the best of my ability realize my intention, as I so mean to do; may that be to the delight of the master and yourself.

With the greatest respect to you and your wife, I remain,

Yours sincerely,

Rainer Maria Rilke

If the master still remembers me, may I ask you to inform him of this letter and assure him of my unchanging admiration? And please be so kind as to pay my respects to his wife, mother, and sister.

Acknowledgments

Two art historians have contributed essays to the catalogue. Drawing on his profound knowledge of Hammershøi's work, Poul Vad has written the general introduction, while Professor Robert Rosenblum of New York University, known among other things for his writings on Scandinavian art, discusses Hammershøi's art within an international context. We offer them both our sincere thanks. We would also like to express our gratitude to Susanne Meyer-Abich, London, who has made available to this project the complete list that she has compiled of Hammershøi's works and the exhibitions in which they have appeared, as well as her Hammershøi bibliography.

Thanks also to the following individuals for their help:

Uffe Andreasen
Adrian Biddell
Henrik Bjerre
Lone Bøgh
Görel Cavalli-Björkmann
Göran Christenson
Anne Christiansen
Judith Cox
James Cuno
Lisa Dennison
Søren Dietz
Jan Drees
Kjeld von Folsach
Stephen Robert Frankel
Finn Terman Frederiksen
Björn Fredlund
Olle Granath
Vivien Greene
Hans Grunnet
Anne C. Haskel
Allis Helleland
Birgitta Hillingsøe
Erik Jacobsen
Kathrine Kampe
Kathrine Lehmann
Teresa Nielsen
Kenno Pedersen
Anne Højer Petersen
Mark Poltimore
Marianne Saabye
Christel Schrøder
Peter-Klaus Schuster
Gail Aidinoff Scovell
Nicolas Serota
Anne-Marie Skov
Jens Erik Sørensen
Merete Soussan
Heinz Spielmann
Lynn Ann Underwood
Gitte Vincent
Mads Øvlisen

Photo credits: Jörg P. Anders, Berlin. Lars Bay Fotografi, Silkeborg. Wermund Bendtsen Fotografi, Odense. Carlo Catenazzi, Art Gallery of Ontario. Ole Haupt, Copenhagen. Geir S. Johannesen, Bergen. Bodil Karlsson, Nationalmuseum, Stockholm. Renate Kühling, Schleswig-Holsteinisches Landesmuseum. Ingrid Nilsson, Malmö Museer. Bent Ryberg / Planet Foto, Copenhagen. Thomas Pedersen, Poul Pedersen, Ole Hein Pedersen, Århus. Hans Petersen, Copenhagen. Photographic Services, Harvard University Art Museums, Cambridge, Mass. Photo RMN, Michèle Bellot. John Webb, Tate Gallery. Ole Woldbye, Copenhagen.